REGULATORY REFORM

REGULATORY REFORM

New Vision or Old Curse?

Edited by
Margaret N. Maxey
Robert Lawrence Kuhn

PRAEGER SPECIAL STUDIES • PRAEGER SCIENTIFIC

New York • Philadelphia • Eastbourne, UK
Toronto • Hong Kong • Tokyo • Sydney

Library of Congress Cataloging in Publication Data
Main entry under title:

Regulatory reform.

   Includes index.
   1. Administrative procedure--United States.
2. Administrative agencies--United States.
3. Consumer protection--Law and legislation--
United States. 4. Trade regulation--United States.
5. Risk management--United States. I. Maxey,
Margaret N. II. Kuhn, Robert Lawrence.
KF5407.R433 1985   342.73'066   84-26261
ISBN 0-03-001473-5 (alk. paper) 347.30266

Published in 1985 by Praeger Publishers
CBS Educational and Professional Publishing
a Division of CBS Inc.
521 Fifth Avenué, New York, New York 10175 U.S.A.

© 1985 by Praeger Publishers

56789 052 987654321

Printed in the United States of America

FOREWORD

Murray L. Weidenbaum

The termination in August 1982 of President Reagan's Task Force on Regulatory Relief has been interpreted by some observers as an acknowledgment that the drive for regulatory reform has run its course. That may not necessarily be the case.

From the viewpoint of the Task Force, however, its initial tasks have been accomplished. First of all, the Task Force reviewed the host of "midnight" rules that the outgoing Carter administration hastily promulgated—rejecting some, approving others, and requiring modifications in still other cases. Most important, the Task Force developed and set into motion a continuing process for reviewing proposed federal regulations, subjecting the major rules to the rigors of benefit/cost analysis. As a result of this process, an estimated $10 billion in capital outlays has been saved, and the annual continuing costs of complying with federal regulations have been cut by about $10 billion. Although such estimates are inherently approximate, they surely indicate that the review process has teeth in it.

The main achievement in regulatory reform since January 1981, however, has involved not so much doing or undoing, but rather *not* doing. That is, for the first extended period in decades the federal government has not launched a major new regulatory activity. To use the terms of the Sherlock Holmes story, the federal regulatory dog has not barked since January 1981.

It is the area of statutory reform that has been the source of greatest disappointment to the supporters of regulatory reform. Few changes have been made in the underlying regulatory statutes. For example, updating the Clear Air Act, which had been identified as the highest priority change in the apparatus of social regulation, has not been accomplished. This has not, however, resulted from any lack of effort by the Task Force, especially its chairman, Vice President George Bush.

The sad fact of the matter is that, from the outset, the Task Force's efforts in the environmental area have been overshadowed by other members of the administration, especially by the statements and actions of former Secretary of the Interior James Watt. In the process, many people in the environmental movement were alienated, including those who had previously avoided engaging in political controversies.

In any event, a political climate has been created in which there is little likelihood, at least in the short run, of significant change in regulatory legislation. There surely appears to be little public support for major departures from the status quo. In fact, a national public opinion poll taken in April 1982 reported that 58 percent of the sample surveyed agreed with the following statement:

> Protecting the environment is so important that requirements and standards cannot be too high and continuing environmental improvements must be made regardless of cost.

That was up from 45 percent favoring the statement in September 1981.

All this seems to explain why the line of mourners at the Task Force's demise was so short. Yet, there may be good reason to believe that any requiem for regulatory reform is premature. First of all, the regulatory review process continues. But, perhaps far more important, changing economic conditions may result in yet another shift in public attitudes and support for regulatory reform.

Looking back over the past two years, it is clear that this period coincided with a decline in the pace of new industrial construction. In such a situation, the obstacles to new facilities represented by the array of environmentally oriented and other regulatory hurdles is not a key factor in the course of the economy. But, in contrast, the coming year or two seem likely to be a time of industrial expansion. Thus, the thicket of regulatory permits and approvals will once again become a serious obstacle to economic growth—and the public likely will react to that turn of events.

A new Task Force on Regulatory Reform might well be required in that new environment. Personally, I prefer the term *reform* to *relief* for a very basic reason. The fundamental concern is not necessarily to lighten the compliance burdens placed on business. Rather, regulatory reformers are motivated by the desire that the citizen-taxpayer-consumer receive the benefits of a more enlightened, more cost-effective system of regulation. Just as it is the consumer who receives the basic benefits of regulation, so it is the consumer who bears the ultimate costs. This explains, of course, why economists are so fond of benefit/cost analysis as a guide to a more effective regulatory regime. Such analyses do not assure that the existing regulatory apparatus will be reduced, but that any change will promote a more efficient functioning of regulatory activity.

The present is the appropriate time for developing the groundwork for a new phase of regulatory reform, one that focuses on revising and updating the substantive laws governing the regulatory process. Preparing the proper foundation of information and analysis necessary to regain the earlier momentum of positive public support is indeed a challenge to economic education and to education generally.

In developing public support for regulatory reform, it will be vital to distinguish between merely reducing the burdens on business and the positive approach of seeking more efficient and more effective modes of regulation. As long as regulatory changes are seen as primarily conferring benefits on business, quite properly there will be limited public support for reform. I must admit that I share the public attitude that business executives are paid to deal with difficult problems, including the ones that arise in complying with regulation. Rather, regulatory reform is fundamentally a consumer issue. It is the consumer who ultimately pays the costs of regulation and it is the consumer who will be the key beneficiary of regulatory reform.

This volume of essays raises key questions about why and how a more enlightened, cost-effective system of regulation would result in greater benefits to the citizen-taxpayer-consumer. It contributes a needed conceptual framework for developing a new phase in regulatory reform.

PREFACE

The centennial celebration of the founding of the University of Texas at Austin has provided a fitting occasion on which to inaugurate a series of policy studies on the proper relationship between governmental institutions and the private sector.

In his provocative book, AMERICA'S TECHNOLOGY SLIP,* Simon Ramo explores in great detail a key premise—namely, that universities and private industry constitute the principal sources of expertise in innovation, whereas government policies of overregulation, overtaxing, and a general weakening of the motivational environment in our nation impose serious constraints on the prudent development of innovative technology. If the private enterprise sector is to be freed to pursue a proper role in technological advance, Ramo urges the university to engage in serious consideration of its responsibility in laying the groundwork for a higher quality of creativity in matching science and technology to social needs and in making the tradeoffs required to meet them. As the embodiment of a free marketplace of ideas, the university must assume leadership in clarifying confusion about the optimum roles of government agencies and private enterprise initiatives.

The College of Engineering at the University of Texas recognizes its responsibility for leadership in this difficult task. The Chair of Free Enterprise, endowed by private donors in 1976, is dedicated to exploring innovative policies for restructuring the relationship of government to the private sector. This volume of essays—a product of a Centennial Faculty/Executive Seminar held in April 1983—takes an initial step toward rethinking a new policy.

The generosity, foresight, and dedication of an anonymous donor has made this undertaking possible. Standing on the threshold of its second century, the University and the College of Engineering hope to continue to express gratitude to their generous donors through publications such as this.

Earnest F. Gloyna

---

*New York: John Wiley & Sons, 1980.

AN EDITOR'S OVERVIEW

Conflicting claims provide the energy of scholarly existence, the engine of human progress. Truth will eventually emerge, no matter the current constraints or values imposed as long as all viewpoints are expressed freely and exposed widely. The criticism that academics argue both sides from the same facts is confirmation of the gravity of the problem not the comedy of intellectual endeavor. Form is as important as content. By allowing opposing opinions to clash in controversy, we enrich substance and ensure continuance.

Too often, however, the pendulum swings too far. Hard debate is stifled, real choice choked off. When parochial position masquerades as a priori assumption, honesty and momentum are sacrificed on the altar of custom and inertia.

Before the middle 60s environmental issues had minimal impact hardly worth the bother of the media or scholar. A decade later we were inundated, deluged, and swamped. It was downright dangerous not to voice alarm. Was there anything more important, more vital for human survival? Not in the early 70s.

The flip side, of course, was perception, not reality. Truth, whatever it was (or is), hadn't changed during those intervening years, only opinion had. Yet the form of fancy seemed to transform the substance of fact. (Berkeley would have loved it—that's the bishop not the university.) Recently, the swing has been arcing back; but since the driving mechanism is more economic necessity than analytical accuracy, we are no closer to truth.

This book should be read in the spirit of free inquiry. If propositions espoused are controversial, even offensive, that's good. If positions are founded on faulty data, or constructed with illogical reasoning, that's bad. The reader remains judge.

Robert Lawrence Kuhn

ACKNOWLEDGEMENTS

This volume of essays and its potential readers are beneficiaries of the commitment, competence, and dedication of several persons.

Without the generosity of an anonymous donor the University of Texas Centennial Faculty Seminar, from which this publication is derived, would never have been possible.

Without the editorial competence and generosity of Robert Kuhn, Senior Research Fellow in creative and innovative management at the University of Texas, and my co-editor, all our efforts would have been in vain. His patience and faith in the importance of the ideas contained here are a valued tribute.

Thoughtful suggestions and constructive criticisms were kindly offered by George W. Pickering and George H. Blank.

With high skill, diligence, and meticulous attention to detail, Betty L. Dees has fulfilled the most intemperate expectations throughout innumerable revisions of manuscripts. Frances Croy and Esther Moore have also generously assisted in the preparation of manuscripts.

To the contributing authors and participants in this first seminar, our esteem and gratitude.

Margaret N. Maxey
Austin, Texas
January, 1984

CONTENTS

Introduction

Margaret N. Maxey

> Unlike any other type of society,
> capitalism inevitably and by virtue of
> the very logic of its civilization
> creates, educates and subsidizes a
> vested interest in social unrest.
> —Joseph Schumpeter

The tendency of any generation to believe that its dangers are utterly unique, unprecedented, and irreversible appears to rest on firm psychological foundation. After all, each individual acquires experience by a process which resists sameness and complacency. We seek simplicity yet learn to mistrust it. Sooner or later, our quest for certainty becomes confounded by the certitude of skeptics. Prophets of doom may be honored by instant success in garnering public attention, but they eventually become dishonored as false prophets when human innovation averts their predictions.

In 1798 British economist Thomas Malthus predicted that the world was on the brink of starvation due to a tragic imbalance between food production and exponential population growth. His so-called "iron law" turned out to be neither iron nor law in the wake of innovations in mechanized agriculture and a revolution in chemical fertilizers. His underestimation of the power of human intelligence did not extend to his own. In short, the unique aspect of hazards confronted by each generation appears to derive justification from the subjective conditions under which different personalities experience anew the realities of the world.

However sound in theory, a psychological account of claims that present dangers are unique does not satisfy. Some dangers may well reside in the eye of the beholder. But when beholders multiply, mobilize, and express moral indignation about the presumed legitimacy of an established social order, clearly more is required. Piecemeal efforts to focus the lens of beholders is insufficient.

Mounting concern among American citizens about unprecedented threats to our health and safety—indeed to the genetic inheritance

1

and even survival of the human species—has increased dramatically in but one generation. Analysts of Western industrialized economies express amazement at a puzzling anomaly:[1] Citizens whose standard of living ranks among the highest in today's world, who enjoy political freedoms and social amenities unparalleled in human history, have nevertheless developed strongly negative attitudes toward the quality of their lives and their environment. Public confidence in human control over the physical world through time-honored sources of safety—science and technology—has been transformed into skepticism and doubt in a remarkably brief period of 15 to 20 years. Confidence in social institutions has undergone a dramatic decline. Fears and fantasies have multiplied. Scare tactics have all but obliterated a civil exchange of reasonable arguments. As in previous times of deep historical change (the end of the Middle Ages, the end of the last century, post-World War I Germany), we now witness an eruption of superstition, a withdrawal into mysticism, a surge of emotionalism and fascination with disaster movies. The desire for a simpler life, for a return to a low-energy and low-consumption society, are commonly expressed. This desire becomes linked with an anti-technology sentiment, a mounting distrust of specialists engaged in applying advanced technologies in society. An anti-expert attitude calls in question the credibility of anyone who appears to have a stake in scientific research or technological applications.

Of what are Americans fearful? Mary Douglas and Aaron Wildavsky offer an ironic response: "Nothing much really, except the food they eat, the water they drink, the air they breathe, the land they live on, and the energy they use." Their answer leads to a key question: "How can we explain the sudden, widespread, across-the-board concern about environmental pollution and personal contamination that has arisen in the Western world in general and with particular force in the United States?"[2]

We cannot understand our situation if we cling to the view that real knowledge of an external world should be allocated to experts in the physical sciences, while illusions or mistaken perceptions pertain to the realm of personal psychology. Given this faulty division, dangers are assumed to be inherent in a physical situation, and the risks they pose are objectively ascertainable by experts. When perceptions or attitudes toward risk among non-experts appear to be out of conformity with "actual risks," it is assumed that the gap "ought to be closed in only one direction—toward the opinion of experts. . . ."[3] According to this view, subjective personality traits presumably account for a bias toward risk as a whole: An individual is either a risk-taker or a risk-avoider. Unfortunately, a subjectivist account cannot explain two critical problems: Why is it that experts disagree? Why does one and the same individual fear environmental dangers to the exclusion of others which are more immediately life-threatening?

A subjectivist and individualistic account of risk perception will not answer these questions. We need a cultural approach as proposed by Douglas and Wildavsky in *Risk and Culture*. A cultural approach begins with a simple question: On what basis do people decide that certain risks are worth taking, while others should be relegated to secondary consideration? In view of statistics dramatizing the premature loss of life from fire, why are alleged cancer-causing agents such as asbestos or tris judged more fearsome than fire which both substances were developed to prevent? If indeed the prevention of cancer in all its forms is of paramount concern, why is public concern not mobilized to prevent leisure-time sunbathing which induces skin cancer? Is our primary moral concern to prevent the most people from suffering a premature mortality or debilitating morbidity? Then should not public concern about starvation in third world countries take moral precedence over the fate of the snail darter or the Furbish lousewort or the El Segundo Blue butterfly? Neither a subjectivist approach nor a moral calculus can do justice to these questions.

Douglas and Wildavsky maintain that only a cultural theory of risk selection as a product of cultural bias and social criticism can account for the anomalies we encounter in Western industrialized economies. "Only a cultural approach can integrate moral judgments about how to live with empirical judgments about what the world is like."[4] A cultural theory of risk selection is wholistic: the social environment, the perceiving subject, and risk selection principles are integrated in one system. The risks we choose to control or mitigate, individually and collectively, are integral to the choices we make with respect to the best way to organize social relations, to protect shared values, and to devise institutional mechanisms for formulating public policy.

In the current risk versus safety debate, each side accuses the other of serving the vested interests of preferred social institutions. Whether the arguments originate from the "industrial establishment" or the "danger establishment," each side accuses the other of irrational bias, of misperceptions of real risks, of subversion of the public interest. Given this impasse, Douglas and Wildavsky observe that it would be a serious error to treat questions about "acceptable risk" as if they could be answered by calculationg the actual versus perceived probability of danger (risk) "out there" resulting from man's interaction with nature, in contrast to determining what level of uncertainty is acceptable "in here" within the rational person's mind. From the perspective of cultural analysis, the primary task is not one of devising a philosophy of risk based on technical estimations of how nature and technology may (or may not) interact to produce latent risks of contamination to ecosystems or endangered species, including man. The problem for cultural analysis is, first and foremost, to learn how to recognize cultural bias toward preferred forms of social organization as a precondition for recognizing risk selection as the instrument for inducing wanted and rejecting unwanted forms of social organization. There can be no reconciliation of disagreements about levels of "acceptable risk" until there is clear recognition that differing political agendas for changing present social institutions and policies underlie the selection of physical risks for public concern and governmental control.

The essays comprising this volume have not been developed with reference to any overarching theory about cultural bias as the source of risk selection for precipitating social change. Nevertheless, they reflect an underlying and unifying theme—one which suggests that present forms of social organization no longer elicit public trust and legitimacy for reasons that are normative and moral, rather than merely economic and technical. Consequently, these essays might well be read as preliminary and unintended tests of the validity of a cultural theory about how democratic social change in a modern technological society is occurring—for better or worse.

To establish some background for examining a cultural theory, three preliminary questions are in order. First, what cultural climate of opinion has given shape to public attitudes over the past 20 years, with the result that there are now widely diverse value judgments about threats to the quality of public health, safety, and the environment? Second, does "public interest regulation," enacted in response to these alleged threats, reflect a change in physical realities or a transformation in political alignments? Third, what indications emerge from these criticisms that might point toward a new agenda for social change?

In the first section of these introductory remarks we examine several major ideas with significant influence on public opinion, bearing in mind three cultural phenomena, namely that 20 percent of the population is identifiably phobic, hence a ready constituency for regulating life to "perfect safety"; second, that a large segment of the population has become super-affluent while making only marginal contributions to social and economic well-being; and third, that the teenage population, although not yet economically productive, represents a $50 billion a year market. In a second section, we examine theories attempting to account for the relation between the emergence of a new political class and a cacaphony of calls for regulatory reform as an ambivalent instrument for managing technological risk. A third section suggests how the major problems of regulatory reform are being raised by the essays in this volume, indicating the emergence of a new political agenda.

A CULTURAL CLIMATE OF OPINION

Nearly 60 years have elapsed since the eminent mathematician and philosopher Alfred North Whitehead pointed out that it is inherent in the very nature of modern science with "its progressive thought and progressive technology" to impose on humanity the necessity for wandering, for making "the transition through time, from generation to generation, a true migration into uncharted seas of adventure." Far from being a fearsome liability to be avoided at any cost, Whitehead suggests that "the very benefit of wandering is that it is dangerous and needs skills to avert evils. . . . It is the business of the future to be dangerous."[5]

Even to suggest that what is dangerous might actually call forth skills with enduring benefits to humanity comes as a shocking proposition in today's cultural climate. It would appear that the business of the present is being transacted in the coin of apocalyptic predictions. Influential scientists, philosophers, and political leaders warn that science and technology will have adverse consequences of cosmic proportions: the human race is rapidly poisoning itself with chemical pollutants; the social order is being weakened through indiscriminate growth in prosperity to the point of "growthmania"; the essential nature of the human species is endangered by overbreeding and by tampering with its genetic inheritance.

An influential body of literature has reinforced the conviction that planetary impacts will result from faulty technological choices.

Vance Packard's best seller *The Waste Makers* warned Americans in 1960 that precious limited resources were being squandered by technologists deliberately trained to design consumer products for planned obsolescence.[6] Two years later, *Silent Spring* by Rachel Carson used a powerful literary metaphor, an apocryphal fable about a silent spring in anytown of America's heartland, to dramatize her message. By introducing chemical pesticides into the food chain, she warned, we are irreversibly destroying our natural world and planting seeds of disease and death for future generations. Invoking Robert Frost's familiar poem, she concluded by exhorting us to take the other fork of the road, the one "less traveled by," as nothing other than our last and only chance "to reach a destination that assures the preservation of our earth."[7]

Subsequently, a decade of literature reiterating the theme that a technological imperative would have dire cosmic consequences reached its climax in 1972. A study commissioned by the Club of Rome, aided by voluminous computer printouts, offered four possible scenarios for reaching the "limits to growth." On the basis of its extrapolations, the report was almost universally interpreted to conclude that a rapid depletion of finite resources, destruction of the life-sustaining biosphere from air and water pollution, starvation and economic collapse from a population explosion would inevitably, by default of human response, lead to the catastrophe of "overshoot and collapse."[8] Commenting on the report, William Tucker observes:

> . . . the MIT experts published a book saying that, because the model had been unable to avoid the overshoot-and-collapse scenario, *the world itself would be unable to avoid it as well.* This became one of the stories of the decade, and the foundation for the environmental movement's argument that stopping growth was the only way to avoid a world collapse.[9]

The authors of *The Limits to Growth*, as well as *Blueprint for Survival*,[10] and such writers as economist Herman Daly (who coined the term growthmania)[11] followed a simple logical deduction: since an eco-catastrophe will result from exponential growth in a finite world, ecological salvation lies in the stationary state allowing only small increments within a carefully planned equilibrium. Daly concluded that "the stationary state economy is, therefore, a necessity."[12]

While Daly believes that growth can be contained in a steady-state economy, Nicholas Georgescu-Roegen takes a more dire view of growth itself on apparently metaphysical grounds.[13] In Georgescu-Roegen's view, Daly is as mistaken as Malthus. Not only was Malthus too optimistic, but he also made a fundamental error, because he thought some growth was still possible before disaster would befall:

> This error is the assumption that population may grow beyond any limit both in number and time *provided that it does not grow too rapidly.*[14]

According to Georgescu-Roegen, the law of entropy demands not only that current growth must come to a halt; it must be reversed. He maintains that the favorite thesis of both standard and Marxist economies (i.e., that the power of technology is without limits) is confounded by the law of entropy—namely, the incontrovertible fact that every transaction man makes with nature entails an irrevocable dissipation of matter and energy, coupled with a natural entropic degradation. An ensuing social disorganization is inevitable, as competing patterns of consumption aggravate pollution of the environment by "garbojunk" which is not "recyclable" as *available* matter but only as dissipated matter.[15]

Technology cannot repeal the essence of the second law of thermodynamics: ". . . that in an isolated system, available matter-energy is continuously and irrevocably degraded into the unavailable state."[16] Based on the premise that the earth is not an open, but a closed system which exchanges only energy with its environment, Georgescu-Roegen argues that the entropic problem of mankind cannot be resolved by such specious ideas as the expectation that technological creativity can and will improve exponentially, nor by the "fallacy of endless substitution" which amounts to an economist's conjuring trick.[17] Instead, Georgescu-Roegen exhorts mankind to adopt a minimal bioeconomic program—namely, a discontinuation of the production of all instruments of war, international aid to underdeveloped nations enabling them to arrive as quickly as possible at a good (not luxurious) life, lowering population to a level which can be adequately fed with organic agriculture alone, the abandonment of energy from coal and uranium in favor of direct use of solar energy, and curing ourselves of the disease of fashion and morbid craving for expensive gadgets such as second cars and golfcarts.[18] He expresses pessimism that mankind will ever adopt a bioeconomic program that constricts human comfort. His conclusion is lugubrious:

> Perhaps, the destiny of man is to have a short, but fiery, exciting and extravagant life rather than a long, uneventful and vegetative existence. Let other species—the amoebas, for example—which have no spiritual ambitions inherit an earth still bathed in plenty of sunshine.[19]

It is neither insignificant nor incidental that Georgescu-Roegen makes reference to the absence of "spiritual ambitions" as decisive in precluding a more noble destiny for mankind. Garrett Hardin has not hesitated to identify ecology with "the Death of Providence," nor to interpret the struggle between ecologists and anti-ecologists as a religious struggle. According to his interpretation of the theological concept of Providence, Hardin declares that the equation God = Providence = Progress must be dethroned and displaced by "The Religion of Ecology."[20] He asks, "Why are ecologists and environmentalists so feared and hated?" In part it is because they are advocating ideas new and alarming to the public; but major opposition must be attributed to the fact that ecology is seen as an attack on widely held religious values, expressed in political and economic faiths which an ecological program subverts. Some measure of anti-ecology sentiments can be taken, says Hardin, by their selection of literary titles—*The Disaster Lobby: Prophets of Ecological Doom and Other Absurdities*, or *The Doomsday Syndrome* described as "an attack on pessimism," and *Models of Doom*—as well as intemperate invectives hurled at ecologists: "crackpots, ecofreaks, neo-Luddites, pessimists, bird watchers, pansy pluckers, merchants of doom, spoilers."[21]

Whether transcendent or immanent, the God of Progress and its religious dogmas are bound to be displaced by the Religion of Ecology ("a set of beliefs that binds us"). For Hardin, this religion must be built on two dogmas contradicting traditional beliefs. Instead of "*The Dogma of Aladdin's Lamp*: If we can dream of it, we can invent it," ecological religion proclaims "*The Dogma of Limits*: Not all things are possible (though death is!)" Instead of "*The Dogma of the Technological Imperative*: When we invent it, we are required to use it," a religion of ecology substitutes, "*The Dogma of*

Temperance: Every 'shortage' of supply is equally a 'longage' of demand; and, since the world is limited, the only way to sanity ultimately lies in restraining demand."[22]

Confronted as we are in today's world with enormously complex problems, Hardin observes that it is entirely natural to believe in, and expect help from, a benevolent God—transcendent or immanent; but when optimism and the pleasant reassurance of divine benevolence become criteria for progress in a limited world, the religious idea of "benevolent progress" becomes pernicious. Hardin expresses hope that when people recognize that the conflict of our time is fundamentally a religious one, then it may be possible to solve it. Meanwhile, the Religion of Ecology must be clear about two aspects of progress qualified by Hardin as *"properly understood:"*

> Progress will no longer be equated with technological progress alone, and the concept of progress must be divested of the illusion of Providence. 'Man makes himself,' Jean Paul Sartre said, and it is high time that we try to reshape human beings into mature creatures who no longer depend on the support of a benevolent Providence (under any name).[23]

Hardin is not alone in recognizing the primacy of religion. Herman Daly considers religion to be the Ultimate End and final Ordering Principle for defining both intermediate ends (ethics) and intermediate means (political economy). In setting priorities, Daly distinguishes the moral science of political economy from "politic economics." The latter is an amoral game which "tries to buy off social conflict by abolishing scarcity—by promising more things for more people, with less for no one, forever and ever—all vouchsafed by the amazing grace of compound interest."[24] Orthodox and Marxist growth economists have been bemused, he says, by a visionary expectation that present constraints will be superseded by future evolutionary capabilities; in short, "Infinite means plus infinite ends equals growth forever."[25] Since they believe that continual economic growth is biophysically possible, "politic economists" manifest an arena of moral concern that does not take seriously the poor, nor subhuman life, nor future generations. Only bioeconomists are going to succeed in cracking "the nut of growth mania." However, to do so, says Daly, they must adopt a more enlightened strategy. Hammering from above with moral arguments alone can be deflected by optimistic biophysical assumptions, while hammering from below with biophysical arguments will be absorbed with an elastic morality. (For example, "Man's manifest destiny is to colonize space" or "Growth itself is the Ultimate End.") Daly is explicit and forceful in recommending the proper strategy for bioeconomists:

> Growth chestnuts have to be placed on the unyielding anvil of biophysical realities, and then crushed with the hammer of moral argument. The entropy law and ecology provide the biophysical anvil. Concern for future generations, subhuman life, and inequities in current distribution of wealth provide the moral hammer.[26]

The persuasiveness of such a strategy seems abundantly evident in light of the widespread influence of environmental thinkers over the past 20 years. Moral concern for future generations has been amplified through the multiplication of uncertainties regarding technical and ethical aspects of disposal programs for radioactive wastes.[27] Concern for subhuman life and "endangered species" has been manifest in costly delays or cancellations of projects for energy resource development or flood control or irrigation.[28] Inequities attributed to a maldistribution of wealth, and to uncompensated suffering from fear of risks, have become the focus of public debate about a decontrol of natural gas, acid precipitation, and radiation exposures from nuclear technologies.[29]

Activists as well as scholars have come to see a religious issue in these ecology questions. David Pesonen is a case in point. Giving up his position with the Sierra Club, he led the opposition in the Battle of Bodega Bay against a proposed nuclear power plant over a period from 1958 to 1964 when delays and public opposition caused the project to be abandoned. Pesonen himself reports that he was changed dramatically: "From fighting to preserve a patch of shoreline," he was "converted to opposition to nuclear power." His description of that conversion experience conveys its mystical and religious dimensions:

> It was a beautiful evening, a touch of fog. I had a feeling of the enormousness of what we were fighting; that it was anti-life. I had an insight into the mentality of it. I began to see it as the ultimate brutality, short of nuclear weapons.[30]

It is arguable that Hardin's Religion of Ecology, and the Entropist Paradigm of Georgescu-Roegen and his followers have not emerged as mainstream influences shaping cultural attitudes. However, there is reason to suspect that this is only a question of time. Growing public attention to the books of Jeremy Rifkin, especially the reception given *Entropy: A New World View* and the acclaim accorded it by such opinion leaders as Senator Mark Hatfield, Hugh Downs, Hazel Henderson, and Samuel Epstein among others, indicates that the public may have only begun to appreciate the cultural power exerted by a paradigmatic idea.[31]

With such powerful ideas shaping a cultural climate of opinion over the past 20 years, it is to be expected that they have spawned a virtual torrent of new versions of "public interest regulation"—for pollution control, occupational safety and health, consumer product quality, and safety. They have also raised in a new way certain perennial issues of ethical and political thought which have been clearly expressed by George Pickering: ". . . the nature of the state (responsible control), the nature of citizenship (rights), the nature of social power (fairness), and the nature of human well-being, material and otherwise (purpose)."[32] Underlying these perennial issues is the ultimate issue of American political life, currently distilled into the meaning and fate of another powerful idea: liberal democracy—commonly referred to as private or free enterprise—the marriage of a market economy with representative political institutions.[33]

PUBLIC INTEREST REGULATION AND POLITICAL TRANSFORMATIONS

David Vogel reminds us that "the public-interest movement . . . represents a historically conditioned response to the problems posed for the American politics by the rise of the large business corporation in the latter third of the nineteenth century."[34] The movement was nurtured by the ethos of the Progressive era—tracing its lineage to Lockean notions of reason, science, growth, properity for all, the rule of law, the idea of progress—providing coherence to basic values of the liberal tradition. Around the turn of the century, what is called the Old Regulation took shape as progressive and populist political compromises were blended into a coherent body of political views. Whereas the older regulatory agencies established between 1887 and the outbreak of World War II were organized cartel-like on an industry-by-industry basis (transportation, airlines, banking, telecommunications), the new regulatory agencies have been deliberately organized along functional lines, with their jurisdictions cutting across industry boundaries. Despite this clear and distinct difference, the "iron triangle" theory—that is, that a regulatory agency, the regulated industry, and Congressional oversight committees form an unholy trio to protect special interests—continues to be the chief critical tool in the armamentarium of social science and journalistic literature on regulatory agencies.[35]

Paul Weaver has expressed considerable dismay that this literature continues to perpetuate two profound misconceptions: that regulation is primarily an instrument of economic policy, and that it is a manifestation of interest-group politics at the expense of the public interest.[36] Such literature either ignores the fact that "iron triangle" theories purporting to explain why regulatory malfunctions are due to "special interests" happen to be mutually inconsistent; or it seems ignorant of the truth that any such iron triangle "was and is a political coalition like any other—sometimes successful, at other times not, and always dependent over the long run on the good opinion of the people."[37] Old regulatory agencies were mandated by law to prevent monopolies, promote competition, and protect the economic well-being of small businesses subject to their jurisdiction. New regulatory agencies are for the most part explicitly forbidden by law to protect economic interests, either of consumers or of small businesses, by a consideration of economic costs and consequences of foregone benefits (for example, when banning suspected carcinogens under the Delaney amendment, or when establishing and enforcing ambient air-quality standards).

Defenders have justified government regulation as a means for remedying "market imperfections" and for "internalizing externalities." Critics have ridiculed the economic absurdities that are everywhere in evidence as studies multiply. However, Weaver insists that both arguments are beside the point:

> The real purpose of government regulation is not to correct the deficiencies of markets but to transcend markets altogether—which is to say, government regulation is not economic policy but social policy. It is an effort to advance a conception of the public interest apart from, and often opposed to, the outcomes of the marketplace and, indeed, the entire idea of a market economy.[38]

Economists with widely divergent political views think regulatory policy should make economic sense, but it was never intended to, and therefore rarely does. Being social policy, government regulation is a manifestation not of special interests but of class politics, that is, of values held by "groups that possess a distinctive 'culture' and relationship to the means of production, and intend to dominate and define the society, i.e. to rule."[39]

Technological risk and its regulation have become primary objects of class politics in the new cultural climate. How one goes about characterizing class politics in general, and the emergence of a new political class in particular, seem to be the key to understanding why a cacophony of calls for regulatory reform does not a symphony make.

There is little dispute about the genesis of a new political class. In the period after World War II, a growing majority of America's population entered higher education producing citizenry with talents for mobilizing words and people. As a consequence the United States economy of necessity shifted its weight in the direction of the service sector.[40] This shift explains, in part, the change in direction taken by the public interest movement. The economic boom and the educational boom worked together to produce a broad class of articulate and critical "service intellectuals."[41] They appear to be uncommitted to commerce and industry, since these boundaries have become irretrievably blurred. With a level of education as high if not higher than the old captains of industry, service intellectuals have been less disposed to suffer subordination.

> Where before, engaged in production, educated people could see why collective constraint might be necessary, working in the service sector suggests such subordination is unnecessary. Removed from the 'firing line,' not having to meet the 'bottom line,' the boundary between service and production becomes one between border and center. The more the means of production are ideas rather than things, the less the hiearchical organization of production appears essential.[42]

Be this as it may, opinions are very much divided on how to characterize the new political class.

Several theorists seem to suggest that an easy distinction to make—one that can account for much of the political turmoil and erosion of public confidence in social institutions—is that an "Old Business Class" has become pitted against a "New Class" whose

power base lies in "the knowledge industry" where statist instruments of reform are easily wielded in an adversarial struggle for
power.[43] The very simplicity of this distinction reminds us of
Whitehead's admonition to mistrust it.

Price's Four Estates

In *The Scientific Estate*[44] Don K. Price outlines three ways in
which an original understanding of liberal democracy, embodied by
the Founding Fathers in our constitution, has been substantially
changed by the development of scientific technology. First, the
public and private sectors have moved closer together; second, a new
order of complexity has been introduced into public affairs; third,
the original scheme of checks and balances in government has
undergone significant change. Power is now exercised in a
technological society in a manner that Price calls "a diffusion of
sovereignty" throughout "four estates": the political estate (elected
political leaders), the administrative estate (managers and administrators) in both private and public corporations), the professional estate (medicine, engineering, law, education, the media), and
the scientific estate (scientists doing pure research in universities, corporations, and government). The original diffusion of power
established by the constitution has been altered by circumstances.
According to Price:

> The process of responsible policy making . . . is a process of in-
> teraction among the scientists, professional leaders, ad-
> ministrators and politicians; ultimate authority is with the politi-
> cians but the initiative is quite likely to rest with others, in-
> cluding scientists in our government."[45]

Dividing lines between estates are anything but hard and fast. "Every
person, in his actual work, is concerned to some extent with all four
functions."[46] Consequently a new system of checks and balances
now operates within society as a whole, and not merely within the
government. This amounts to a new democratization of knowledge.
Correspondingly it alters our former notions of power and property,
of capitalism and democracy. Price says: "We are now obliged to
think about the political functions of various types of people not on
the basis of the property they own but of what they know, and of the

professional skills they command."[47] In short, the four estates have redeployed concentrations of power in ways that both safeguard and strengthen private enterprise and democratic political institutions.

Winner's Technological Politics

Among those who refuse to interpret this development as a positive gain for liberal democracy, Langdon Winner is representative. He complains that Price's model of contemporary politics with its "fortuitous rise of a new pluralism" does not rescue us from the rule of "faceless technocrats."[48] At best, liberal democracy has won a Pyrrhic victory, since the system actually works by maintaining a delicate balance among the estates, and goes out of kilter if and when "an aroused public" demands more participation. Moreover, Winner complains that "Price begins his analysis of political power after a great deal of the available power has already been meted out and the possible problems associated with it simply dismissed."[49] In other words, in the political game among the four estates, Winner thinks that democracy plays only at halftime.

For Winner the source of domination and oppression ruling all forms of modern thought and activity is "autonomous technology."[50] His basic premise is that a technology-out-of-control is self evident and that it cannot be mastered by philosophies content with thoughtful passivity or by a "new ethic" of noble sentiments. Although he does not explicitly characterize a new political class, he nonetheless builds up his case about the political dominance of an autonomous technology (in contrast to its tool-use function in solving problems) in such a way that a theory of "technological politics" enables him to collapse the distinction between who governs and what governs in an advanced technological society. He finds no compelling evidence to support a power elite thesis which would simplify attempts to control technology's ubiquitous oppression. However Winner finds John Kenneth Gailbraith's description of the components and values embodied in an autonomous "technostructure" in *The New Industrial State*[51] a much more enlightened and credible portrait of the power relationships in modern American society than the Four Estates of Price.

Nevertheless, Winner prefers to develop his own theory of *technological politics*. He derives it from "a theory of culture, a theory of the patterns human institutional life, structures of consciousness and conduct, take in advanced technological societies. It is . . . a theory of culture with teeth."[52] Due to the technological imperative and reverse adaptation (i.e. ends are transformed to suit the available means), Winner articulates his key notion: "The influence of socially necessary technical systems begins to constrain rather than liberate political choice."[53] Initially a technical system is intended as a means to an end, but then requires its own means (resources, laws, regulations), eventually leading society to decisions and actions far removed from its original purpose.

Decision makers may appear to bow to "indelible pragmatic necessity" but have actually succumbed to technological politics. He recognizes that Price and Gailbraith were unable to locate a distinctive role for political actors, or a single and cohesive technical elite. However, they do locate the basis for an increasingly dominant mode of enfranchisement in the authority of scientific and technical knowledge. Winner claims superiority for his approach because it "traces the fundamental source of important decisions in matters involving technology beyond the role of any particular class or elite—technical, scientific, administrative, or political—to the configuration of technological conditions themselves." [54] His theory is neither elitist nor has it eliminated the position of the traditional political actor. Instead it embraces a much broader vision: prior to any real act of political determination, the central agenda of political problems and even their solutions are largely predetermined by technological circumstances.[55]

Winner's theory of technological politics does not end the matter of building support for his case about autonomous technology. He not only goes on to evaluate this theory against expectations of controlling technology found in orthodox Marxism and Leninism, but he also considers expectations that eventually we shall develop tools of intellectual synthesis which will deal effectively with extreme complexity and information overload—for examples; by systems theory and analysis or by artificial intelligence or by a science of sciences.

Through default of intellectual capacities to deliver on these expectations, alternative strategies have surfaced. Among them Winner finds Charles Lindblom's philosophy of "disjointed incrementalism" to be of interest. According to this strategy, a decision maker need not have some all-encompassing, rational-comprehensive understanding of how an entire system works down to its intricate complexities. Since his moves can and should be small ones, he need only anticipate the consequences of changes made step by step with reference to existing conditions and policies. In Linblom's words, "Only those policies are considered whose known or expected consequences differ incrementally from the status quo."[56] Winner interprets this strategy as an elaborate justification for ignoring concerns about the values of society, indeed for ignoring the public once and for all.[57] He draws no comfort from Lindblom's description of how a system of multiple, overlapping government regulatory agencies comes closest to assuring that this division of labor provides a watchdog for the important interests and values of society. In "The Science of Muddling Through" Lindblom argues that our system works because a pluralism of organized interests in the polity is best protected by a pluralism in the government bureaucracy.

> Without claiming that every interest has a sufficiently powerful watchdog, it can be argued that our system often can assure a more comprehensive regard for the values of the whole society than any attempt at intellectual comprehensiveness.[58]

Winner concludes, however, that the apparent strength of the Lindblom theory of disjunctive incrementalism becomes a source of an intriguing puzzle. If "the intelligence of democracy"[59] (in Lindblom's phrase) consists in keeping civic bafflement over society's unintelligibility isolated from the ability of each group and individual to take proper care of their own little spheres of activity, what can account for a harmonious outcome? Winner asks whether interventions of a *deus ex machina* can be expected to bring about beneficent results from disjointed incremental actions of individuals and groups who have little knowledge of or concern for the good of each other—much less of society as a whole.

The skepticism implicit in Winner's question leads him to consider how his idea of autonomous technology merges with Adam Smith's classic formulation about "the invisible hand."[60] Smith wrote that, when the individual intends only his own security, works industriously to produce what is of greatest value, and intends only his own gain, he is nonetheless "led by an invisible hand to promote an end which was no part of his intention. Nor is it always the worse for society that it was no part of it. By pursuing his own interest he frequently promotes that of society more effectually than when he really intends to promote it."[61] According to Linblom's updated version of the Invisible Hand, complex societies "can avoid dissolution or intolerable dislocation only by meeting certain preconditions, among them that certain kinds of change are admissable only if they occur slowly."[62] With undeterred consistency, Winner presses his case for autonomous technology on two fronts: "Is there a level of complexity or rapidity of change (or the two combined) in which the beneficence of the aggregate process is no longer insured?" Observing that modern technological society appears at times to have gone incrementally mad, and that one finds in a modern city confusion and social ills on a colossal scale, Winner asks: "Which of two invisible hands—the benevolent or malevolent—has the firmest grasp? Which hand is more likely to thrive in a situation of increasing confusion?"[63]

When all is said and done, Winner's portrait of the political landscape is peopled not so much with a "new political class" in responsible control of a technological Leviathan, as with a populace of somnambulists unaware that "technology is itself a political phenomenon" because it "now legislates the conditions of human existence."[64]

Those working in a utilitarian-pluralist framework with the expectation that they can devise ways of regulating technology (environmentalists, Naderites, technology assessors, public-interest scientists) do not ask whether they will more likely succeed in "putting a more elegant administrative facade on old layers of reverse adapted rules, regulations, and practices," since they nourish a hope of new modes of implementing technology. These utilitarian-pluralists do not realize that laws and regulations are actually a form of technology itself—a technique or apparatus or organization for having something and *having it over with*, thereby giving humankind *"a license to forget."*[65]

In conclusion, Winner modestly declines from offering a positive course of action, much less a grand strategy for subverting an ubiquitous technology. Instead he recommends an updated Luddism —not wielding a sledgehammer to smash machines but instead asking Socratic questions that will induce "appropriate technologies." The most effective among Luddite alternatives would be to refuse to repair the technological infrastructure (freeways, centralized power and water supplies, sewers) so as to "let dying artifice die."[66]

Pickering's Agenda-Setting Classes

Among those unwilling and unable to settle for an account of the current plight of liberal democracy in terms of a simplistic polarity (Old Business versus New Class) or a pansophic abstraction (autonomous technology), George Pickering introduces some penetrating real-world insights.[67] He locates the anguish of contemporary political conflict in a bifurcation, that is, in the unresolved and problematic aspects of affluence and technology, not in the elevation of one aspect of modern life to the exclusion of others. He focuses attention upon the concept of "political classes" as loose collections of social groups whose more or less common set of interests, values, and concerns in a given period define a "political agenda." In his view, contemporary political conflicts compel us to consider first the relationship of politics to social change, second the characteristics of an agenda-setting political class, and third how personal conceptions of a good life in a time of affluence are related to technological issues.

Pickering observes, with Samuel Lubell, that the dissolution of the Old Roosevelt Coalition during the late 1960s was accompanied by a radical shift in the role played by public opinion. Instead of being limited to the power to say yes or no, voters as well as presidents and other social managers were no longer content to channel their wishes through political parties. The public's demand for political visibility and control has had profound repercussions, reflected in Lubell's sobering comment:

> One of the most fearful aspects of our whole crisis is that the relationship of government and the governed is becoming a psychological contest, in which manipulation tends to eat away the principles on which men must agree if they are to be able to govern themselves.[68]

In the decade of the 1970s, a spate of "public interest lobbies" were organized from left to right on the political spectrum.[69] They introduced a new idea and strategy for achieving significant reform. In contrast to the reliance of progressives and New Dealers on a powerful executive branch to enact reforms in a neutral scientific manner, the leaders of public interest groups formed ad hoc coalitions with which to exert pressure on executive and legislative branches alike. Pickering emphasizes that the underlying source of this pressure has been an emerging theory of representation which Andrew McFarland has called "the theory of civic balance" nourished by "civic skepticism." It implies that "unless citizens form new institutions for representation, American government will have an elitist character, in that economic, political, and bureaucratic leaders will control public policy for their own benefit, rather than for the benefit of the public."[70]

Pickering identifies the emergence of a "new agenda-setting class" by distinguishing it from those of previous sociopolitical periods in American life. Using Everett Ladd's terminology,[71] Pickering notes that in the period of the Rural Republic (1790-1860) it was the independent land-owning farmers who set the political agenda. During the period of the Industrializing Nation (1865-1925) it was the entrepreneurial businessman. During the period of the Industrial State (1929-1970) it was the working class constituting the Roosevelt Coalition. The decade of the 1970s marks the beginning of a new sociopolitical period best characterized as a Technological Society. Ladd calls the new agenda-setting class of this period "the brain workers" or "the professional and managerial stratum."[72]

In tracing the history of the formation of this class, Pickering singles out statements of Christopher Lasch as especially illuminating.[73] One of the hallmarks of this class arises from the conflict between its professed vocation for social criticism, hence political detachment, yet its social engagement through attempts "to see society from the bottom up, or at least from the outside in."[74] Lasch explains:

> Because his vocation is to be a critic of society, in the most general sense, and because the value of his criticism is presumed to rest on a measure of detachment from the current scene, the intellectual's relation to the rest of society is never entirely comfortable; but it has not always been as uncomfortable as it is today in the United States.[75]

From its vantage point in the mid-1960s, says Lasch, this class saw itself "not simply as individuals involved in a common undertaking, the somewhat hazardous business of criticism, but as members of a beleaguered minority."[76]

To the extent that this is the case, Pickering sees an additional reason for locating the source of anguish in current political conflict not only in the problematic aspects of affluence and technology, but also in a struggle within the agenda-setting political class to define a majoritarian agenda, form coalitions, and appeal to the rest of the nation for support. Pickering insists—contrary to simple polarities pitting the Old Business class against a New Intellectual class—that "a Ralph Nader, a John Gardiner, and an Amory Lovins are as much a part of this class as a James Schlesinger, and Bernard Cohen, or an Alvin Weinberg."[77] To interpret the polarization within this class as a struggle for power between two antagonistic classes, observes Pickering, would be "one of the most deceptive, least substantial, and potentially damaging of the political perceptions which might come to prevail."[78] Given an internal division about what this dominant class can and ought to offer to the future of a technological society, Pickering remarks that this is a novel situation which will require a great deal of adjustment, adding civic bafflement to civic skepticism. "Another novelty is that we can expect the conflicts within this class, rather than the conflicts between this class and other classes in society, to set the issues, the tone, and the ultimate political agenda for a period of time."[79] Since there are no defenders of the status quo in the current lineup of conflicts, all the contenders exchange arguments about which kinds of change are most desired and most feared. Yet hope prevails "even when they include strains of nostalgia for a lost communal dimension or a lost corporate or scientific autonomy."[80]

Pickering echoes Price in his emphasis on the political transformation of scientific and professional expertise. Price observed that the new political role of scientific powers of knowing and acting could be mutually endangering, that is, scientists might use them to gain a dangerous control over traditional political institutions; conversely, political forces might attempt to govern or restrict the pursuit of scientific truth. Price has counseled that the Political Estate and the Scientific Estate should remain separate yet collaborative. "The scientists and professionals, in order to do their jobs, must be involved in the formulation of policy, and must be granted wide discretion in their own work."[81] Similarly, "politicians and administrators must control the key aspects of technological plans if they are to protect their own ability to make responsible decisions."[82] Price was confident that the checks and balances among the four estates had been effectively established and that a "pluralist consensus" could be counted on.

Writing some 15 years after Price, Pickering is less sanguine. The new political role of scientific and professional experts seems to be causally related to the erosion of public trust in corporate, governmental, and professional institutions. Pickering maintains that this distrust is structural, not irrational, and must be treated with respect by seeking structural solutions instead of rhetorical dissimulation. Pickering cautions:

> The public at large perceives the power which inheres in professional and scientific expertise even if the holders of it do not. Therefore the disputes between professional and scientific experts have taken on a public meaning which far surpasses the standing of merely intellectual or ivory tower disputes. For better or worse, they have become the stuff of public policy and, therefore, a proper object of public concern.[83]

Pickering foresees that the politically salient issues for a considerable time are going to be questions of knowledge, expertise, and bias. He reminds us of Ladd's comments in 1970:

> In a technological society, the exponential growth of bodies of expert information, increased complexity of problems as they are defined before society, and the emergence of a large class of high status 'brain workers' committed to styles and orthodoxies of rationality and expertise elevate science to the status of a principal ideology offering systematic analyses and prescriptions as to the issues of public life."[84]

What troubles Pickering is a common failure to appreciate the dual function of scientific language and, therefore, the two sets of problems this failure poses for the future. On the one hand, scientific discourse is a language of truth-seeking rationality, while on the other hand, it functions as the language of policy legitimation. Pickering warns that this duality raises problems for the general public "the vast majority of whom do *not* use the language of scientific rationality for their daily discourse"; but it also raises problems for professionals "who *are* accustomed to the use of that language but are not accustomed to the duality of its functions." The social consequences of public misunderstanding and of demagogic mischief, says Pickering, are very great.[85]

As if quantum shifts in the composition of a new agenda-setting political class were not problematic enough, the fruits of affluence have made possible massive shifts in the rules governing personal lifestyles. More and more of the populace has had the leisure to become preoccupied with questions of self-fulfillment, threats to personal freedom, and vulnerability to what appear to be unnecessary technological risks. Preoccupation with self has been substituted for questions of practical economic survival. Americans think little or nothing of undertaking risky experiments in their personal lives, yet strongly resist paying realistic attention to, much less taking, socially imposed risks. Pickering observes that this inconsistency and reluctance to accept any socially imposed risks has been interpreted by some to be an unrealistic craving for "zero risk." To the contrary, he suggests that it may simply be a matter of "selective risk attention" on the part of the general populace whose self-preoccupation makes them "more concerned with the personal than the social, and irritated that issues of collective life keep intruding into the struggle against personal vulnerability."[86] To the extent that this is the case, the crucial question for Pickering is:

> whether this new political class will lead with its competence or with its grievances, will look out upon the world and ask what can be done to improve our common lot, or will look in upon itself and ask what new private enjoyments the world can be made to yield them—whether this class will seek its own liberty at the expense of others' well-being.[87]

INDICATIONS OF A NEW POLITICAL AGENDA

The ways in which "public interest regulation" has come under attack during the past decade can all too easily be interpreted in simple terms as an antagonistic confrontation between the "Old Business Class" defending its values and unparalleled achievements against a "New Intellectual Class" pursuing a self-appointed vocation for social criticism. However, a more complex interpretation of an underlying conflict in political philosophy emerges if one contrasts the cultural theory proposed by Douglas and Wildavsky with the theory of culture proposed by Langdon Winner. An even more fruitful interpretation results if one combines Price's description of a "diffusion of sovereignty" among Four Estates with Pickering's description of the emergence in a Technological Society of a new agenda-setting political class struggling to resolve its internal conflicts.

In the essays which follow, each author is representative of one of Price's Four Estates. Each considers one or another aspect of the

social and cultural bases for an environmental critique of a Technological Society from the vantage point of membership in Pickering's
new Agenda-Setting Class. Each reflects a particular cultural bias
which elicits a fundamental criticism of modern society's risk-taking
strategies and institutional mechanisms for selecting and managing
technological risk. Each raises substantive questions pertaining to the
political and moral legitimacy of public-interest regulation, especially
its cost-effectiveness if and when calculated by those who must
ultimately pay for it—consuming, taxpaying voters.

Merril Eisenbud reflects upon the historical evidence and shows
that contemporary environmentalism can hardly be regarded as a
new cultural phenomenon nor without precedent in its concern for
sustaining a proper balance between human well-being and the environment. He raises several significant questions about the counterproductive consequences of polarization and politicization in the environmental field which effectively prevent environmental protection
from evolving gradually with a program of well-ordered priorities,
based on sound scientific evidence instead of political extremes locked
in adversarial confrontation.

Julian Simon examines cross-cultural evidence of aggregate
trends indicating that health, pollution, natural resources, food,
agricultural productivity, species extinction and deforestation—even
such nonmaterial aspects of life as education, travel, and crime
rates—warrant the conclusion that our common life has shown and
will continue to show steady improvement. Claims that more government intervention is urgently necessary to reverse trends alleged to be
destructive of the environment and health, he avers, cannot be sustained by historical evidence nor scientifically established data.

After reviewing the regulatory system which has evolved during
the 1970s and its perturbation by the advent of "adversarial
science," Thomas McGarity examines proposals that might more effectively resolve the most crucial problem—restoration of the public
trust in institutions contributing to the public policy risk assessment
process. To mitigate the burden placed on humans and the environment by liberal democracy and a free enterprise economy, the university must exercise its dual role: its research arm should conduct
trustworthy risk assessments which could legitimate an appropriate
degree of regulatory intervention into market mechanisms; its educational arm should play a more important role through risk education
for the general public.

Edwin Zebroski carries these reflections further, focusing attention on the broader social costs and consequences of a failure to conduct a proper ranking of risks. This failure results in an excessive allocation of resources for control of less important risks which, in turn, starves the resources available to control more important risks and to reap the benefits of innovation. The university's dual role as "keeper of culture" and "seekers for truth" can be expressed not only in broad terms, by contributing a healthy skepticism to a current mythology of exaggerated risk, but also in specific scholarly disciplines.

Robert Benne guides our attention to the need for a resurgence of creative political thought and policy making on the part of centrist groups who have the best chance of combining three essential values —efficiency, decentralization, and justice—in creative new ways that will succeed in persuading the electorate of their merits. Among three competing theoretical models of political economy—the commercial republican, the social democratic (or democratic socialist), and the democratic capitalist—Benne develops a persuasive case for the democratic capitalist integration of the best aspects of the other models without their liabilities. His proposals for regulatory reform follow those of Charles Schultze and Alfred Kahn.

William Tucker argues a startling proposition, namely that "it is not a *lack* of government interference in the marketplace that has led to environmental problems. Rather, government intervention in the marketplace has *caused* most of the environmental problems we have today." The free market and the search for profit protects the environment. Popular belief that advances in technology have caused a host of unique and unprecedented environmental problems, Tucker observes, is plainly wrong. He reminds us that Adam Smith posited three players in the economic game—laborers, capitalists, and landlords—each making his contribution to the "wealth of nations" in a different way and through differing reward mechanisms. The problem today is that "public ownership" of lands and general resources has displaced the private interests and incentives of the landlord to protect and preserve the environment. Tucker concludes that we must find ways of instituting environmental reforms through economic means. The role of government is to set the rules of game and to function as umpire. It must not play the game.

In his concluding essay, Aaron Wildavsky moves us to a philosophical level of discourse where we come to the heart of the matter.

Granted that we must have some rationale for government intervention and for implementing its regulation of risk, which strategy for risk reduction best serves the public interest: anticipation or resilience? The former strategy entails a rationale and a policy of "no trial without prior guarantees against instituting error," thereby instituting uniformity and inflexibility, and decreasing safety by increasing vulnerability. Control by anticipation requires centralized bureaucracy to enforce standards. Contrary to the facile assumption that the best way to protect people is to reduce the risks they face, Wildavsky argues that justice, safety, and freedom are best served by enabling people to overcome dangers with strategies of resilience. The anticipatory strategy breeds lack of trust, because its demand for no trials without prior guarantees against error lowers the resilience of institutions to deal with problems effectively and flexibly as they emerge. A strategy of resilience requires public trust in organizational ability to adapt quickly and effectively. Resilient institutions require high legitimacy. Wildavsky concludes that mounting concern has concentrated upon alleged risk to human bodies and a natural environment, but it is actually our institutions that are at risk.

It should be clear from a careful reading of these essays that a new agenda for our technological society has already begun to take shape.

REFERENCES

1. A. Wildavsky, "Richer Is Safer," *The Public Interest* 60 (June, 1980) pp. 23–39; M. Douglas and A. Wildavsky, "How Can We Know the Risks We Face? Why Risk Selection Is a Social Process," *Risk Analysis* 2/2 (1982), pp. 49–51. M. Douglas and A. Wildavsky, *Risk and Culture* (Berkeley: Univ. of California Press, 1982).

2. Douglas and Wildavsky, *Risk and Culture*, p. 10.

3. Douglas and Wildavsky, "How Can We Know the Risks," p. 50.

4. Ibid. p. 51.

5. A. N. Whitehead, *Science in the Modern World* (New York: Mentor Books, 1949), pp. 207–208.

6. V. Packard, *The Waste Makers* (New York: David McKay, 1960).

7. R. Carson, *Silent Spring* (Boston: Houghton-Mifflin, 1962).

8. Dennis Meadows, Donnella Meadows, et al., *The Limits to Growth: A Report for the Club of Rome's Project on the Predicament of Mankind* (New York: New American Library, 1972).

9. W. Tucker, *Progress and Privilege: America in the Age of Environmentalism* (Garden City, NY: Anchor Press/Doubleday, 1982), p. 205 (emphasis in text).

10. The Ecologist, *Blueprint for Survival* (New York: New American Library, 1972).

11. H. Daly, *Steady-State Economics: The Economics of Biophysical Equilibrium and Moral Growth* (San Francisco: W. H. Freeman, 1977); cf. also F. Daly *Toward a Steady-State Economy* (San Francisco: W. H. Freeman, 1983).

12. H. Daly, *The Stationary-State Economy,* Univ. of Alabama Distinguished Lecture Series, No. 2, 1971, p. 5.

13. N. Georgescu-Roegen, "The Entropy Law and The Economic Problem," *Economics, Ecology, Ethics: Essays Toward a Steady-State Economy* ed. by H. E. Daly (San Francisco: W. H. Freeman, 1980. pp. 49–60) (appeared previously in The University of Alabama *Distinguished Lecture Series,* No. 1, 1971); cf. also "Selections from 'Energy and Economic Myths,'" op. cit. pp. 61–81.

14. Georgescu-Roegen, p. 66. Georgescu-Roegen remarks in a footnote: "Joseph J. Splenger, a recognized authority in this broad domain, tells me that indeed he knows of no one who may have made the observation." (p. 75, n. 12).

15. N. Georgescu–Roegen, "The Steady State and Ecological Salvation: A Thermodynamic Analysis," *Bioscience* 27, 4 (April 1977), p. 269.

16. Ibid., p. 267.

17. Ref. 13, p. 64.

18. Ibid., pp. 73–74.

19. Ibid., p. 74.

20. G. Hardin, "Ecology and the Death of Providence," *Zygon* 15, 1 (March 1980), pp. 57–68.

21. Ibid., p. 63.

22. Ibid., p. 66.

23. Ibid., p. 67.

24. H. Daly, "Entropy, Growth, and the Political Economy of Scarcity," *Scarcity and Growth Reconsidered,* ed. by V. Kerry Smith (Baltimore: Johns Hopkins University Press, 1979), p. 67.

25. Ibid., p. 71.

26. Ibid., p. 72.

27. R. and V. Routley, "Nuclear Energy and Obligations to the Future," *Inquiry* (Universeitetsforlaget, Oslo) 21 (1978), p. 133–179; R. E. Goodin, "Uncertainty as an Excuse for Cheating Our Children: The Case of Nuclear Wastes," *Policy Sciences* 10 (1978) pp. 25–43; R. E. Goodin, "No Moral Nukes," *Ethics* 90 (April 1980), pp. 418–419; E. Partridge ed., *Responsibilities to Future Generations: Environmental Ethics* (Buffalo: Prometheus Books, 1981).

28. W. Tucker, "The Sinking Ark," *Harpers* 258, 1577 (January 1979) pp. 17–20; W. Tucker, *Progress and Privilege,* ref. 9, *passim.*

29. D. L. Gibbons, "Acidic Confusion Reigns," *Sciquest* (January, 1982), pp. 10–15; K. McKean, "Hothouse Earth," *Discover* (December 1983), pp. 99–102; G. M. Woodwell, et al., "Global Deforestation: Contribution to Atmospheric Carbon Dioxide," *Science* 222, 4628 (12/9/83), pp. 1081–1086; J. W. Gofman, *Radiation and Human Health* (San Francisco: Sierra Club Books, 1981); A. B. Lovins and J. H. Price, *Non-Nuclear Futures: The Case for an Ethical Energy Strategy* (New York: Ballinger 1975).

30. S. Novick, *The Electric War: The Fight over Nuclear Power* (San Francisco: Sierra Club Books, 1976), p. 241.

31. Commenting on Jeremy Rifkin and Ted Howard's book, *Entropy: A New World View* (New York: Bantam, 1981), Senator Mark Hatfield states, "It has compelled me to re-evaluate much of the safe and comfortable thinking which governs our day to day lives." Hugh Downs states, "For a long time I've been aware of the pervasive error in overlooking or denying the Second Law of Thermodynamics in dealing with the Earth environment. . . ." Hazel Henderson does not hesitate to say that the authors of the book have "written the epitaph of economics. This brilliant work will strike terror into the heart of every economist. It is a major reconceptualization which will help shape the public debate of the 1980's." Samuel Epstein states, "This is an important book of truly cosmic dimensions. . . ."

32. G. W. Pickering, *An Analysis of Social and Ethical Issues in Energy Use: The Case of Nuclear Power* with Ian Forbes. (Waltham, Mass.: Energy Research Group, Inc. January, 1982), revised draft p. 147.

33. "Liberal democracy" should be understood in this text to designate a set of philosophical principles, and not a commitment to a particular set of social policies (e.g. civil rights, redistribution of wealth, etc.). In addition, its meaning should be distinguished not only from *classical liberalism* (i.e. that of English parliamentarians of the seventeenth century, John Locke and Adam Smith) but also from *contemporary liberalism* (i.e. the theories of John Dewey, John Kenneth Galbraith, et al.). The usage intended here refers to *essential liberalism* as developed by Edward Walter in *The Immorality of Limiting Growth* (Albany: State University of New York Press, 1981), pp. x–xi.

34. D. Vogel, "The Public Interest Movement and the American Reform Tradition," *The Political Science Quarterly* 95, 4 (Winter 1980–81), pp. 607–627, citation p. 608.

35. P. H. Weaver, "Regulation, Social Policy, and Class Conflict," *The Public Interest* 50 (Winter 1978), pp. 45–63. Weaver shows by argument and illustration that the "iron triangle" theory, even when applied to old regulatory agencies, bears little resemblance to reality. However, he is quick to say in fairness that the theory was an honest mistake advanced by scholars on the basis of careful research; but it was conducted, nonetheless, on misleading literature describing how the regulatory establishment operates (pp. 47–50).

36. Ibid., pp. 56–57. Weaver refers to several theories attempting to account for "special interest" control of regulatory policy. The "capture" theory of Huntington, the "life-cycle" theory such as Bernstein's, the "original intent" theories of Kolko and Stigler are all variations on a common theme. Jaffe and Wilson advance a competing theory that the real "special interests" served by regulatory agencies are not the regulated businesses or industry, but rather the professionals involved in perpetuating the regulatory process itself—lawyers, environmental consultants, judges, business lobbyists, et al. (pp. 46–47).

37. Ibid., p. 50.

38. Ibid., p, 56.

39. Ibid., p. 57.

40. Douglas and Wildavsky, *Risk and Culture,* p. 159.

41. Ibid.

42. Ibid., p. 160.

43. M. Novak, *The American Vision: An Essay on the Future of Democratic*

Capitalism (Washington, D.C.: American Enterprise Institute, 1978); I. Kristol, *Two Cheers for Capitalism* (New York: Basic Books, 1978).

44. D. K. Price, *The Scientific Estate* (Cambridge, Mass.: Harvard University Press, 1965).

45. Ibid., p. 68.

46. Ibid., p. 135.

47. Ibid., p. 56.

48. L. Winner, *Autonomous Technology: Technics-Out-of-Control as a Theme in Political Thought.* (Cambridge, Mass.: The MIT Press, 1977); p. 157.

49. Ibid., p. 161.

50. Winner tells us: "In the present discussion the term *autonomous technology* is understood to be a general label for all conceptions and observations to the effect that technology is somehow out of human control by human agency. . . . The theories I will examine here all maintain, in one way or another, that far from being controlled by the desired and rational ends of human beings, technology in a real sense now governs its own course, speed, and destination." Ibid., pp. 15–16.

51. J. K. Galbraith, *The New Industrial State* (New York: New American Library, 1968).

52. Winner, p. 237.

53. Ibid., p. 258.

54. Ibid., p. 261–262.

55. Ibid.

56. D. Braybrooke and C. Lindblom, *A Strategy of Decision* (New York: Free Press, 1963), p. 85.

57. Winner, p. 292.

58. C. E. Lindblom, "The Science of Muddling Through," *Public Administration Review* 19 (Spring 1959), p. 80.

59. C. E. Lindblom, *The Intelligence of Democracy* (New York: The Free Press, 1965).

60. A. Smith, *An Inquiry into the Nature and Causes of the Wealth of Nations* (Indianapolis: Liberty Classics, 1981 edition of Oxford University Press 1979 edition).

61. Ibid., p. 456.

62. Lindblom, p. 73.

63. Winner, p. 293–294.

64. Ibid., pp. 323–324.

65. Ibid., p. 315, 319–320.

66. Ibid., p. 333.

67. Pickering and Forbes, pp. 147 ff.

68. Samuel Lubell, *The Hidden Crisis in American Politics* (New York: W. W. Norton, 1970), p. 12.

69. Pickering lists the Nader organizations, The Sierra Club, Friends of the Earth, Natural Resources Defense Council, League of Women Voters, NOW, various 'Right to Life' lobbies, Heritage Foundation, American Enterprise Institute, and many others. Some have been around a long time, while others were organized in the 1970s. (p. 150).

70. A. McFarland, *Public Interest Lobbies: Decision Making on Energy* (Washington, D.C.: American Enterprise Institute, 1976), p. 9.

71. E. C. Ladd, Jr., *American Political Parties: Social Change and Political Response* (New York: W. W. Norton, 1970).

72. Ibid., p. 277.

73. C. Lasch, *The New Radicalism in America: 1889–1963* (New York: Alfred A. Knopf, 1965).

74. Ibid., p. xv.

75. Ibid., p. ix.

76. Ibid., p. x.

77. Pickering, p. 154.

78. Ibid.

79. Ibid., p. 155.

80. Ibid.

81. Price, pp. 147–148.

82. Ibid., pp. 148–149.

83. Pickering, p. 156.

84. Ladd, p. 227.

85. Pickering, p. 157.

86. Ibid., p. 165.

87. Ibid., p. 167.

Part I
New Rationales for Risk Selection

1

HEALTH RISKS AND ENVIRONMENTAL REGULATIONS: A HISTORICAL PERSPECTIVE

Merril Eisenbud

The word *environment* is a recent entry into the public vocabulary and has taken on new meaning during the past 15 years. Moreover, there are highly subjective differences in how the environment is perceived and defined. The principal environmental problem of the trout fisherman may be that his stream has become overfished or polluted, while someone else may be concerned about air pollution, the existence of nuclear reactors, or the need to conserve wild species. However, the environment is everything about us. The contemporary narrow perception of the subject has even bound itself into law: thus, the wide-ranging activities of the Environmental Protection Agency do not include such fundamental environmental influences on our lives as the quality of housing, traffic congestion, or the deteriorating infrastructure of our older cities.

A recent edition of *Webster's New Collegiate Dictionary* defines environmentalism as "a theory that views environment rather than heredity as the important factor in the development, and especially the cultural and intellectual development, of an individual or group." It defines environment as "the aggregate of social and cultural conditions that influence the life of an individual or community." These are definitions from an edition of the mid-1970s.[1] It is to be assumed that future editions will reflect the more modern meaning of these words, which will be unfortunate because by emphasizing those aspects that seem most important to contemporary environmentalists, we may be neglecting other environmental problems of greater importance.

To understand the subject of "environment" in an historical context we must first recognize that throughout the earth's history, millions of living species have not only adapted to their environment, but have also modified it and, particularly in the case of humans, have controlled it to some extent. Life has existed on earth for about 3 billion years, during which time humans have existed for only about the last 2 million years. Recorded history covers only about 4,000 years, which means that the total sum of human knowledge has been accumulated during a period of time that is no more than a flash in the total span of biological history. In fact, most of our collective knowledge has been accumulated in this century!

Society today is properly concerned about the environmental impact of its technological developments, but we should not be misled into believing there are no precedents for major environmental changes caused by other species. Life processes, from the very beginning of the existence of life on earth, have produced many major geophysical changes. Even gaseous oxygen, that most essential constituent of our environment, did not exist in the primordial atmosphere, but was produced by the photosynthetic activity of algae and higher plants from the earth's crustal materials. Our atmosphere, which is today rich in nitrogen and oxygen, is believed to have originally consisted mainly of methane, ammonia, vapor, and hydrogen, but has been altered by biological processes. The great beds of limestone that exist all through the world were produced by the gradual accumulation of the calcareous remains of sea organisms in ancient ocean sediments. Other examples of major environmental impacts by simple life forms could be given, such as the creation of coral reefs and atolls, and the damming of streams by beavers.

The course of biological evolution has been influenced by thousands of geophysical and geochemical characteristics of our environment. Among these are the distance of the earth from the sun, the characteristics of the earth's perisolar rotation, the composition of the sun's radiations, the thermodynamic characteristics of the atmosphere, the remarkable chemical properties of carbon and water, and an endless list of other fundamental properties of the environment as it exists on earth. The physical and chemical factors vary only within relatively narrow limits, which must not be exceeded if life is to continue. An infinite variety of environments exist within these limits, and over many millions of years, such disparate places as the muds at the bottom of lakes, mountain crags, deserts, and ocean islands, have provided hospitality for the diverse life forms that have evolved. Among these species, man has proved to be the most adaptable, at least so far as the terrestrial environments are concerned. However, man is a latecomer to the scene and, unless one believes that our predominance as a species is foreordained as part of a divine plan, we must accept the premise that for human society to survive, we must conduct our affairs in such a way that we do not impose so great a burden on our environment that we cause the ecosystem of which we are a part to collapse. We must maintain the delicate balance of environmental factors in order to survive.

The relationship between our species and our environment is reciprocal, in that our actions have an impact on the environment while at the same time the environment has an impact on us. However, this was not always so. For almost the entire time during which the human species has existed, about 2 million years, people have lived as wandering hunters and pickers. Primitive people had no more impact on their environment than most other species. But, like other species, mankind was subject to predation and the effects of natural disasters. In short, primitive man lived in a threatening environment that he did not affect, and over which he had essentially no control.

It was only about 10,000 years ago that humans constructed their first primitive settlements and began the practice of agriculture and animal husbandry. People then began to live in a less hostile environment but new environmental problems began to develop. Even as late as Roman times, an account of the winter habitations in England describes them as "deep caves, dug into the earth, where the inhabitants resided, surrounded by their provisions for the winter, almost concealed from casual view, and suffocated by smoke".[2]

Primitive societies, from prehistory to the present, have seriously degraded land in many ways. Many of the present deserts and semideserts in countries along the Mediterranean coasts once supported dense populations. Now, they are no longer capable of doing so. The predominant opinion of climatologists is that there has been no marked change in the climate of the Mediterranean basin during the past 2,000 years. The extensive desertification of these areas is probably due to the fact that the once-fertile soils were eroded because of unrestricted practices of clearing forests, poor tillage of soil, and the introduction of grazing animals, particularly the goat.[3,4,5] This process was well advanced by the time of the classical Greek civilization, and Plato gave us an excellent description of the damage done:

By comparison with the original territory, what is left now is, so to say, the skeleton of a body wasted by disease; the rich, soft soil has been carried off and only the bare framework of the district left. At the time we are speaking of these ravages had not begun. . . . What we now call the plains of Phelleus were covered with rich soil, and there was abundant timber on the mountains, of which traces may still be seen. . . . Not so very long ago trees fit for the roofs of vast buildings were felled there and the rafters are still in existence. There were also many other lofty cultivated trees which provided unlimited fodder for beasts. Besides, the soil got the benefit of the yearly "water from Zeus," which was not lost, as it is today, by running off barren ground to the sea.[6]

Fortunately, at least some of the land so wasted is capable of restoration in a relatively short period of time, using modern agricultural methods. The situation in Palestine, the biblical land of milk and honey, had deteriorated to such an extent by 1937 that the British Royal Palestine Commission found only 76 square miles of forests and farms out of 6,250 square miles of land fit for such purposes.[7] Whereas only 1.2 percent of the land was fit for forestation or cultivation in 1937, about 20 percent of modern Israel is now under cultivation.

One of the earliest environmental impacts of the human settlements was that the filth in which people lived bred communicable diseases that were the major environmental problem until this century. The pre-Neolithic human wanderers moved in small groups of 50 to 60 people, who rarely came in contact with other humans. It is thought that prior to the establishment of permanent dwellings, the human race was relatively free of most pathogenic organisms specifically adapted to the human species.[8,9] Many of the communicable diseases require the existence of clearly defined ecological relationships among the external environment, the host, the pathogen, and in some cases an intermediate organism such as an insect or rat.

Evolution of the towns and cities created new ecological niches for a wide variety of organisms. Even under the relatively hygienic conditions of modern suburban living, man has involuntarily domesticated such species as the robin, housefly, cockroach, and bluejay, among many others that could be cited. Most of these are probably harmless, and some, like the songbirds, add to the pleasures of life. Under conditions of congestion and filth, the domesticated species are less desirable, for they include the obnoxious and disease-carrying organisms generally classed as vermin. For some of these organisms, the relationships to man are highly intimate, as those of lice and fleas that can live on the body surface or the worms that can infest the intestines and liver. Most of the diseases that have devastated mankind during the course of history depend on delicate ecological relationships that have been facilitated by the practice of living in communities.[10]

Epidemic disease that was largely due to a lack of personal and community hygiene ravaged Europe all through the Middle Ages, giving rise to generations of people who were obsessed with death and the superstitions associated with it. It is a remarkable fact that it was not until 1842 that modern concepts of the relationship between health and the environment were first defined. The British Parliament became so concerned with the high death rates from infectious disease in the working class districts, that an inquiry was initiated into the conditions under which the laboring population lived. The report of the investigation, "On an Inquiry into the Sanitary Conditions of the Labouring Population of Great Britain," written by Sir Edwin Chadwick[11], a well-to-do lawyer and student of life insurance, for the first time set forth in detail the conditions of life in the English slums, the sanitary deficiencies that existed, and their effects on the statistics of sickness and death. With this report, a turning point in the history of public health, the relationship between the environment and human health was first described and thus began what has been called the Sanitary Revolution, which was the first environmental movement.

As has been true of the contemporary environmental movement, the driving forces during the early nineteenth century Sanitary Revolution were often amateurs such as Edwin Chadwick, his mentor Jeremy Bentham, whose work led to the establishment of the first Ministry of Health, and a wealthy mill owner Robert Owen, who wrote prolifically about the responsibilities of mill owners for the well-being of their employees.[12] It will be recalled also that it was through the writings of Charles Dickens and other authors of the period that the need to improve the conditions of the working poor, orphans, and widows was first brought to public attention. One cannot fault the writers of that period for the vivid language they used. Conditions in the homes of working class people, in the mines and in the mills, had become so intolerable that drastic corrective action was required and finally came in the form of legislation that provided the basis for the sustained improvement in living and working conditions that has since taken place.

I should note in passing that the strident language of those writers was not without political impact. Among the most sensational was the work by Friedrich Engels, who later became an important collaborator of Karl Marx and who, at the age of 25, published the widely read book *Condition of the Working Class in England*.[13]

For reasons not well understood, there were already signs that health of the general population had been improving for about a century, at least insofar as Western Europe and North America were concerned. This seems to have been due in part to improvements that were taking place in the level of nutrition made possible by the first applications of applied science in the field of agriculture. Thus the weight of cattle sold at London market doubled in the eighteenth century.[14] The improvement in nutrition may have been due in part to the gradual improvement in climate that was taking place during that period. Modern climatological studies have concluded that Europe was just emerging from a "Little Ice Age" which had persisted for about 300 years and which had resulted in, on average, a reduction of 1 °C in average temperature.[15] One cannot rule out the possibility that the improvement in nutrition that took place was the result of better growing conditions made possible by the rise in temperature. If so, this is a clear example of the elegant balance that exists between our species and its environment. The ability of the environment to provide food in sufficient quantities is greatly influenced by minor climatic changes. This becomes particularly worrisome when we consider that in 1982 the Food and Agricultural Organization records indicated that the world stocks of excess grain were only sufficient for about 55 days of consumption.[16]

I wish I could give the free enterprise system more credit for the reforms that have been undertaken since the early nineteenth century. The conditions that existed and the attitudes of various segments of early nineteenth century society are well documented in a series of reports, the "Blue Books" released by Parliamentary investigatory commissions in England. The earliest of these inquiries were concerned with the conditions of child labor,[17] a subject of singular ugliness without which no description of the human environment during the Industrial Revolution would be complete. At the start of the nineteenth century, it was not uncommon for children to be sold into apprenticeships in the mills and mines when they were only five or six years old, and there is evidence that children as young as four years of age were apprenticed to the master chimney sweepers, who found the diminutive size of the children to be advantageous.

In the early days of the Industrial Revolution, the children accompanied their parents into the mines and factories much as they would have done if the parents worked in the fields. Since it was the custom in rural England for children to help their parents plant and harvest at the earliest possible age, it did not seem unusual at first for wives and children to accompany their husbands and fathers to the mills or mines.

Employment of children was widely believed to be socially desirable in the early nineteenth century. A Connecticut textile mill owner in 1808 was granted tax exemption because, according to the state legislature, "he had put the energies of women and children to good use".[18] The mill owner himself was reported to have believed that by giving the children employment, he had rescued them from a life of poverty and crime. Earlier, Noah Webster had made a similar proposal. "The children wander the streets," he said. "It would be best for them and the communities if they were put to work in the factories".[19]

This was a period in history when people who could not look after their needs were sent to workhouses scattered across the countryside. Orphaned infants, the infirm aged, the crippled, the blind, and the mental defectives would live together in common quarters that came into being out of the well-intentioned but ill-conceived laws that had evolved during the eighteenth century. The conditions in many of the English workhouses were so bad that it was easy to understand how a mill or mine owner could believe factory employment was a superior choice to the workhouse—the only alternative at that time for poor people, children, and adults alike.[20]

The situation with respect to orphaned children was not destined to change quickly. In the United States it was not until the end of the nineteenth century that children in need would be treated differently from adults in the poorhouses. Until then, the children were confined not only with people whose incapacity arose from their poverty, but also with the criminals, the insane, and the depraved. It was not until

1874 that New York State took its orphans out of the poorhouses and placed them in separate facilities or arranged for their adoption.[21]

The early reformers asked for little in the way of legislation to limit the employment of children, but the few laws proposed were resisted strenuously by the mill and mine owners. A bill failed passage in England that would have excluded children younger than nine years of age from employment in the mills. Children in the age group between nine and 16 would have been limited to no more than 13 hours per day, including one and a-half hours for meals and recreation. A similar bill was finally enacted, the Factory Act of 1835, which excluded children under nine from employment, limited the hours of work to eight hours a day for children nine to 13, and to 12 hours a day for those aged 14 to 18.[22]

Other sad chapters in the early history of environmental legislation were the attempts to establish systems for the compensation of workers injured in industrial accidents.

Workmen's compensation legislation was first passed in the United States by the federal government in 1908, but it was applicable only to federal employees. Several states subsequently passed compensation laws (Montana in 1909; New York in 1910; and Kentucky in 1914), but these were repeatedly declared unconstitutional until Wisconsin succeeded in establishing the first permanent law in 1916. It was not until the 1940s that the last of the states adopted systems of workmen's compensation. Thus, for more than 150 years after the Industrial Revolution, society was satisfied to allow the costs of industrial injuries to be paid by the injured employees. However, it was only the personal hardship that was borne by the employees and their families; the financial costs were ultimately paid by the community because the injured workman and his family often became public charges.

With the passage of the workmen's compensation laws there developed various systems of providing insurance for the employers. In the United States, this kind of insurance coverage has been provided mainly by private companies operating according to the laws of the various states. The costs paid by the employer are higher or lower, depending on the accident experience of his company. The insurance system thus provides economic incentives for the employer to reduce the number of accidents.

Workmen's compensation laws were originally drafted to provide compensation to victims of accidents but not to those who suffered from occupational disease. Illinois amended its workmen's compensation laws to provide coverage for occupational disease as early as 1911, but other states were slow to follow suit and the amendments were restrictive in that certain occupational diseases were compensable but others were not. The restrictions have gradually been eliminated, however, and all states now provide for such protection.

Although the modern environmental movement can be traced to concerns about population growth and land abuse early in this century, and the movement as we now know it was probably inevitable, it might not have developed when it did were it not for a series of events that occurred in the 1950s and 1960s.[23] There is no question but that many of the most vocal individuals of the period were motivated by their understandable concern about the dangers of radioactive fallout from nuclear weapons testing. But fallout also alerted the world to the complexities and subtleties of the ecosystem: it came as a shock to many people that a nuclear weapon detonated in the atmosphere in Las Vegas, Bikini, or Siberia would result in contamination of milk throughout the world by radioactive forms of iodine, strontium, and cesium.

Atmospheric testing of nuclear weapons was curtailed in 1962, with the adoption of a test ban agreement among the three nuclear powers of that period. However, no lull in concerns about the environment occurred because in the same year Rachel Carson published her book *Silent Spring.*[24] Her book was concerned with the use of the organic pesticides, mainly DDT, and their effects on life forms higher than the insects for which the pesticides were intended. Like radioactive fallout, the use of DDT taught scientists, government officials, and the public that the biological environments was an elaborate integrated network, and that a substance introduced into one part of the environment could pass to other parts by complex pathways that were not fully understood. Rachel Carson has been widely criticized because of her extensive use of literary license, but the means used by more moderate writers could never have achieved the ends she sought. The time had certainly come to alert the world that some toxic chemicals were persistent in the environment, that many could be concentrated biologically, and that we were largely ignorant of the manner in which transport of these chemicals occurred within ecosystems.

Following the 1962 publication of *Silent Spring,* and continuing to the present, wave after wave of excitement about environmental matters have spread across the United States and other countries. Ever since the mid-1960s, the public has been bombarded with a steady stream of environmental crises which, in almost 20 years, have included sulfur oxides, lead, carbon monoxide, noise, PCBs, mercury, low-level radioactivity from nuclear reactors, and asbestos, among others.

A unifying factor in many of these concerns was the 1964 publication of a report by World Health Organization that 60-90 percent of all cancers were due to environmental factors.[25] Among these, the WHO identified cigarette smoking, exposure to carcinogens in the workplace, carcinogens that occur naturally in food, and a number of other factors, mostly unknown, generally related to cultural practices. The public, and many of its elected officials, were misled into believing that 60-90 percent of cancers were due to industrial pollution. There is no evidence that this is so. We do know that cancers have been produced among industrial workers exposed to such carcinogens as radium, chromium, asbestos, and vinyl chloride. Fortunately, cases such as these, which are largely preventable by application of standard industrial hygiene techniques, have not been sufficiently numerous to affect the national statistics of cancer morbidity or mortality. Contrary to public belief, there is no cancer epidemic in this country except for lung cancer, which is attributable almost entirely to cigarette smoking. As a matter of fact, there have been remarkable reductions in the incidence of cancer at two important sites, the stomach and the uterus. The trends of cancer mortality during the past 50 years are shown in Figures 1.1 and 1.2. The time trends of cancer incidence tend to parallel the mortality trends.[26]

Nevertheless, many people are concerned that cancer has become a more common cause of death in recent decades. Thus, cancer was eighth on the list of major causes of death early in this century, but is now second only to death due to cardiovascular disease. The reason for this is that the communicable diseases are no longer major causes of death. There is a higher probability nowadays that people will die of cancer in their later years because they no longer die early in life from diseases such as tuberculosis and diphtheria.

Public interest in pollution reached a high point in the late 1960s as a result of widespread concerns that we were facing an environmental crisis. The mid- and late 1960s were a turbulent period

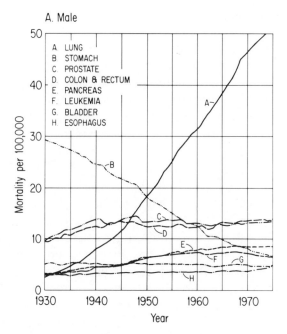

FIGURE 1.1. Cancer Mortality among U.S. Males for Selected Anatomical Sites, 1930–1975.

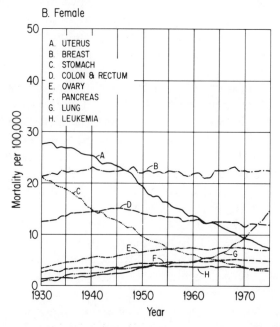

FIGURE 1.2. Cancer Mortality among U.S. Females for Selected Anatomical Sites, 1930–1975.

in the United States, in which many cities were aflame because of racial confrontations and the country was badly divided over the Vietnam issue. Yet, the public information polls of the period placed the subject of environment uppermost among the concerns of the American public. One cannot help but wonder whether, in one way or another, the subject of environment served the public consciousness as an analgesic that could numb the pain of more troublesome issues.

It seems strange in retrospect that prior to the late 1960s, the federal government was hardly involved in control over environmental pollution. The limited involvement that did exist was discharged mainly through the U.S. Public Health Service (USPHS). This then-prestigious organization functioned under the leadership of the surgeon general of the United States for more than a century, but had no power to set standards or regulate pollution. These powers traditionally resided with the states, which could call upon the USPHS only for technical assistance. By the mid-1960s, complaints were heard that the USPHS had not done a satisfactory job. There is no question but that it could have done more, but its work was commendable considering the absence of authority over the states and the meager budgets of the period. One thing in its favor was the high quality and excellent esprit of the scientists, physicians, and engineers who worked within the bureaus concerned with occupational health, air pollution, water pollution, and radiation.

Federal involvement in pollution control moved very slowly. In 1962 President Kennedy requested that Congress pass a bill of modest content, introduced two years earlier, that would authorize the USPHS to hold hearings on interstate air pollution. This resulted in the Clean Air Act of 1963, which also authorized the Department of Health, Education and Welfare to hold exploratory conferences and hearings and make funds available to assist local governments to establish air pollution control departments.

The automobile then began to attract attention as an important source of air pollution, and the first Motor Vehicle Air Pollution Control Act was passed in 1965. It authorized the secretary of HEW to establish emission standards applicable to new cars. This had already been done in the state of California, for application to the 1967 models. It was the original intent of HEW to apply the California standards nationally by 1968.

A further step was taken with the Air Quality Act of 1967, which established air quality regions and laid the groundwork for the promulgation of state standards, subject to the approval of HEW.

When the authorizations contained in the Clean Air Act of 1967 expired in 1970 they were replaced by the Clean Air Act of 1970—overwhelmingly passed by Congress—which, among other stipulations, required that automobile emissions in the 1970s be reduced by 90 percent no later than 1975. This was an expensive decision, the cost-effectiveness of which remains debatable.

The Clean Air Act amendments of 1970 also required that the newly established Environmental Protection Agency (EPA) establish national standards of air quality—primary standards to protect health and secondary standards to protect property, vegetation, and atmospheric visibility.

This was a period when there was great public concern about air pollution. Thus, Senator Muskie, chairman of the Senate Public Works Committee, in reviewing the basis for the 1970 Clean Air Act amendments, stated that "the air pollution problem is more severe, more pervasive and growing at a more rapid rate than was generally believed."[27] This statement, made in late 1970, could not then be supported by the facts. Many of the most polluted cities in this country, notably Pittsburgh, St. Louis, New York, and Chicago, had made gratifying progress in cleaning their air. The major exceptions were western cities, notably Los Angeles, where a combination of bright sunlight, heavy automobile traffic, and local topography resulted in visibility-reducing, eye-irritating photochemical smog. The local governments were making substantial progress, but could have done more with financial and technical assistance from traditional sources within the federal government. Instead, at a time when the federal government had need of its experts more than ever before, the USPHS was disrupted by a series of transfers of responsibilities to newly established federal agencies.[28]

I believe it fair to say that there is now (1983) less concern about the health effects of the levels of air pollution than existed in 1970. For example, many of us felt intuitively at that time that there was probably a relationship between lung cancer and air pollution, but extensive epidemiological studies have not sustained this view.[29] Whereas it was demonstrated clearly that the high levels of sulfur oxide and particulate pollution that then existed were associated with impairment of respiratory function among the residents of London during the mid-1950s, that association disappeared following implementation of pollution control measures adopted in the late 1950s and early 1960s. No such clear epidemiological findings have been reported in the United States. A 1970 EPA study known as the Community Health and Environmental Surveillance System (CHESS), in which studies of the relationship of air pollution to respiratory tract disease were undertaken in seven cities, purported to demonstrate impairments in lung function, but those conclusions have not stood the test of time, have been widely repudiated by the scientific community, and are no longer used as a basis of federal policy formulation.[30,31]

Whereas we hear relatively less about the health effects of air pollution at the present time, there is much more attention given to acid rain, a subject that has monopolized recent attention and has been the subject of acrimonious debate not only within our own country but between the U.S. and Canadian governments and among several governments of Western Europe. There is no question but that the acidity of rain water has increased as the result of introduction of acidifying substances such as sulfur and nitrogen oxides. In certain areas where the soils do not have the ability to neutralize the effects of the acidic deposition, effects on fish life and possibly certain types of vegetation are reported to have occurred. The problem is complicated technically by the fact that sulfur and nitrogen oxides can be transported for thousands of kilometers before they produce these effects. In the northeast United States, for example, it is said that the acidic desposition originates in the Ohio Valley.

Present EPA regulations require that most of the sulfur oxides be removed from the flue gases of newly constructed power plants by installation of scrubbers. It has been estimated that during the decade 1979–88, electric utilities will spend $121 billion on air pollution abatement, over and above the costs that would be incurred in the absence of federal regulation. Most of these costs will be for installation and operation of desulfurization equipment. This equipment, for a modern 1000-megawatt generating station, can cost more than $100 million. The operating costs of the scrubbers, in addition to the cost of amortizing the capital investment, can add up to 30 percent to the cost of generating electricity.

It seems strange in retrospect that the strenuous efforts made during the past 20 years to control sulfur oxides have been based on shifting rationales. The original emphasis was on the need to prevent respiratory disease that resulted from exposure to sulfur dioxide from local sources. This rationale gradually gave way, so that by the late 1970s the emphasis was on the sulfates formed by the interaction of sulfur dioxide and trace metals in the course of long-range transport through the atmosphere, but the effects of sulfates were almost as unequivocal as the effects of SO_2. During the past few years there has been another shift in rationale for sulfur control, and the emphasis is now on acid rain. The basic problem is that the subject of acid rain has been under study for a relatively short time, and there are many unanswered questions, but as in the case of many other environmental problems, political pressure is building up to do something. The general impression that has been created is that the effects of acid rain are causing conditions to deteriorate so rapidly that action must be taken quickly. There is no reason to believe that this is so. Sulfur oxide emissions have remained the same or decreased somewhat during the past decade. The exact mechanisms by which the acidic pollutants cause ecological damage are not known, but could probably be understood quantitatively as the result of five years of intensive research.

In addition to the need for a better understanding of the mechanisms of atmospheric transport and transformation, we need to know much more about the effects of the acid deposition and the means by which those effects can be mitigated short of installation of scrubbers. For example, just as it has long been known that the effects of excessive acidity can be mitigated on lawns and farmlands by the spreading of lime, so it has been demonstrated that lakes can be limed as well. The nature of the problem is such, in my opinion, that little would be lost and possibly much gained if it were to be decided that regulations for control of sulfur oxide emissions would not be made more stringent pending the results of five years of investigation. However, this will be a difficult consensus to reach in the face of the enormous pressure that has developed, because of the general belief that the situation is deteriorating rapidly.

A considerable portion of this discussion is being spent on the subject of air pollution because it is in many ways the most controversial area of environmental protection and has received a major part of the attention given to the subject by environmentalists, the media, the legal profession, and both the legislative and executive branches of government.

Water pollution control has a similar history.[32] As in the case of air pollution, the Public Health Service was the original center for technical expertise in the federal government, but it was powerless to do anything except advise the states on request. It was not until 1948 that the first Federal Water Pollution Control law was passed. It was a weak law, designed to provide loans to municipalities for the construction of sewage treatment plants, but funds for the loans were never provided! In 1965, because of criticism of the USPHS for being too conservative, and for being concerned with human health to the exclusion of wildlife, Congress passed the Water Pollution Control Act of 1965, which relieved the USPHS of its responsibilities and transferred its functions to a new Federal Water Pollution Control Administration (FWPCA), which was organized as a separate unit within HEW. There was also a requirement that the states establish water pollution standards that would be acceptable to HEW. About a year later, Congress again became dissatisfied with the lack of progress, and transferred the FWPCA to the Department of Interior. The two transfers, within about a year, resulted in demoralization of the staff, and many of the senior technical personnel formerly with the USPHS retired from government.

Early in 1979, an oil-drilling rig in the Santa Barbara channel began to leak about 20,000 gallons of oil per day into the surrounding waters. About 20 miles of California shoreline had become heavily polluted with oil by the time the leak was controlled several weeks later. This incident increased the clamor for clean water, and early in 1970 President Nixon sent a special message on the environment to Congress in which he recommended that federally approved standards be required for all industrial and municipal pollution sources. This led to the Water Pollution Control Amendments of 1972, which mandated elimination of discharges into navigable waters by 1985. Despite the report of the President's Council on Environmental Quality that it was not feasible to eliminate all discharges, the bill was passed unanimously by the Senate and by a vote of 380 to 14 in the House. It was then vetoed by the president, but his action was overwhelmingly overridden by both houses.

One development that took place in New York served to illustrate the unreasonable and illogical attitudes that existed at that time.

In the mid-1960s, a long-needed sewage treatment plant was designed to treat the effluents from the west side of Manhattan. The plant was to be constructed at a cost of about $200 million, and its design was based on an understanding of the ability of the lower Hudson estuary to assist, without detriment, in the final "polishing" of the sewage treatment process. The plant would not discharge water of potable quality, nor did it need to, into the reasonably well oxygenated and brackish receiving water. In the parlance of the engineer, the plant was designed for 67 percent removal of biochemical oxygen demand. Under pressure from environmental groups in 1966, two local politicians who were running for office clamored for more complete oxidation of the residual before discharge and, in fact, asked that the best treatment plant that technology could design be provided. As a result, the plant was redesigned for 90 percent removal of biochemical oxygen demand which, because of the much larger size of the plant, required that a new site be selected. At the present time, more than 15 years since the decision was made, the plant has not yet been completed because it will cost more than $1 billion to fulfill the original design requirements, and the money simply is not available. A huge sum of money has been wasted, and many years of additional pollution added to the river, because of the impractical though well meaning demands that were made at the time.

It has been estimated that air and water pollution control for the decade 1979–1988 will cost nearly $600 billion over and above what would have been spent were it not for the intervention of the federal government.[33] Many of us believe that these and other costs that could be identified are excessive in relation to the benefits that will be achieved, and some say that costs are contributing to inflation, although I do not believe that this is so to a significant extent.

I believe that when the history of the late twentieth century environmental movement is finally told from the perspective of the next century, one of its saddest chapters will be the divisive effect that the subject has had on American society. The high degree of polarization of views about environmental matters and the extremes of advocacy that exist in the environmental field are everywhere in evidence. Polarization has developed hand-in-hand with politicization and together they have often prevented programs of environmental protection from evolving along rational lines. The environmental movement has produced a major revolution in the way our economy operates. I wish it would have been possible for the changes that have taken place to have been brought about gradually by a program of well-ordered priorities, based on careful analysis of the environmental needs. Unfortunately, this is not the way American society operates. It took the Santa Barbara channel blowout to bring about much-needed water pollution control laws, but when the laws came into being, they tried to do too much too soon, and the laws were drafted with an inadequate sense of technical or historical perspective. The pace of air pollution legislation was likewise disastrously frenetic.

We now see that the same pattern is developing in connection with the need to clean up the accumulation of chemical wastes. In the northeast where I live, health departments have been concerned about groundwater contamination by chemical wastes since the mid-1940s. By the time widespread interest in the environment began to develop in the mid-1960s, it was clear that better methods had to be devised for either the recycling or permanent disposal of chemical wastes. It was finally the Love Canal episode that provided the necessary stimulus, but only after the health implications of the Love Canal episode were greatly exaggerated by the environmentalists, the press, and many government officials. I would have wished that before the Love Canal episode came to public attention, the chemical industry had taken some initiative in calling to the attention of government that they would like to cooperate in developing a plan for the better management of their wastes. Many members of the chemical industry seemed to believe they escaped responsibility when they transferred responsibility for disposal of their waste materials to licensed scavengers, even though it was generally known that they sometimes did not always conduct their affairs in a socially responsible way. An intolerable situation has been developing for many years, and industry was in the best position to develop the remedial actions that should be required. But industry in general did not approach the problem of chemical wastes in a way calculated to serve its own best long-range interests. Instead, it continued on a year-to-year basis to follow its short-sighted policies that eventually led to the complexities currently associated with the national effort to correct the poor practices of the past.

Beginning with opposition to child labor legislation in the early years of the last century, and continuing to the present problems with solid waste, there has been a steady pattern of resistance by industry to badly needed environmental legislation. Unhappily, what industry would not do voluntarily, it is now being required to do by law. It is required to do too much, too soon. As often happens, when the pendulum finally swung, it swung too far.

REFERENCES

1. *Webster's New Collegiate Dictionary* Springfield, Mass: G. & C. Merriam Co., 1977).

2. Malcolm, J.P., *Anecdotes for the Manners and Customs of London from Roman Times to 1700* (London, 1811).

3. Marsh, G.P., *The Earth Modified by Human Action* (New York: Scribners, 1874).

4. Osborn, F., *Our Plundered Planet* (Boston, Mass: Little, Brown and Co. 1948).

5. Darby, H.E., "The Clearing of the Woodland in Europe," in *Man's Role in Changing the Face of the Earth*, W.L. Thomas, ed. (Chicago, Ill: University of Chicago Press, 1956).

6. Plato, *The Collected Dialogues*, E. Hamilton and H. Cairns, eds. (New York: Bollingen Series LXXI, Pantheon Books, 1966).

7. Lowdermilk, W.C., *Palestine: Land of Promise*, 2nd ed. (London: Victor Gollancz, Ltd., 1946).

8. Burnet, MacF., *Natural History of Infectious Disease* (London: Cambridge University Press, 1966).

9. Cockburn, A., "Paleoepidemiology," in *Infectious Diseases: Their Evolution and Eradication*, A. Cockburn, ed. (Springfield, IL: Charles C. Thomas, 1967), Ch. 5.

10. Zinsser, H., *Rats, Lice and History* (Boston, Mass: Little, Brown & Co., 1935).

11. Chadwick, E., *Report on the Sanitary Condition of the Labouring Population of Gt. Britain* (1842), ed. with intro by M.W. Flinn Edinburgh: Edinburgh University Press, 1965).

12. Owen, R., *A New View of Society & Other Writings* (London/Toronto: J.M. Dent & Sons, New York: E.P. Dutton & Co., 1927).

13. Engels, F., *The Condition of the Working Class in England* (Oxford: Blackwell, 1945; (trans. and ed. by W.O. Henderson and W.H. Chaloner, New York: Macmillan Co., 1958).

14. Trevelyan, G.M., *English Social History* (London: Spottiswoode, Ballantyne & Co., Ltd., 1944), p. 116.

15. National Research Council, *Climate and Food. Rept. of Comm. on Climate and Weather Fluctuations and Agricultural Production* (Washington, D.C.: National Academy of Sciences, 1976).

16. Food and Agriculture Organization of the United Nations, *Monthly Bulletin of Statistics*, Vol. 5, No. 10 (Oct., 1982).

17. British Parliamentary Papers, *First Report of the Commissioners—Mines.* Children's Employment Commission, 1842. Reprinted by Irish University Press, Shannon, Ireland (1968).

18. Kuczynski, J., *The Rise of the Working Class* (New York: McGraw-Hill, 1967).

19. Warfel, H.R., *Noah Webster: School Master to America* (New York: Octagon Books, 1966). (First printing: Macmillan Co., New York, 1936.)

20. Longmate, N., *The Workhouse* (New York: St. Martin's Press, 1974).

21. Trattner, W.I., *Homer Folks: Pioneer in Social Welfare* (New York: Columbia University Press, 1968).

22. British Parliamentary Papers, op. cit.

23. Eisenbud, M., *Environment, Technology, and Health* (New York: New York University Press, 1978).

24. Carson, R., *Silent Spring* (Boston, Mass: Houghton Mifflin Co., 1962).

25. World Health Organization, *Prevention of Cancer: Report of a WHO Expert Committee.* Technical Report Series No. 276. Geneva (1964).

26. American Cancer Society, *1982 Cancer Facts and Figures.* ACS 81-(500M)-No. 5008-LE. New York (1981).

27. Burger, E.J., *Protecting the Nation's Health* (Lexington, Mass: D.C. Heath, 1976).

28. Eisenbud, op. cit.

29. Ware, J.H., Thibodeau, L.A., Speizer, F., Colome, S. and Ferris, B.G., "Assessment of the health effects of atmospheric sulfur oxides and particulate matter: Evidence from observational studies," *Environ. Health Perspectives* 41: 255–276 (1981).

30. Eisenbud, op. cit.

31. Burger, op. cit.

32. Ibid.

33. Council on Environmental Quality, *Environmental Quality.* Eleventh Annual Report. U.S. Govt. Printing Office, Washington, D.C. (1980).

2

NATURAL RESOURCES AND POPULATION: WHAT ARE THE PROPER ROLES OF PUBLIC AND PRIVATE SECTORS?

Julian L. Simon

Those who call for more government involvement in the spheres of natural resources, environment, and population almost invariably base their call on the assertion that things are not only bad but are getting worse. If government does not step in to reverse these trends, they say, our future is gloomy indeed.

But if we raise our gaze from the usual frightening articles in the newspaper, and instead look at life around us as well as statistical data, we can see that life, at least in its more important aspects, has been getting better over the last centuries and decades, here in the United States as well as in the rest of the world. And there is no persuasive reason to believe that these trends will not continue indefinitely. I focus mostly on the United States, because more data are available. But the picture is much the same for less-developed countries (LDCs) as for more-developed countries (MDCs). The picture portrayed exposes as false the proposition that the outlook for the world is grim in the absence of more government intervention.

THE SETTING

Not long ago I was riding in a hotel's van from Newark Airport to Springlake, New Jersey on the Jersey shore, along with other

The author appreciates useful suggestions from Peter Lindert and Daniel Primont, as well as the opportunity to present some of this material to the UC-Berkeley-Davis-Santa Cruz demography group, Southern Illinois University, and Manhattan College.

conference goers. I mentioned to the person next to me that my paper was concerned with how natural resources have gotten less scarce, and how the U.S. environment has been getting cleaner. He found those notions difficult to believe, and he expressed the view that life has been getting worse rather than better.

That conversation caused me to look out the window and to reflect on our trip to the Jersey shore. When I was a child my parents owned two little cottages in the town of Bradley Beach, which we rented out for the summer. We usually went to the shore in the spring to fix up and rent them, and in the fall to clean them up and to vacation if the weather was still warm. During the summer we sweltered in the city. I remembered, however, one early July when we had not yet rented one cottage and therefore went for a weekend during the vacation season. That trip was literally a nightmare for a child, going in both directions. The traffic on each alternative road was bumper-to-bumper most of the 45 miles. Cars overheated then stalled. Tempers exploded at drivers trying to beat the crowd by driving up the gravel shoulder and then cutting in. Worst of all, collisions—including head-on crashes in the undivided roads—caused horrible injuries as people without seatbelts were catapulted through windshields with nonshatterproof glass. The trip might take four or more hours for the 45 miles. And waiting until 1 A.M. Friday night or 3 A.M. Monday morning seldom was a worthwhile ploy for the husbands who left their families at the shore during the week to escape the hot city apartments.

Now here we were breezing down the New Jersey Turnpike in an air-conditioned, reasonably safe van on a comfortable highway, at a speed discreetly above the 55 MPH limit, having a ball. And city residents don't even have to make the trip to escape the heat of summer anymore, because they can switch on the air conditioners that virtually all can now afford.

Has U.S. life really gotten worse since 1940?

I wish there were time to show you some pictures from a book called *The Good Old Days—They Were Terrible* by the famous archivist Otto L. Bettman. The historical photos and drawings make horribly vivid the tragedies of life at the turn of the century that we never think of: For example, the fact that "Between 1870 and 1906 four American cities—Chicago, Boston, Baltimore, and San Francisco burned to the ground" (p. 39), a world record; the slum children who slept on the streets; the bums; the loneliness of the prairie farm family who could go nowhere and had no one to talk to, not even a telephone; as well as other horrors of "horse pollution," overcrowded and unsafe tenement housing, crime, financial insecurity, bad food, and much much more. Bettman's pictures make this all very real and very believable.

Before moving on from anecdotes to data, I wish to stress a qualification that should not be overlooked: I do not say that all is well everywhere, and I do not predict that all will be rosy in the future. Children are hungry and sick; people live out lives of physical or intellectual poverty and lack of opportunity; war or some new pollution may finish us. What I *am* saying is that for most relevant economic matters, aggregate trends are improving rather than deteriorating.

Also, I do not say that a better future happens automatically or without effort. It will happen because men and women will struggle with problems using muscle and mind, and will *probably* overcome, as they have in the past. This needs to be emphasized because there are many people who assume that if the *government* is not doing something about a matter, nothing is being done. If you suggest that the market will provide natural resources in quite satisfactory fashion, many people say: "Oh, you mean to say the situation will take care of itself?" Yes and no. If you include the efforts of people struggling with might and main as part of your concept of a market— and that is exactly what underlies every market—and if you assume that that happens "automatically," then yes, it is reasonable to say that the situation will take care of itself. But we need to remember that it is *people* who are taking care of the situation, and it surely does not seem automatic to them. But if you mean by *automatic* that the fine results descend from heaven, then no, it won't occur automatically. The issue is not government action versus benefits descending from heaven, but government action versus private action.

LIFE AND HEALTH

Speaking literally of life now, it seems reasonable to say that life can't be good unless you are alive. The fact that your chances of living through any given age now are much better than in earlier times must therefore mean that life, at least in this basic definition, has gotten better. Relatively good data show (Figure 2.1a) that female life expectancy in France rose from 25.7 years in 1740/49 to 75.4 years in

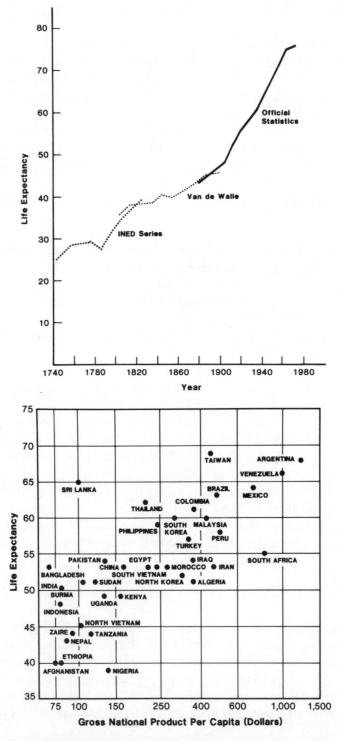

FIGURE 2.1a and FIGURE 2.1b Female Expectation of Life at Birth, France
Source: Reproduced from Demeny, 1974, p. 155.

1966/70 (Lee, 1979, p. 142). And we see this history being recapitulated in a cross section of the countries of the world (Figure 2.1b).

This gain in life expectancy has not been limited to rich countries. For example, life expectancy in less-developed regions rose from 42.6 years in 1950/55 to 53.4 years in 1970/75 (the rise in Asia being even greater), a much bigger jump than the rise from 65.2 years to 71.2 years in the more-developed regions (Gwatkin, 1980, p. 62). And this phenomenon has not yet run its course, the gains having been more rapid in recent years in the United States, more than twice as fast (2.1 years) between 1970 and 1976 than in the entire decade of the 1960s (0.8 years).

But, you ask, what about the increase in cancer? In return I ask, *what* increase in cancer? In fact, the data show no such increase, despite popular belief, except for deaths due to smoking-caused lung cancer (see Table 2.1). As the late Philip Handler, then-president of the National Academy of Sciences, said:

> The United States is not suffering an 'epidemic of cancer,' it is experiencing an 'epidemic of life'—in that an ever greater fraction of the population survives to the advanced ages at which cancer has always been prevalent. The overall, age-corrected incidence of cancer has not been increasing; it has been declining slowly for some years.

One of the few things that we might consider worse than our own death and nonlife is the danger of death to our loved ones. Infant mortality is a reasonable measure of child mortality generally. In the 1700s and 1800s about 20 percent of all children died before the age of one in Europe. The figure was still that high in Spain, Russia, Germany, and Hungary, among other European countries, as late as 1900. Now it is about 1.5 percent or less in a great many countries (Mitchell, pp. 42–43).

Think how it was for parents a short 50 to 60 years ago, even in a rich country, when there were no miracle drugs against infection. Each time a child got a strep throat the result might be scarlet fever and then death or a rheumatic heart. Nowadays, it's penicillin and back to school after one day, with little risk.

Think also about the possible death of the main breadwinner in the family when life expectancy was lower and there were no public assistance programs. Betty Smith's *A Tree Grows in Brooklyn* tears at the heartstrings.

TABLE 2.1 Cancer Incidence and Mortality

Primary Sites	Incidence per 100,000 White Survey Population*			Death Rate per 100,000 United States White Polulation*		
	1947	1969-71	Percent Change	1950	1970	Percent Change
		White Male				
All sites†	282.2	296.2	+ 5	144.5	170.4	+ 18
Lung and bronchus	29.5	64.3	+118	28.5	52.2	+ 83
Prostate	34.8	45.9	+ 32	15.0	14.7	− 2
Colon	26.2	28.5	+ 9	14.6	15.9	+ 9
Bladder	18.6	20.3	+ 9	6.0	6.0	—
Rectum	22.1	15.5	− 30	8.2	5.6	− 32
Lymphomas‡	10.8	14.8	+ 37	6.6	10.4	+ 58
Stomach	34.1	12.0	− 65	20.2	8.7	− 57
Leukemia	9.1	11.4	+ 25	7.1	8.1	+ 14
Pancreas	9.3	10.5	+ 13	7.2	9.8	+ 36

White Female

All sites†	293.9	247.5	− 16	130.3	116.6	− 11
Breast	72.8	72.0	− 1	24.2	25.2	+ 4
Colon	27.8	25.3	− 9	16.2	14.1	− 13
Uterus (total)	56.3	37.7	− 33	18.7	9.0	− 52
Corpus uteri	10.3	20.0	¶	9.1§	4.0§	− 56
Cervix uteri	32.8	15.5	¶	9.6	5.0	− 48
Ovary	14.7	13.6	− 7	7.5	8.5	+ 13
Lung and bronchus	6.5	13.5	+ 108	4.5	10.3	+ 129
Lymphomast‡	7.5	10.1	+ 35	4.1	6.9	+ 68
Rectum	15.2	9.4	− 38	5.5	3.3	− 40
Leukemia	6.3	6.8	+ 8	5.1	5.2	+ 2
Pancreas	5.5	6.2	+ 13	4.8	5.7	+ 19
Stomach	18.3	5.7	− 69	10.9	4.2	− 61
Bladder	8.0	5.3	− 34	2.5	1.8	− 28

*Adjusted on basis of age distribution of the United States total population, 1950.
†Excluding cancer of the skin.
‡Including Hodgkin's disease and multiple myeloma.
¶Not precisely comparable—see text.
§Including "uterus, not otherwise specified."

Source: Prudential Insurance. Statistical Bulletin, October 1975, Vol. 56. Source of basic data: *Morbidity from Cancer in the United States*, 1947, and *Third National Cancer Survey: Incidence Data*, 1968–71. National Cancer Institute: reports of Division of Vital Statistics, National Center for Health Statistics.

Health has improved, too. There was a decrease in loss of work days per year between 1961–65 and 1971–75, mostly in persons 45 and over, coming mostly from a decrease in loss due to chronic conditions. Table 2.2 shows that the average number of acute conditions per year also has declined (though days of bed disability and of restricted activity have not fallen, which casts some doubt on the conclusion, however; *Prudential Statistical Bulletin*, July-September 1978, p. 4).

POLLUTION

It is possible that life expectancy would rise even while pollution-caused ailments would also be rising, if cures of these and other diseases were improving rapidly. In this sense, life expectancy is only one boundary to an estimate of pollution's effects, rather than an unbiased estimate. But at least in the United States, we see no independent evidence of such a countervailing pollution effect. Direct evidence on air and water pollution has shown them to be on the decline in the United States since the early 1960s when the data begin. The new Pollutant Standard Index available shows this neatly for the last few years (Figure 2.2).

Pollution in the less-developed countries is a different sort of story, but not necessarily a discouraging one. Despite claims by the Global 2000 Report and others that pollution is worsening in the LDCs, no worldwide data are available, and not even regional data has been presented. Nevertheless, it is reasonable to assume that pollution of various kinds has increased as poor countries have gotten somewhat less poor and have bought pollution-creating industry and consumer goods. Industrial wastes are indeed an evil for air and water, but they do not arise in preindustrial countries. And in the early stages of industrialization, countries and people are not yet ready to pay for cleanup operations. So pollution must rise during the early stages of industrialization. The same is true of consumer pollution—junked cars, plastic wrappers, and such oddments as old vials from antibiotics which I saw on the ground by the hundreds around a primitive stall in an isolated Iranian village a decade ago. But further increases in income almost as surely will bring about industrial pollution abatement.

I am not saying that government should let businesses alone with respect to pollution. Whenever there is a commonly owned good

She said she is a "water person" who loves to swim, water ski, and sail. She lives at Lakeway because of Lake Travis. I then asked if, by any chance, Lake Travis is man-made. She said that it is. So we see that human beings, and population growth, do good things to the environment as well as bad things. But such positive effects of people tend to be overlooked, while the negative effects—which tend to be more temporary—are highlighted. (Just *why* people are attracted to the negative is an interesting question beyond the scope of this discussion.)

NATURAL RESOURCES

What about the more material base of life? Though natural resources are a less important part of our economy with every succeeding year, they are still important, and cause grave concern to many. Following on Barnett and Morse, I have written about natural resources at length: Scarcity—as measured by the economically meaningful indicator of cost or price—has been decreasing rather than increasing in the long run for all raw materials except lumber and oil. Figures 2.3 and 2.4 show this effect for copper, which is representative of all the metals.

The available data are for the United States, but the story is not essentially different for the LDCs. The price of raw materials in labor time in LDCs has not fallen as markedly as in MDCs because income has not risen as markedly in LDCs; but that price surely has fallen somewhat because the world market price is much the same everywhere and income has risen in LDCs. And there is reason to suppose that the price of raw materials relative to consumer prices has fallen even more sharply in LDCs than in MDCs because the production of other goods has not improved as sharply in LDCs as in MDCs (though services temper the story).

Let's consider the two exceptions I've mentioned, oil first. The long-run picture is in Figures 2.5 and 2.6, the shorter-run picture in Figure 2.7. The recent price rise is purely political, of course, the cost per barrel in the Persian Gulf still being perhaps $.15-.25. Because I've dealt with it at length elsewhere, I'll not talk about energy in general except to say that there is no reason to believe that the supply of energy is finite, or that prices will not continue their long-run decrease.

Lumber is unusual because for decades trees were disposed of as a nuisance to farmers clearing land. As lumber came more to be a

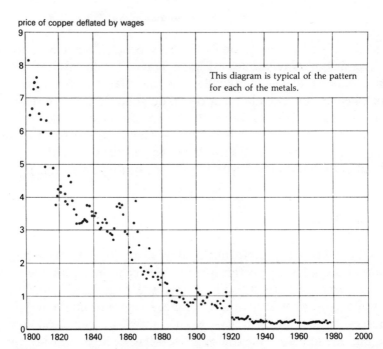

price of copper deflated by wages

This diagram is typical of the pattern for each of the metals.

FIGURE 2.3. The Scarcity of Copper as Measured by Its Price Relative to Wages.

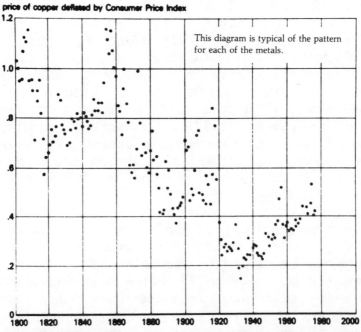

price of copper deflated by Consumer Price Index

This diagram is typical of the pattern for each of the metals.

FIGURE 2.4. The Scarcity of Copper as Measured by Its Price Relative to the Consumer Price Index.

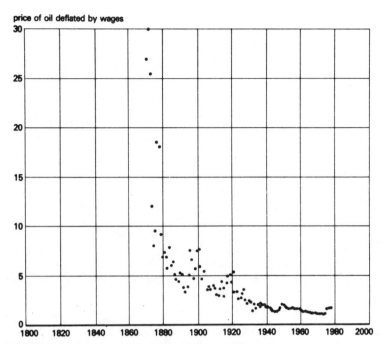

FIGURE 2.5. The Price of Oil Relative to Wages

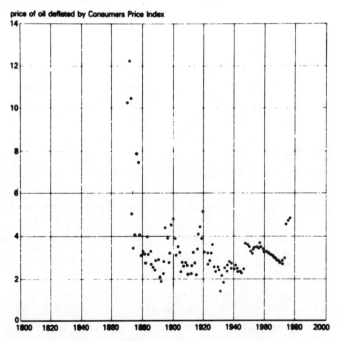

FIGURE 2.6. The Price of Oil Relative to the Consumer Price Index.

65

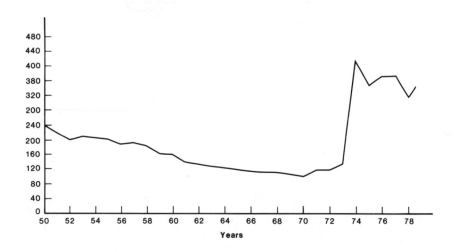

FIGURE 2.7 OECD–Europe Prices of Imported Petroleum (Deflated).
Source: Reproduced from Bannett et. al., 1981, p. 6.

commercial crop and a good for builders and railroad men, its price rose. But it seems reasonable to expect prices to hit a plateau and then follow the course of other raw materials as the transition is completed. Evidence consistent with this view is the increase, rather than the popularly supposed decrease, in the tree stock in the United States (Figure 2.8).

A third resource about which particular concern has been expressed recently is fish, as for example by Paul Ehrlich, Lester Brown, and the recent Global 2000 Report. This was one of the very few topics for which Global 2000 presented trend data, though that report claimed to be based on trend data. And their figures showed that in the few years prior to the last date they showed, the catch had apparently stagnated (Table 2.3 and Figure 2.9).

Now look at more recent data, as collected by John Wise (Table 2.4). This is still another illustration of how one often reaches wrong conclusions by extrapolating the experience of a few recent years rather than the long-run trend, when there is no compelling reason to

FIGURE 2.8 Net Annual Growth of Growing Stock and Sawtimber on Commercial Timberland, by Softwoods and Hardwoods, and by Section[1]

Section	All species			Softwoods			Hardwoods		
	1952	1962	1970	1952	1962	1970	1952	1962	1970
				Growing stock—billion cubic feet					
North	4.1	4.9	5.5	1.1	1.2	1.4	3.0	3.6	4.2
South	6.3	7.5	8.6	3.6	4.5	5.4	2.7	3.0	3.2
Rocky Mountain	1.2	1.3	1.4	1.1	1.2	1.3	.1	.1	.1
Pacific Coast	2.3	2.7	3.1	2.0	2.3	2.6	.3	.4	.5
Total	13.9	16.4	18.6	7.8	9.3	10.7	6.1	7.1	7.9

[1]Data may not add to totals because of rounding.

Note: Data for 1952 and 1962 differ from data published in earlier reports because of adjustments based on newer information from remeasured Forest Survey plots. Data for all years are "trend level" estimates.

Source: Perspective on Prime Lands, U.S. Department of Agriculture. Background papers for Seminar on the Retention of Prime Lands July 16–17, 1975, sponsored by the USDA Committee on Land Use, p. 21. Originally from U.S. Department of Agriculture, Forest Service 1973. *The Outlook for Timber in the United States.* For. Res. Rpt. No. 20.

TABLE 2.3 Total World Catch and Selected Categories (millions of metric tons)

	Total	Freshwater and Diadromous	Marine Fish	Crustaceans and Mollusks	Mollusks
1953	—	—	19.1	2.6	—
1954	—	—	20.3	2.9	—
1955	28.9	—	21.3	2.8	—
1956	30.8	—	22.7	2.9	—
1957	31.7	5.1	22.8	3.0	—
1958	33.3	5.6	24.1	3.0	—
1959	36.9	6.1	26.8	3.3	—
1960	40.2	6.6	29.2	3.6	—
1961	43.6	7.0	32.2	3.5	—
1962	44.8	6.8	35.6	3.8	—
1963	46.6	7.0	36.4	4.1	—
1964	51.9	7.2	40.9	4.0	—
1965	53.3	7.8	39.6	4.1	2.9
1966	57.3	8.1	43.0	4.3	3.0
1967	60.4	8.2	45.9	4.5	3.2
1968	63.9	9.3	48.7	5.0	3.5
1969	62.6	9.8	47.2	4.7	3.2
1970	69.6	11.6	52.7	5.1	3.4
1971	70.9	12.2	52.5	5.1	3.4
1972	66.2	12.4	47.2	5.3	3.6
1973	66.8	12.8	47.1	5.4	3.5
1974	70.4	12.6	50.8	5.5	3.5
1975	69.7	13.4	49.3	5.8	3.8

Source: Food and Agriculture Organization. *Yearbook of Fishery Statistics: Catches and Landings,* vols. 16, 24, 32, 40. Reproduced from Global 2000, p. 105.

believe that there has been a structural change that would reverse the long-run trend.

Food is an especially important resource, and the evidence is especially strong that we are on a benign trend despite rising population. The long-run price of food relative to wages, and even to consumer products, is down (Figures 2.10a, 2.10b and 2.10c). Famine deaths have decreased even in absolute terms, let alone relative to population, in the past century, a matter which pertains particularly

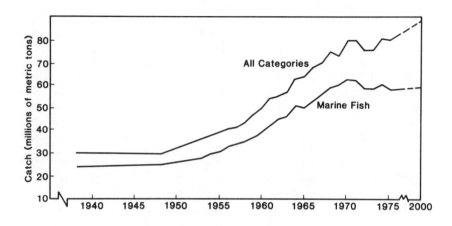

FIGURE 2.9 Annual Catch of Marine Fish and of All Marine Animals, Showing the Downward Trend in Marine Fish since 1970.
Source: Reproduced from *Global 2000*, p. 106.

to the poor countries. Per capita food consumption is up over the last 30 years (Table 2.5). And there are no data showing that the bottom of the income scale is faring worse, or even has failed to share in the general improvement, as the average has improved. Africa's food production per capita is down, but no one thinks that has anything to do with physical conditions, but instead rather clearly stems from governmental and other social conditions.

The biggest food production problem in the United States today is too much production, that is, falling prices due to high production, falling consumer demand for meat in the United States, and increased foreign competition in such crops as soy beans. Farmers then complain, and ask government for help in reducing production. As of October 1, 1981,

. . . the Reagan administration has just proposed a new wheat set-aside program, similar to those used in 1979 and before.

TABLE 2.4 World Fisheries Catch Statistics, 1938-79, Treated Various Ways (in million metric tons)

Year	a	b	c	d	e	f	g	h	j	k	l	m
1938	21.0	21.0	2.2	18.8	.0	18.8	.6	1.2	1.8	19.2	17.0	17.0
1948	19.6	19.6	1.8	17.8	.0	17.8	.6	1.3	1.9	17.7	15.9	15.9
1950	21.1	21.1	2.4	18.7	.0	18.7	.7	1.6	2.3	18.8	16.4	16.4
1951	23.5	23.5	2.6	20.9	.0	20.9	.7	1.8	2.5	21.0	18.4	18.4
1952	25.1	25.1	2.8	22.3	.0	22.3	.7	1.9	2.6	22.5	19.7	19.7
1953	25.9	25.9	3.0	22.9	.0	22.9	.8	1.8	2.6	23.3	20.3	20.3
1954	27.6	27.6	3.2	24.4	.0	24.4	.9	1.9	2.8	24.8	21.6	21.6
1955	28.9	28.9	3.4	25.5	.0	25.5	.9	1.9	2.8	26.1	22.7	22.7
1956	30.8	30.7	3.5	27.3	.1	27.2	.9	1.9	2.8	28.0	24.5	24.4
1957	31.7	31.4	3.9	27.8	.3	27.5	.9	2.1	3.0	28.7	24.8	24.5
1958	33.3	32.5	4.5	28.8	.8	28.0	.9	2.1	3.0	30.3	25.8	25.0
1959	36.9	34.9	5.1	31.8	2.0	29.8	.9	2.3	3.2	33.7	28.6	26.6
1960	40.2	36.7	5.6	34.6	3.5	31.1	1.0	2.6	3.6	36.6	31.0	27.5
1961	43.6	38.3	5.7	37.9	5.3	32.6	1.0	2.5	3.5	40.1	34.4	29.1
1962	44.8	37.7	5.8	39.0	7.1	31.9	1.1	2.7	3.8	41.0	35.2	28.1
1963	46.6	39.4	5.9	40.7	7.2	33.5	1.1	3.0	4.1	42.5	36.6	29.4
1964	51.9	42.1	6.2	45.7	9.8	35.9	1.2	2.7	3.9	48.0	41.8	32.0
1965	53.2	45.5	7.0	46.2	7.7	38.5	1.2	3.0	4.2	49.0	42.0	34.3
1966	57.3	47.7	7.3	50.0	9.6	40.4	1.3	3.0	4.3	53.0	45.7	36.1
1967	60.4	49.9	7.2	53.2	10.5	42.7	1.4	3.2	4.6	55.8	48.6	38.1
1968	63.9	52.6	7.4	56.5	11.3	45.2	1.5	3.5	5.0	58.9	51.5	40.2
1969	64.4	54.7	7.6	56.8	9.7	47.1	1.5	3.2	4.7	59.7	50.4	42.4
1970	65.6	52.5	8.4	57.2	13.1	44.1	1.6	3.4	5.0	60.6	52.2	39.1
1971	66.2	55.0	9.0	57.2	11.2	46.0	1.7	3.4	5.1	61.1	52.1	40.9
1972	62.2	57.4	5.7	56.5	4.8	51.7	1.8	3.6	5.4	56.8	51.1	46.3
1973	62.8	61.1	5.8	57.0	1.7	55.3	2.3	3.7	6.0	56.8	51.0	49.3
1974	66.6	62.6	5.8	60.8	4.0	56.8	2.5	3.7	6.2	60.4	54.6	50.6
1975	66.5	63.2	6.2	60.3	3.3	57.0	2.5	4.1	6.6	59.9	53.7	50.4
1976	69.9	65.6	5.9	64.0	4.3	59.7	2.5	4.4	6.9	63.0	57.1	52.8
1977	69.2	69.4	6.1	63.1	.8	62.3	2.8	3.5	6.3	62.9	56.8	56.0
1978	70.5	69.1	5.8	64.7	1.4	63.3	2.9	4.8	7.7	62.8	57.0	55.6
1979	71.3	69.9	6.1	65.2	1.4	63.8	3.1	5.0	8.1	63.2	57.1	55.7

[a] Total catch
[b] Total catch, excluding Peruvian anchovy
[c] Freshwater catch
[d] Marine catch
[e] Peruvian anchovy catch
[f] Marine catch, excluding Peruvian anchovy
[g] Crustacean catch
[h] Mullusc catch
[j] Invertebrate catch
[k] Finfish catch
[l] Marine finfish catch
[m] Marine finfish catch, excluding Peruvian anchovy

Note: Includes in recent years some 6 million tons of aquaculture production, 65% finfish (almost all fresh water), 15% molluscs, 15% seaweeds, 5% other (FAO Fisheries Circular No. 704, 1977).

Source: John Wise, Personal Communication. Originally from FAO Yearbook of Fishery Statistics, Volume 48 and preceding volumes (values shown are latest available revisions).

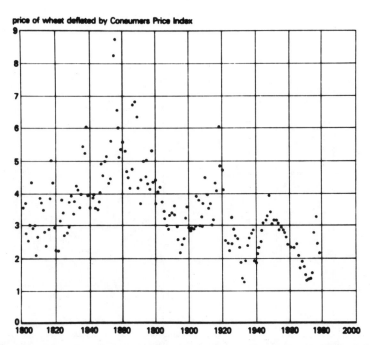

FIGURE 2.10a. The Price of Wheat Relative to Wages in the United States.

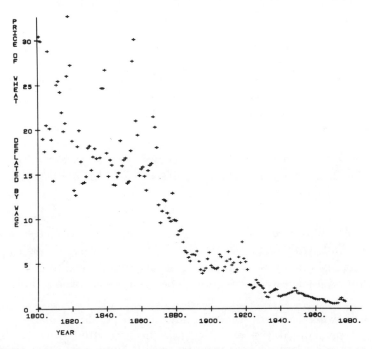

FIGURE 2.10b. The Price of Wheat Relative to the Consumer Price Index.

71

1967 dollars per bushel

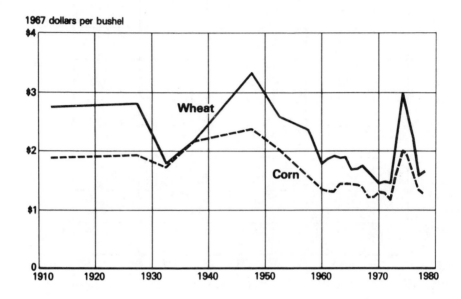

FIGURE 2.10c Export Prices of U.S. Wheat and Corn in Constant 1967 Dollars.

> Under the program, wheat growers who left 15% of their land idle could participate in government price-support and loan programs if prices fell below a minimum level. The administration hasn't proposed a corn set-aside, although Agriculture Secretary John Block says he's thinking about it. (*Wall Street Journal*, October 1, 1981, p. 1)

Set-asides would repeat the cycle which begins with restricted production and ends with fears of world inability to produce enough food when there is a bad year worldwide, because some flexibility to meet temporary shortages has been lost when American production goes down.

A growing food insurance policy should be mentioned: at present, 35 percent of the world's grain in 1980–1981 goes to feed animals for meat (Hudson, 1981). The growing consumption of meat

TABLE 2.5 Index of World Food Production per Capitia

Year	Excluding Mainland China (1952–56 = 100) UNFAO	Including Mainland China (1961–65 = 100) UNFAO	USDA	Combined Index (1948–52 = 100) UNFAO	USDA
1948–52	93			100	
1952	97			104	
1953	100			108	
1954	99			106	
1955	101			109	
1956	103			111	
1957	102			110	
1958	106			114	
1959	106			114	
1960	107			115	
1961	106			114	
1962	108			116	
1963	108			116	
1964	109	102		118	
1965	108	100		116	
1966	111	103		119	
1967	113	105		121	
1968		106		123	
1969		105		119	
1970		106		123	
1971		107		125	
1972		104		120	
1973		108		126	
1974		107	113	125	132
1975		108	113	126	132
1976		110	117	128	136
1977		110	118	128	137
1978			122		142
1979			118*		137

*Preliminary estimates

Sources: UN Food and Agriculture Organization, *Production Yearbook*, 1968, 1975, 1976, and *World Agricultural Situation*, January 1980.

Note: I am more inclined to believe USDA figures for the years since 1974 because they are more recent and because the USDA has no institutional stake in showing a relatively poor world food situation, whereas the UNFAO does. The likeliest source of the difference is in population estimates rather than in aggregate food production estimates.

per person* as income rises leads to increased grain production capcity (as well as to increased grain prices, other thing being equal). In time of dire need, this grain could be diverted to feed humans.

AGRIGULTURAL PRODUCTION

Various writers see danger clouds for the continuation of these trends in the United States, in crop yields, soil erosion, and farmland loss to urbanization. Let us therefore look at these issues. My colleague Earl Swanson has for more than a decade studied the economics of soil erosion in great detail. He has found that from the point of view of the farmer and landowner, and taking a reasonable economic horizon as defined by a range of realistic discount factors, soil conservation practices that are markedly different than present common farm practice do not pay, from a private point of view. And even when the public costs of soil erosion are also taken into account, the conclusion changes little. In three of the six watersheds he studied, silting up of the drainage ditches is important enough so that changes in present conservation practices would be economic from a social point of view; in the other three, not. But this has nothing to do with the loss of top soil for future farm operations that so excites conservationists. And improvements in drainage ditch technology could further reinforce the conclusion that current practices are economic.

The purported decreasing gains in agricultural yields is another apparently unfavorable change that has frequently been warned about recently. Again, Swanson has studied the matter. In Figure 2.11a we see his corn yields in the last four decades; the trend is at least linear in absolute gains, and may be faster than linear. And close examination of corn and soybean yields in Illinois holding weather and other factors constant confirms the impression given by the figure that

> Both corn and soybean yields in Illinois are still trending upward. Nothing in this study indicates that there is a leveling off, contrary to predictions a few years ago. As long as producers continue to adopt favorable production practices, which stem

---

*Meat consumption may also drop again with still higher income, and with changing tastes and perceptions about health. This seems to be happening already in the United States.

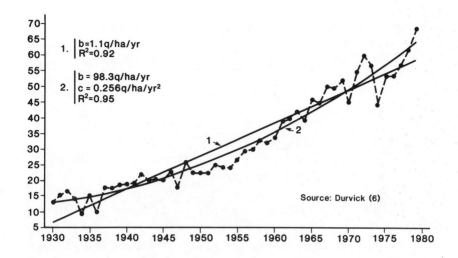

FIGURE 2.11a. Average Corn Yields in U.S. 1930–1979
Source: Reproduced from Swanson, 1981, Durvick (6).

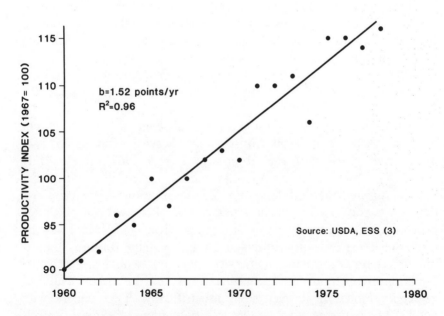

FIGURE 2.11b. U.S. Agricultural Productivity 1960–1980.
Source: Reproduced from Swanson, 1981, USDA, ESS (3).

largely from research efforts, then yields should continue to rise for some time. Only if the research base for developing future management practices declines will there be a leveling off of corn and soy-bean yields." (1980, p. 9).

Overall U.S. agricultural productivity continues to increase at the same absolute rate, too (Figure 11b).

The agriculture-connected scare that has gotten the most publicity lately has been the purported yearly "loss" of 3 million acres of farmland to "urbanization," an assertion proclaimed widely by the National Agricultural Lands Study of the Carter administration and given support by present Secretary of Agriculture John Block. I've worked on the matter for some months, and if it will give you some comfort, I can assure you that that claim is as preposterous as any so-called "official" statistic that has ever been rushed into print. The true figure is roughly one-third or less of the publicized 3 million-acre figure. This is at or below the average for the decades since 1950 of about 1 million acres a year. And only a portion of that 1 million acres is cropland, the rest being pasture, wasteland, and so on. Furthermore, this represents only a microscopic proportion of U.S. land. *Total* urbanized land in the United States is less than 3 percent. And we are making more new cropland from irrigating deserts and draining swamps (wetlands) each year than we are "paving over." Most improtant, total U.S. cropland has been going up and not down since the 1960s, due to increases in demand for food.

The 3-million-acre figure is a political scam. Its only apparent support was a faulty Soil Conservation Service resurvey in 1975 of a small portion of the observations in a 1967 survey. Only about 55 observation points represented agricultural land that became urbanized, and less than 20 observations were cropland that were converted to urban uses. And there were other huge problems with that resurvey stemming from the fact that the original survey was not intended to throw light on this matter, but rather on conservation practices. It is most conclusive that the 3-million acre figure is contradicted by all the other available evidence, much of it very solid scientifically. Two papers with details ad nauseam are available upon request (Simon, 1981; Simon and Sudman, 1981).

SPECIES EXTINCTION AND DEFORESTATION

Another fear among environmentalists is that the earth is losing large numbers of its species, largely as a result of world deforestation. For example, the *Global 2000 Report* to the president expressed concern over the possible loss of species between now and the year 2000. Its "Major Findings and Conclusions" section says: "Extinctions of plant and animal species will increase dramatically. Hundreds of thousands of species—perhaps as many as 20 percent of all species on earth—will be irretrievably lost as their habitats vanish, especially in tropical forests" (U.S., 1980, I, p. 3). *Global 2000* also expressed concern about deforestation, especially in the tropics, both for itself and as related to the loss of species. "The projections indicate that by 2000 some 40 percent of the remaining forest cover in LDCs will be gone" (U.S., 1980, I, p. 2). And the concern is "official": *Global 2000* "was the U.S. government's analysis of probable changes in world population, resources, and environment through the end of the century" (U.S., 1981, p. iii). I submit that this is an egregious case of a far-reaching prediction based on virtually no evidence.

Let's start with the loss of species itself: the proximate source of these assertions is a book by Norman Myers, *The Sinking Ark* (1979; see also Ehrlich and Ehrlich, 1981), from which we may extract these key points:

1. The estimated extinction rate of known species is about one every four years between the years 1600 and 1900.
2. The estimated rate is about one a year from 1900 to the present.
   No sources are given for these two estimates, either on the page from which the quote is taken or on pages 30–31 of Myer's book where these estimates are again discussed.
3. Some scientists (in Myer's words) have "hazarded a guess" that the extinction rate "could now have reached" 100 species per year. That is, the estimate is simply conjecture and is not even a point estimate but rather an upper bound.
4. Even this guessed upper limit in (3) is then increased and used by Myers, and then by Lovejoy, as the basis for the "projections" quoted above. In *Global 2000* the language has become "are likely to lead" to the extinction of between 14 percent and 20 percent of all species before the year 2000 (U.S., 1980, II, p. 328). That is, an upper limit for the present which is pure guesswork has become the basis of a forecast for the future, and one which has been published in newspapers to be read by tens of hundreds of millions of people and understood as a scientific statement.

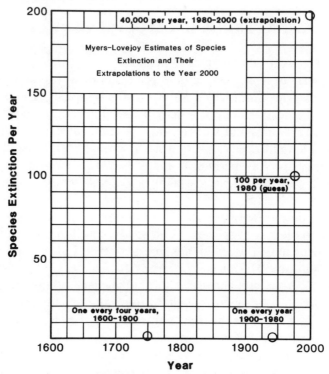

FIGURE 2.12 Myers-Lovejoy Estimates of Species Extinction and Their Extrapolations to the Year 2000.

The two historical rates stated by Myers, together with the yearly rates implied by Lovejoy's estimates, are plotted together in Figure 2.12. It is clear that without explicitly bringing into consideration some additional force, one could extrapolate almost any rate one chooses for the year 2000, and the Lovejoy extrapolation would have no better claim to belief than a rate, say, one hundredth as large. Looking at the two historical points alone, many forecasters would be likely to project a rate much closer to the past than to Lovejoy's. Such a projection is based on the common wisdom that in the absence of additional information, the best first approximation for a variable tomorrow is its value today, and the best second approximation is that the variable will change at the same rate in the future as it has in the past.

Projected change in the amount of tropical forests implicitly underlies the differences between past and projected species-loss rates in Lovejoy's diagram. But to connect this element logically, there must be systematic evidence relating an amount of tropical forest removed to a rate of species reduction; no such empirical evidence is given by Lovejoy, Myers, *Global 2000*, the Ehrlichs, or other sources I have checked.

We might logically stop here, with the case considered complete. Let us go further, however. Lovejoy asserts that there is now, and will be in the future, a rapid rate of deforestation (though we must say again that even if the rate of deforestation were indeed rapid, there would still be little or no basis for inferring a rate of species extinction of Lovejoy's projected magnitude). But in fact there is no historical evidence to support a projection of such rapid deforestation. *Global 2000* says "Significant losses of world forests will continue over the next 20 years. . . " (U.S. 1980, I, 2). But *Global 2000* presents no time-series data on such losses. (And please keep in mind that only a historical series of comparable observations can scientifically and statistically establish the existence of a trend. Observation at one given moment can convey only impressions about a trend. The impressions may be sound because they are made on the basis of first-hand contact, previous wide experience, and wise judgment. But this is a very different basis for policy decisions than are well-grounded statistical trend estimates.)

Global 2000's main reference is Persson (1974). But Persson's study was a one-time survey, following in the path of prior FAO work. I therefore arrayed the FAO data plus Persson's data in Table 2.6. From that table I draw two conclusions: First, the data are too crude and irregular to show any trend with any reliability. And second, there is no obvious recent downward trend in world forests— no obvious losses at all, and certainly no "near catastrophic" loss. And this is so even though the long-run historical trend must be downward at the beginning of human settlement in an area. Data from *World Wood Review* for the countries with the largest forests shows much the same story of irregular inconclusive data as does Table 2.6.

Recent papers by Lugo and Brown (no date) and by Allen and Barnes (1981) look at some additional data and arrive at the same conclusion—the data do not support the worried statements about the pattern of deforestation.

WORK AND INCOME

Now let us get down to the nitty-gritty: work and income. One of the great trends in historical economics is the decline in work hours

TABLE 2.6 World Forest Area, 1947–1974 Millions of Hectares of Forest

	1947 FAO: World Forest Inventory			1953 FAO: World Forest Inventory			1958 FAO: World Forest Inventory			
	productive	other	total	accessible	inaccessible	total	accessible	inaccessible	total	in use
North America	507	221	728	312	344	656	400	333	733	400
South American and Central America	664	91	775	329	561	890	332	699	1031	90
Europe and USSR	727	319	1046	558	321	879	1269	3	1272	594
Asia (excl. USSR)	358	162	520	311	214	525	326	194	520	236
Africa	306	543	849	284	517	801	380	373	753	125
Oceania	50	30	80	20	66	86	26	70	96	20
Total	2612	1366	3978	1814 in use	2023 inexploited	3837	2733	1672	4405	1465
				1140	2697					

Productive in this report means accessible, and so is subject to change over time. This means that the category "other" land may or may not be usable land.

The information was gathered by survey, and responses covered about 62% of the surface area of the earth, (excl. Greenland and Antartica). The rest of the world was estimated from other records.

Comparison of this data to the 1947 inventory would be invalid since: (1) data have improved somewhat; (2) changed definitions; (3) effects of rebuilding from WWII made 1947 estimate provisional for some countries.

In this survey, 73% of world forested area responded to the questionnaire.

Comparison with 1958 inventory is again difficult because statistics provided by countries improved somewhat.

In this survey, accessible land was defined as actually (currently) accessible, as opposed to previous surveys where accessible also included potentially accessible areas.

The survey responses covered 88% of world forest area.

	1963 FAO: World Forest Inventory				1974 Persson: World Forest Inventory			
	productive	unproductive	total	Forest Land	closed	open	total	Forest Land
North America	420	290	710	750	630	0	630	630
South America and	371	530	901	996	590	152	742	795
Europe & USSR	832	44	876	1054	905	144	1049	1089
Asia (excl. USSR)	340	160	500	550	400	60	460	530
Africa	300	400	700	710	190	570	760	800
Oceania	52	40	92	96	80	105	185	190
Total	2315	1464	3779	4156	2800	1000	3800	4030

Improved statistics again make comparison to previous inventories difficult.

The classification of land into accessible or inaccessible was dropped.

Forest land without forest can be found by comparing forest land area to actual forested area.

No data on forest area in use was available, but a breakdown of forest in industrialized versus less industrialized areas is available.

83% of world forest area was covered by the response to this survey.

Closed forest is defined as forest area with crown density of more than 20% of surface area.

Open woodland is forest area with crown density between 5% and 20% of surface area.

The total of open and closed forest area corresponds to the total of productive and unproductive in the 1963 FAO report.

This report was based on surveys of Africa and Europe, and used other sources to supplement the survey results. While comparison with the 1963 survey is still strained, it is the best comparison available with this information.

TABLE 2.6 (Continued)

Note: In general, the difficulties in interpreting and comparing the data shown in this table are glaringly obvious from the data themselves, and become even more obvious when the original sources are examined. The 1947 Inventory made explicit in its table that many important countries did not report their situations, and "For this reason the staff of FAO has searched all available records bearing upon the forest resources of countries which have not yet replied, and has prepared tentative estimates for each of them" (p. 6) and the reporting changed from Inventory to Inventory. The definitions and categories have changed, for example, from "productive" to "accessible" to "productive," and then to "closed" in Persson. There were gross errors in the data, some of which were so obvious that they could be repaired. And then there is the fundamental issue that (from the world-production point of view, though not from the point of view of species extinction) it is net growth that is of interest rather than acreage, and the former rises relative to the latter as forests are brought under rational maintenance.

The main purpose of displaying this table here is to show what *cannot* be shown, the trend of forest areas over recent decades.

82

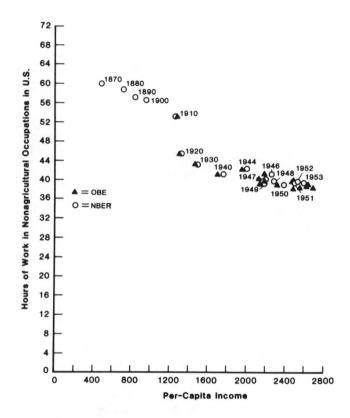

FIGURE 2.13 The Relationship of Per-Capita Income to the Length of Work Week in Non-Agricultural Occupations in the United States, 1870–1960.

Source: *Work week,* De Grazia, 1962, Table 1; per-capita income, *Historical Statistics of the U.S.*

per week with increasing income, which is an increase in a person's freedom to dispose of his or her most treasured possession—time—as he or she wishes. We see this decline in the United States (Figure 2.13) and we see it also in a contemporary array of countries by income (Figure 2.14). If that isn't a benign trend, I don't know what is.

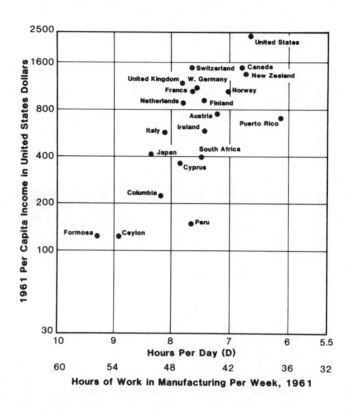

FIGURE 2.14 Hours of Work in Manufacturing per Week in a Cross-Section of Countries, 1961.

Source: Kindleberger, 1965, p. 6.

Another trend that most of us would consider benign is the increase in the proportions of students who obtain various levels of education (Figures 2.15a and 2.15b). In 1860, 56.2 percent of persons aged five to 19 were in school in the United States; in 1970, it was 88.3 percent. For blacks, the figures were 1.8 percent in 1850, 9.9 percent in 1870, 33.8 percent in 1880 (a peculiar jump in the figures occurs between 1870 and 1880), 31.1 percent in 1900, 53.5 percent in 1920, and 85.3 percent in 1970 (*Hist. Stat.*, p. 370).

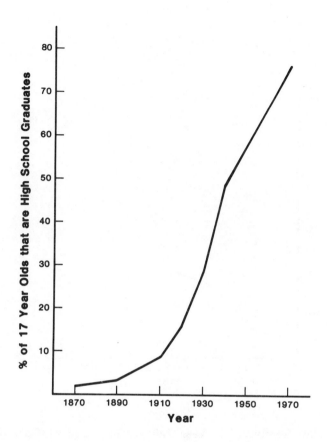

FIGURE 2.15a Percent of 17 Year Olds as High School Graduates.

In 1940, 79 percent of persons 14 to 17 were in school in the United States, and 94 percent in 1970; for persons 18 to 19, the percentage went from 29 percent to 47.7 percent (50.2% in 1969) (*Hist. Stat.,* pp. 370, 372). The percentages of 17 year-olds that were high school graduates in various years were as follows: 1870, 2 percent; 1890, 3.5 percent; 1910, 9 percent; 1920, 16 percent; 1930, 29 percent; 1940, 49 percent; 1970, 76 percent (*Hist. Stat.,* p. 379). For 23 year-olds with BA or first-professional degrees the percentages were: 1900, 1.9 percent; 1920, 2.6 percent; 1930, 5.7 percent; 1940, 8.1 percent; 1950, 18.2 percent; 1970, 22.3 percent (*Hist. Stat.,* 385–386).

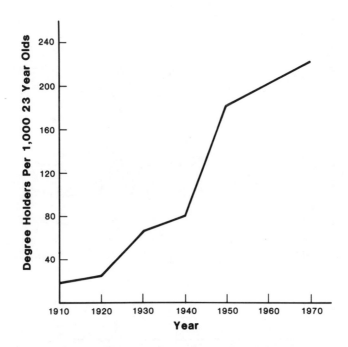

FIGURE 2.15b Number of 23 Year Olds per Thousand with BA or First Professional Degree.

The pupil/teacher ratio in U.S. public secondary education went from 27.8 in 1910 to 14.4 in 1970 (*Hist. Stat.,* p. 368). The average length of school term went from 132 days in 1870 to 157.5 days in 1910, to 175 days in 1940, to 179 days now. The average number of days attended school per year per enrolled pupil went from 78 in 1870, to 113 in 1910, to 152 in 1940, to 162 in 1970 (*Hist. Stat.*, pp. 375–376).

The proportion of persons receiving education also has boomed phenomenally in the less-developed countries in recent decades. All this increased education is an indication of an increase in individuals' occupational and social mobility, and of their increasing opportunities to develop their talents in a fashion that is personally satisfying as well as socially useful.

With respect to income, the most straightforward and the most meaningful index, I believe, is the proportion of persons in the labor force working in agriculture. In 1800 the percentage was 73.6 percent (*Hist. Stat.*, p. 139), whereas in 1980 the proportion was 2.7 percent (U.S. Department of Commerce, 1981). That is, standardized for population size, only $\frac{1}{25}$ as many persons today are working in agriculture as in 1800. This suggests that the effort that would produce one bushel of grain or one loaf of bread then, will now produce the bushel of grain or loaf of wheat plus what 24 other bushels or loaves will buy in other goods, equivalent to an increase in income by a factor of 25. Of course this is crude; it does not allow, on the one hand, for the lower earnings of farm workers in 1800 compared to other workers, or the transfer of some functions such as equipment manufacture from the farm to the nonfarm sector. On the other hand, it does not allow for the fact that almost half of farm operators work off the farm, most of them 200 days a year or more (*Stat. Abst.* 1980, p. 689); and it does not allow for the one-third of our crops that are exported (*Stat. Abst.,* p. 713). So this long-run increase by a factor of 25 may be a fair index of the improvement in our standard of living.

Income in less-developed countries has not reached nearly so high a level as in the more-developed countries, by definition. But it would be utterly wrong to think that income in LDCs has stagnated rather than moving ahead. In fact, income per person has increased at a proportional rate at least as fast, or faster, in LDCs than in MDCs since World War II (Morawetz, 1978).

"But in the last few years our income has been falling, not rising," many people in the United States say. If one tries to confront that statement directly, one runs into a bewildering confusion of statistics—family income, personal income, wages, and so on. This is my summary of the U.S. income situation: (1) Just how we've been doing over the past few years is confusing, but we probably haven't lost or gained much. Considering the full decade of the 1970s, we're better off at the end than we were at the beginning. (2) The recent slowdown probably is one of many pauses in the remarkable long-run increase in purchasing power. We only need to reflect on the contents of our homes and public places compared to the contents of homes in 1900 or 1700 or 700 A.D. to realize the enormous sweep of this trend. To focus on five or ten recent years probably is to repeat the worst sort of error in long-run forecasting, looking at one short recent period. It is this error that has led to such incorrect forecasts of resource scarcity as the scares of deforestation in Elizabethan England and Teddy Roosevelt's United States, and the coal scare of Jevons' day 100 years ago in England. (3) When considering short-run and intermediate-run income statistics, it is crucial to remember that improvement in our material life is understated due to the omission of improvements in product quality, and of new products, from the consumer price indexes. A striking example, chosen to bring out this point, is the difference between price and cost trends of tires. "The CPI tire index rose 140% from 1935 to 1978, or an average of 1.9 percent per year. However, had the index been based on cost per tire mile, a far more accurate measure of the product's value to the consumer than price, the index would have reflected a decline of 9% in 43 years, or 0.2% per year" (Moore, 1978). Here are the details of the computation:

Tire Price	*Tire Cost*	
1978 Steel-belted radial:		
approx. price, $68		
Life: 40,000 miles	$0.00170	per mile
Auto wt: 1.95 tons	0.000872	per ton-mile
Road speed: 50 mph	0.0000174	per ton-mile-mph
1935 4-ply cotton:		
approx. price, $13		
Life: 7,000 miles	$0.00186	per mile
Auto wt: 1.45 tons	0.00128	per ton-mile
Road speed: 40 mph	0.0000320	per ton-mile-mph
Price per tire rose 423%, but tire life increased 471%.	Cost per mile fell 9%	
	Cost per ton-mile fell 32%	
	Cost per ton-mile-mph fell 46%	

(A digression on international income comparisons: we're still better off than any other country. We have 79 percent more cars—and of course larger cars—than our closest European competitor, Sweden, and 31 percent more than Canada; 126 % more radios than

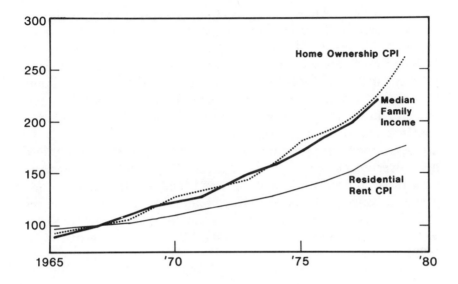

FIGURE 2.16 Home Ownership Costs, Residential Rent, and Family Income (1967 = 100).
Source: Reproduced from Miller, 1980, p. 20.

Argentina—next highest after us except for Canada, which also isn't close to us; 64 percent more TV sets than Sweden; and we use 28 percent more paper than Sweden. Comparisons of per capita income in various countries based upon exchange rates are quite misleading. Much more meaningful are comparisons of the total goods consumed in a pair of countries, figuring with the prices of both countries. Using this method, Kravis et. al. found that if the United States is assumed to have had a standard of living of 100 in 1974, West Germany had 78, France 73, Netherlands 69, Britain 63.5, Japan 59, and Italy 49, while Kuwait had an index of 161 [New York *Times*, November 26, 1978].)

Some of you will say that this is all just damned statistics, and you will mention rising housing and food prices as showing that we are really worse off. But amazing as it may seem, the apparent rise in housing prices is not a fact. Figure 2.16 shows that rent has fallen since 1965, and home prices have stayed about even, as compared to the CPI.

Indications of how our housing has been improving is seen in data on persons per room, and on plumbing: In 1940 in the United States, 20.2 percent of households, but in 1974 only 4.5 percent, had 1.01 or more persons per room (U.S. Department of Commerce, 1977, p. 90). In 1940, 44.6 percent of housing units, but in 1974 only 3.2 percent, lacked some or all plumbing facilities. In 1940, 55.4 percent had all plumbing, whereas in 1974, 96.8 percent had all plumbing (U.S. Department of Commerce, 1977, p. 91).

As to food, the proportion of our incomes spent for food declined from over 20 percent in 1960 to below 17 percent in 1979. (And though the subject of this paper is trends and not intercountry comparisons, some of the latter may be interesting: the proportion the United States spends for food is lower by far than in countries such as France, Germany, and Britain [*Wall Street Journal*, August 16, 1979, p. 36].

What about our consumption of public goods? Paved highways have risen from nothing since the turn of the century in the United States. Natural park areas have been rising (Figure 2.17a). And trips to parks have risen phenomenally (Figures 17b & 18). And population growth is not in the long run antagonistic to these trends.

Employment? One person who wants a job and lacks one is a tragedy. But for perspective, we might keep in mind that in Malthus' day almost one person in nine was on welfare (Peterson, p. 473).

What about the nonmaterial side of life: crime, for example? Long-term trends provide an interesting perspective. Consider the trends in homicide in England from the thirteenth to the twentieth centuries in Figure 2.19. Gurr's assessment—which makes sense to me—is that the long-run trend is downwards, with occasional sustained upsurges following on wars; we are presently in the midst of one such upsurge, in his view.

INTERPRETATION AND CONCLUSION

What is the explanation of our material life getting better in the face of supposed limits to growth? I offer an extended answer in my recent book (Simon, 1981). In short, the source of all benefit is the human mind—and there are more productive minds when there are

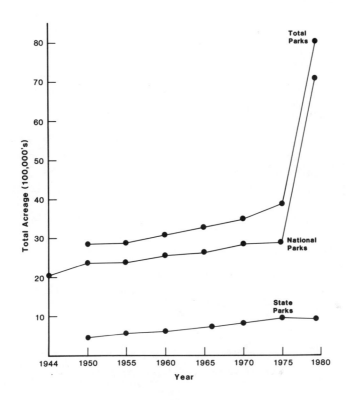

FIGURE 2.17a Land in Public Parks, 1944–1980
  Sources: *Statistical Abstract of the U.S.*, 1973, p. 202; 1980, p. 242 for 1950–79.
Information Relations to the National Park System, United States Department of
the Interior, National Park Service, June 30, 1944, p. 35 for 1944.

more people, other things being equal. That is, population growth
from additional babies being born, or from immigrants, has a
positive effect in the long run upon the standard of living due to the
increased productivity that is caused by more people. The productivity increase comes both from the additional minds that develop productive new ideas, as well as from the impact of the additional demand for goods upon industry productivity. Immigrants are the best

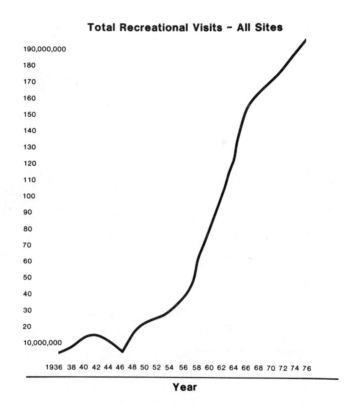

FIGURE 2.17b Total Recreation Visits—All Sites.
Source: Baden, 1980, p. 16.

deal of all because they usually come when they are young and strong, and therefore contribute more to the public coffers in taxes than they take out in welfare services.

The long-run outlook is for a more abundant material life rather than for increased scarcity, in the United States and in the world as a whole. What we need most to speed this process is imagination and enterprise, boldness and will, in order to build and to beautify our economy and our society.

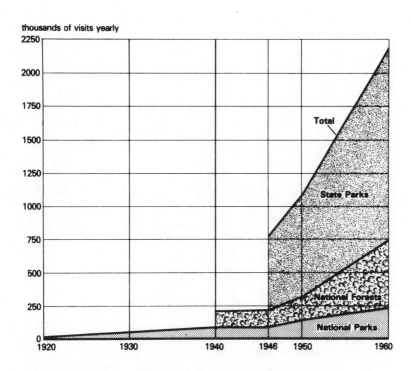

FIGURE 2.18 Visits to Public Parks, 1920–1960.
Source: Simon, 1981, Figure 16-5.

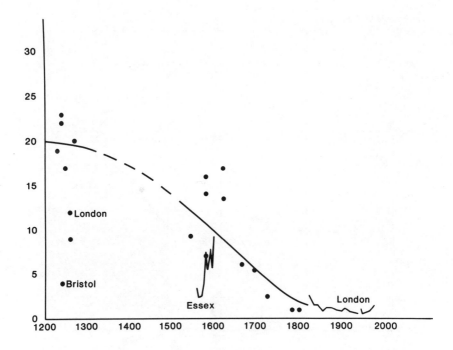

FIGURE 2.19 Estimates of Homicides per 100,000 Population in England from the Thirteenth to Twentieth Centuries.

Source: Reproduced from Gurr, 1981.

REFERENCES

Abramovitz, Moses. "Welfare Quandaries and Productivity Concerns." *American Economic Review* 71 (March 1981) 1-17.

Abrams, Bill. "People Spend Less of Their Income on Food Even Though Its Price Keeps Rising Sharply." *The Wall Street Journal* (August 16, 1976), p. 36.

Allen, Julia C. and Douglas Barnes. "Deforestation, Wood Energy, and Development." Mimeo draft. (Washington: Resources for the Future). September, 1981.

Baden, John, ed. *Earth Day Reconsidered.* (Washington, D.C.: Heritage Foundation, 1980.)

Barnett, Harold J., Gerard M. van Muiswinkel, and Madechai Schechter, "Are Minerals Costing More?" IIASA, February, 1981.

Bettman, Otto L. *The Good Old Days—They Were Terrible.* (New York: Random House, 1974).

Boskin, Michael J. "Prisoners of Bad Statistics." *Newsweek* (January 26, 1981), p. 15.

Brown, Lester R., Patricia L. McGrath, and Bruce Stokes. "Twenty-two Dimensions of the Population Problem." *Population Reports*, Series J, no. 11 (November, 1976).

Demeny, Paul. "The Population of the Underdeveloped Countries." *Scitific American*, 231 (September, 1974), pp. 148-59.

Ehrlich, Paul, and Anne Ehrlich. *Extinction* (New York: Random House, 1981).

Furlow, Robert. "'Real' family income plunges a record 5%." *Newark Star-Ledger* (Friday, August 21, 1981) p. 30.

Giesbrecht, Martin. "The Sad (Statistical) Reality." *National Review* (April 17, 1981), p. 421.

Gurr, Ted Robert. "Historical Trends in Violent Crimes: A Critical Review of Evidence." Mimeo in preparation for *Crime and Justice: An Annual Review of Research*, III, February, 1981.

Gwatkin, Davidson R. "Indications of Change in Developing Country Mortality Trends: The End of an Era?" *Population and Development Review* 6 (December 1980), pp. 615-644.

Heller, Walter W. "Economic Rays of Hope." *The Wall Street Journal* (December 31, 1980), p. 4.

Hudson, William. Personal communication, October, 1981.

Kindleberger, Charles W. *Economic Development.* (New York: McGraw-Hill, 1965), p. 6.

Lee, W. R. ed. *European Demography and Economic Growth.* (New York: St. Martin's Press, 1979).

Lovejoy, Thomas of U.S. Council on Environmental Quality and the Department of State. *The Global 2000 Report to the President,* Vol. II. (Washington: U.S. Government Printing Office, 1980), pp. 328ff.

Lugo, Ariel E. and Sandra Brown. "Conversion of Tropical Moist Forests: A Critique." Mimeo, Institute of Tropical Forestry, Rio Piedras, Puerto Rico, and Department of Forestry, University of Illinois (no date).

Malabre, Alfred L. "Living-Standard Gauge Shows Big Rise Since Carter Became President." *The Wall Street Journal* (December 2, 1980), p. 48.

Metropolitan Life Insurance Company. "Trends in Disability Among Males." *Statistical Bulletin* 59 (July–September 1978), pp. 12–15.

Miller, Glenn H. "The Affordability of Home Ownership in the 1970s." *Economic Review* of the Federal Reserve Bank of Kansas City. (September–October 1980), pp. 17–23.

Moore, F. Lee, Jr. "Index Mischief: Price Versus Cost." *Electric Perspectives* No. 78/5, pp. 8–27.

Morawetz, David. *Twenty-five Years of Economic Development: 1950 to 1975.* (Baltimore: Johns Hopkins, 1978).

Myers, Norman. *The Sinking Ark* (New York: Pergamon, 1979).

"U.S. Is Second-Richest Country, New Survey Finds." The New York *Times* (November 26, 1978), p. 482.

Peterson, William. "Malthus and the Intellectuals." *Population and Development Review* 5 (September 1979), 469–478.

Reynolds, Reid T. "Money Measures." *American Demographics* 2 (February 1980), pp. 34–36.

Simon, Julian L. "The False Religion of Farmland Preservation," *The Public Interest* (forthcoming).

Simon, Julian L. and Seymour Sudman. "How Much Farmland Is Being Converted to Urban Use? An Analysis of Soil Conservation Service Estimates," mimeo, 1981.

Swanson, Earl R. "Agricultural Productivity and Technical Progress: Acceleration or Atrophy?" Mimeo, Working paper no. 81 E-152, Department of Agricultural Economics, University of Illinois (January, 1981).

Swanson, Earl R. and James C. Nyankori. "Influence of Weather and Technology on Corn and Soybean Yield Trends." *Agricultural Meteorology* 20 (1979) pp. 327–342.

Swanson, Earl R. and James C. Nyankori. "Influence of Weather and Technology on Corn and Soybean Yield Trends—Reply." *Agricultural Meteorology* 23 (1981), pp. 175–180.

U.S. Bureau of the Census. "Real Median Family Income Declined, Number of Poor Increased, Reflecting Double-Digit Inflation and Economic Slowdown During 1980." News Release. Washington: U.S. Department of Commerce, August 20, 1981.

U.S. Bureau of the Census. "Nation's 1980 Farm Population Estimated to be 6.1 Million, Census Bureau–U.S.D.A. Report Shows." News Release. Washington: U.S. Department of Commerce, September 2, 1981.

U.S. Council on Environmental Quality and the Department of State. *The Global 2000 Report to the President*, Volumes I and II. (Washington: U.S. Government Printing Office, 1980).

Walker, W. M., E. R. Swanson, and S. G. Carmer. "What yield plateau?" *Crops and Soils Magazine* 32 (November 1980), pp. 7–9.

Part II
New Strategies for Managing Risk

3

RISK ASSESSMENT AND PUBLIC TRUST: THE ROLE OF THE UNIVERSITY

Thomas O. McGarity

INTRODUCTION

During the latter half of the twentieth century it has been apparent that the products and technologies that make all of our lives more comfortable also expose many of us to undesirable risks to our physical well-being. The automobile is perhaps the best example of a beneficial technology that does not come without its attendant risks, and this single technology has had a profound effect upon both private law and public law. In the last 15 years we have also discovered that many of the production processes that yield beneficial products have undesirable side effects that pose risks to human health and to the environment. The environmental movement has turned this simple observation into a powerful political force. To say that a product, by-product, or production technology poses risks to human health and the environment, however, is merely to begin the inquiry into how we should react to those risks. The next logical step in the inquiry is to assess the magnitude of those risks. Only after attempting to assess the nature and potential magnitude of such risks can society rationally begin implementing control technologies and other responses aimed at reducing or eliminating those risks.

The risk assessments that formed the basis for early protective government actions were, by present standards, crude and intuitive. For example, former and current EPA Administrator Ruckelshaus assessed the carcinogenic risks posed by DDT in a subjective and qualitative way. He found as a "fact" that respectable scientists had testified that DDT causes cancer in laboratory mice. He did not embellish this finding with any data or predictions as to the extent of human exposure to DDT other than to point out that DDT was by 1972 ubiquitous in the environment. He made no predictions about the number of human cancers that could be expected from status quo levels of exposure to DDT.

In the intervening years, much intellectual effort has gone into attempts to assess quantitatively the health and environmental risks posed by new and existing technologies and production processes. Prodigious efforts have gone into risk assessments for the nuclear power industry. Huge sums have been expended on studies of the lives that could be saved through the installation of airbags and other passive restraints in automobiles. The EPA has now adopted a policy of quantifying the carcinogenic risks posed by pesticides before considering initiating proceedings to take them off the market. And the Supreme Court has strongly hinted that OSHA must assess risks quantitatively before setting exposure standards for toxic substances in the workplace.

Risk assessment is big business. Even a cursory overview of risk assessment in practice, however, reveals that the "science" of risk assessment is still quite primitive. It is also extremely controversial. Moreover, the huge stakes that often ride upon regulatory decisions based upon risk assessments ensure that the controversy surrounding risk assessment will not disappear.

It is therefore appropriate to examine risk assessment as it is practiced in health and environmental regulatory agencies such as the Environmental Protection Agency (EPA), the Occupational Safety and Health Administration (OSHA), the Consumer Product Safety Commission (CPSC), and the Food and Drug Administration (FDA) to observe the problems that have plagued agency attempts to use risk assessment in regulatory decision making and to suggest some possible reforms. As the name of this chapter suggests, the university may play a role in the way agencies assess risks, and the university can play a role in reform.

I suggest that public trust is the key to the future of the use of risk assessment in the regulatory process. A thorough risk assessment is an extraordinarily complex task, and the speculative nature of the intellectual endeavor ensures that it is shrouded by large uncertainties. The process must depend heavily upon the input of highly trained experts—toxicologists, statisticians, ecologists, chemists, physicists, and many others. In many cases the combined efforts of these experts can lead to more rational choices about risks than the largely uninformed choices of consumers and businessmen operating in an imperfect market. There are, however, important limits on the rationality of expert-derived quantitative risk assessments in the field of health and environmental protection that are dictated by the immature state of the "science" of risk assessment and by the uncertainties that always pervade attempts to predict the future when one of the variables is a human being. Indeed, these limits are so endemic and so profound in scope that they threaten the integrity of the entire risk assessment enterprise. Whether risk assessment will ultimately prove useful will depend upon the legitimacy of its outputs in the eyes of businessmen, consumers, environmentalists, and the general public. And this, to a considerable degree, depends upon the extent to which the public trusts the experts who contribute to those outputs.

Under the traditional paradigm for the regulatory agency, established during the New Deal, the public places a great deal of trust in expertise. The regulatory agency is presumed to be very familiar with the workings of the industry that it regulates, and this special knowledge can be used to ensure that the regulated industry pursues public goals as well as its own narrower private goals. When public and private goals conflict, the agency directs the regulated entity toward the former and away from the latter.

During the 1960s and early 1970s the traditional New Deal paradigm was strained to the breaking point. The Vietnam War made many Americans cynical about the value and neutrality of expertise. We were told once too often by experts that the light was at the end of the tunnel. The statistics compiled by the experts told us that we were winning the war, but the observers who were there told us we were losing.

At the same time the consumer and environmental movements were launching a barrage of probes into the inner workings of the regulatory agencies. Although lacking in technical sophistication, those studies revealed in a way calculated to reach the general public what careful observers of the administrative process had known for a long time—that many of the agencies that were supposed to be protecting the public had in fact become captives of the regulated industries and were more often than not serving their interests rather than the broader public interest.

Finally, the surge of "social" regulation—aimed at protecting public health and the environment—that came about at the end of this period required agencies to address their rules and regulations across-the-board to many different industries. The happy assumption that the experts within a regulatory agency could acquire a familiarity with regulated industry sufficient to enable the agency to guide the industry in socially desirable directions no longer held. No agency could assemble enough experts with sufficient familiarity with all of the varied forms of human conduct that the new social regulatory agencies had to address. In addition, the policy debates that led to the enactment of social regulation made it painfully clear that there was very little consensus within the community of experts as to what the problems were and how to solve them. Disagreement among experts became still another source of uncertainty for the new and rejuvenated agencies.

Moreover, the reform spirit that animated the new agencies took the regulated industries by surprise. Agency attempts to implement the extremely ambitious goals of the early environmental and worker safety statutes soon precipitated a predictable backlash of charges of overregulation and bureaucratic arrogance. Reacting to these complaints the Reagan administration launched a comprehensive "regulatory relief" program that precipitated still another backlash of charges that the agencies consistently placed private greed over the broader public interest.

We find ourselves now in a position where we do not know whether to trust the agencies that have been established to regulate and protect us. Regulated businessmen tell us that senseless and overbearing regulations have caused the prices of their products to increase and have thereby contributed to inflation with little benefit for consumers and the environment. Environmentalists and consumer activists tell us that the agencies are so thoroughly captured by the regulated firms that we can no longer be confident that the food we eat and the water we drink will not cause cancer or some other dread disease. One agency attempts to deprive us of saccharin at the same time that another strikes a "sweetheart deal" with a hazardous waste dump. It is enough to cause one to despair of any solutions to these complex problems.

Still, those of us who produce and consume products and care about the environment cannot do the job individually. We cannot collect and wade through the scientific data, draw inferences from those data and make scientific judgements in accordance with those inferences, choose between competing risk assessment models, and ultimately make the correct individual choice. If we cannot delegate these problems to some institution that is deserving of our trust, the process of making simple day-to-day decisions about what we eat, where we go, and what to do will rapidly paralyze us.

We could have developed a market for professional risk assessors to assess risks for collective consumption or for individual consumption for a fee. A few such institutions (for example, magazines like *Consumer Reports)* have arisen in the recent past, and, not surprisingly, they go to prodigious lengths to inspire public trust. Nevertheless, the most important shield between consumers and the environment is, and will probably continue to be, the regulatory agency. The immediate task is to discover mechanisms for ensuring public trust in the decisions that they reach.

This chapter will examine the regulatory system that has evolved during the 1970s to protect the public from risks to health and the environment. It will identify some of the problems with the system that have reduced the extent to which the public can confidently place its trust in the system's outputs. It will suggest that the nation's universities can be vital repositories of public trust, but only if the scientists and other experts within those institutions retain their traditional neutrality and do not, like many of the regulatory agencies, become the captives of one or another of the interests that joust in the regulatory arena. Finally, I will suggest that even the impact of impartial experts from the university community cannot resolve many of the most important questions that plague health and environmental risk assessment. Many of these questions are technical in nature, but ultimately policy-dominated. The result that the decision maker reaches must therefore depend as much upon public considerations as upon expertise. It is important that the entire enterprise remain completely open to all members of the scientific community and to an informed public. The university can also play an important role in educating members of the public about the risks they face. While allowing all of the relevant players to have a role in an open decision-making process will not guarantee perfect results, it can go a long way toward producing trustworthy decisions.

THE NATURE OF RISK ASSESSMENT

The dominant theme that emerges from a study of risk assessment in regulatory agencies is that of uncertainty. All predictions about the future involve uncertainties, but for health and environmental risk assessment the uncertainties are compounded by our basic ignorance of many of the mechanisms through which technologies and their by-products cause harm. Indeed, the uncertainties that becloud many attempts to assess health and environmental risks are so substantial as to threaten the viability of quantitative risk assessment as a decision-making tool.

By most definitions, risk is a function of two variables—probability and consequences.[1] While some policy analysts might disagree, we will assume that risk is simply the product of probability and consequences. Hence if there is a one-in-ten chance as I drive down the road during the next year that I will have a collision that causes $1 thousand worth of damage to my automobile, the risk to my wallet is $1 hundred. Other things being equal, I should, for example, be willing to spend $95 per year for automobile insurance that protects me from all losses. In assessing health and environmental risks uncertainties arise concerning both of these elements of risk.

Gathering and Evaluating Information

Kinds of Risk Assessment Information. The quality of the information underlying a risk assessment is probably the most important determinant of its value to the decisionmaker. Information on risks can come from various sources, depending upon the kind of risks being assessed and the nature of the regulatory regime. Risk information can be further divided into at least three broad categories: (1) information on the normal risks posed by a product or technology as it is properly used or operated; (2) information on abnormal risks due to human error or negligent misuse of the product or technology; (3) information on abnormal risks due to intentional malfeasance where the product or technology is merely a tool in the hands of a malevolent individual intent upon doing harm. While the former category of information has dominated past risk assessments, society has increasingly placed the burden of producing and evaluating information in the latter two categories on companies and agencies, even though a company is not in a legal sense at fault when its product or technology is negligently misused or abused by a criminal.[2]

Normal Risks. In many regulatory schemes, the regulatory agency performs a gatekeeping function, releasing a technology to the market only after the proponent of the technology has demonstrated to the satisfaction of the agency that the technology is suitably safe. Examples of gatekeeper regulatory regimes include drug, pesticide, and nuclear power plant licensing and, to a more limited extent, product screening under the Toxic Substances Control Act. Typically the technology's proponent has the initial burden of assembling risk information. For drugs, pesticides, and some chemicals, for example, the manufacturer must undertake extensive health and safety testing in laboratory animals to determine the toxic effects of the substances. A potential nuclear power plant licensee must perform elaborate geological and engineering safety studies to demonstrate that the location and the design of its plant is suitable. After the studies are completed by the company itself or by a contract or under its supervision, they are evaluated by the company's scientists and engineers. Their forwarded to the agency which reevaluates the studies and draws its own conclusions. After receiving its initial license, the technology's proponent typically has the continuing burden of providing risk information. If postlicensing information demonstrates that the product, by-product, or technology poses unacceptable risks, then the agency must initiate a proceeding to withdraw the license previously granted.

Other regulatory regimes place more of the burden of producing risk information on the regulatory agency. The Clean Air Act, the Clean Water Act, and the Consumer Product Safety Act, for example, generally place the burden of performing risk assessments upon the relevant agency.[3] The information required to set air and water quality standards and to evaluate consumer product safety is much the same as that required to support the registrants of a drug or the license of a power plant. The relevant agency must commission laboratory animal experiments and engineering studies. Since the agency generally does not take action until the product, by-product, or technology is already on the market or in the environment, the agency can search the scientific and engineering literature for additional studies and can assemble information (for example, from epidemiological studies and product complaint histories) on the harm caused by normal use of the product or technology. Under these statutes, the regulatory agency generally has the burden of demonstrating on the basis of its own risk assessments that the product, by-product, or technology is unacceptably risky.

Abnormal Risks Due to Human Error and Negligent Misuse. Evidence on abnormal risks due to human error and negligent misuse is rarely included in gate-keeping risk assessments. This is not surprising, because it is very difficult to predict in the abstract how the conduct of negligent human beings will combine with products or technologies to create risks. Usually the risky combinations only manifest themselves after the product or technology has been in existence for a while. Gate-keeping risk assessments do make attempts to predict human error for risks involving very large consequences, such as the meltdown of the fuel core of a nuclear reactor. When risk assessors can point to instances in which predictable human error will cause very large damage, the agency typically responds by requiring the installation of redundancies or fail-safe devices that protect against damage even when error occurs. Alternatively, the agency can promulgate regulations aimed at keeping dangerous technologies or products away from humans who are likely to misuse them negligently. Nuclear power plant operators, for example, must be licensed, and some dangerous pesticides may only be used by "certified applicators."

Other health and environmental statutes usually ensure against human error only after one or more accidents have happened. The response is typically ad hoc and it is addressed to the particular risk that has already manifested itself in harm. Interlock devices ensure that automobiles cannot be started until the seat belts are buckled. Childproof caps are required on drugs and other toxic consumer products. In this context, the added protection that an agency can provide probably does not exceed greatly the protection afforded by the tort system under a strict liability regime.

Intentional Malfeasance. Only recently have regulatory agencies devoted substantial attention to risks posed by the interaction of a product or technology with a criminal who malevolently causes harm. Recent concerns for sabotage in nuclear power plants and the tragic murders of innocent consumers of the over-the-counter drug Tylenol have focused public and governmental attention on this problem.[4] Obviously, only rarely will an agency deprive society of a valuable product or technology simply because it may be misused. Knives and guns can and do kill in the hands of miscreants, but so far society has determined that the benefits derived from these products outweigh their risks. Occasionally, however, agencies place restrictions on the availability of products and technologies because of the risk that they will be intentionally misused. Handguns must be registered, dynamite and plastic explosives are not routinely available for purchase, and some weapons, such as bazookas and Num-Chuck sticks, are completely prohibited in many municipalities.

Sometimes the risk of malevolent misconduct can be reduced by control technologies designed to complement the useful technology. Airlines must screen passengers and their luggage for weapons before they board planes. Security technologies in sensitive places like liquid natural gas facilities, petroleum refineries, and nuclear plants can discourage sabotage attempts. Tamper-resistant packaging can be required for drugs, eyedrops, and other commodities.

Another sort of malfeasance that can enter into the risk assessment for a technology is the risk that the company which designs or operates the technology will take safety-threatening short-cuts to reduce expenses. Recent allegations of corner-cutting by nuclear power plant contractors have focused public attention on the nuclear power industry, but the same risk-enhancing conduct could arise in building and bridge construction and product manufacture and design. Regulatory agencies can exert some control over this sort of "white collar" malfeasance through their authority to oversee the development and use of the relevant technologies. Still, since no agency has sufficient resources to ensure perfect enforcement of its regulations, the risk of intentional misconduct by the producer or technology's proponent is another risk that should be factored into the overall risk assessment for that product or technology.

Potential Regulatory Failures. Several severe problems plague the risk assessment efforts of agencies and regulatees. Many of the problems may be endemic in the nature of risk assessment and therefore impossible to cure. Others, however, result from slovenly science and can easily be corrected with adequate regulatory resolve.

Invalid and Fraudulent Studies. Quite often in regulatory debates over risk assessments a party to the debates argues that a study should not be considered because it is invalid. This general indictment can have many causes. The study may have been conducted pursuant to improper protocols. The data may have been handled incorrectly. The observer may have inadvertently biased the study in one direction or another. The study may have relied upon an inappropriate statistical analysis, or the study may have had too few data points to lead to valid statistical conclusions.

While the problem of inadequate data can afflict both gatefold regulatory regimes and schemes that require affirmative government action, the impact of poorly conducted studies can vary depending upon the regulatory framework within which risks are being assessed. For example, many of the most important pesticides currently used in the United States were originally registered by the U.S. Department of Agriculture when protocols for health testing were much less demanding than at present and protocols for environmental risk assessment were virtually nonexistent. The studies that originally supported pesticide registration would be grossly inadequate by today's standards to support those registrations. The public soon realized that it could place very little trust in pesticide decisions that were made long ago on the basis of inadequate data. In a rare attempt to undo the mistakes of the past, Congress reacted to these concerns and mandated that all old pesticides must be reregistered according to modern requirements. Unfortunately, the process got off to a very erratic beginning when EPA refused to evaluate the validity of the old studies in determining whether new studies were required.[5] Hence, new studies were required only for new requirements for which there was a complete absence of data. The agency did not implement the congressional intent that old invalid studies be replaced with new studies conducted in accordance with modern protocols.

The failure to evaluate the validity of existing studies returned quickly to haunt the agency when it was revealed that a major outside consultant for the drug and chemical industry, Industrial Biotest Corporation, had for years been preparing health and safety studies for clients that were very poorly done and, at times, even fraudulent. As the IBT scandal grew, EPA quickly implemented a program of validating IBT-prepared studies and, where necessary, requiring studies to be repeated. The fact that these shoddy and fraudulent studies had for years supported many widely used pesticides does not inspire trust in either the pesticide industry or the EPA and its predecessor agencies.

The problem of inadequacy can be just as disagreeable when an agency attempts to use allegedly invalid data as the basis for imposing new health and environmental requirements on an industry. Since there is no gatefold process under many health and environmental statutes, the agency must either conduct studies itself or depend upon studies done by contractors or independent persons (often university scientists) with outside funds. The agency often has little control over the quality of the information that it must rely upon. Yet the agency has an obligation to protect the public. The problem reaches its enigmatic extreme when a poorly conducted study indicates that a large group of people may be at high risk. Are health and environmentally protective decisions that are grounded in poor data any more trustworthy than decisions to leave a product or technology on the market based upon inadequate studies?

An especially good example of this problem is the attempt by EPA to assess the risks that the chemical wastes buried under Love Canal posed to the surrounding neighbors. The Love Canal issue captured national attention in 1978 when it became evident that chemicals from the old hazardous waste disposal facility buried in Love Canal were leaking into neighboring homes. Many homeowners complained of various illnesses, and amateur attempts were made to draw an association between residency near Love Canal and birth defects and spontaneous abortions. Under extreme political pressure to do something about the perceived crisis, EPA commissioned a "quick and dirty" study to compare chromosome aberrations in Love Canal residents with their incidence in the general population.[6] Although some scientists (including one commissioned by Hooker Chemical Country, the former owner of the Love Canal site) opined that the study was adequate, given the constraints under which the investigator was operating, others felt that the failure to establish a separate control group and observe aberrations in that group undermined the integrity of the entire study.[7] EPA and state agencies had to decide whether this study warranted evacuating the Love Canal area.

EPA and other health and environmental agencies have often been criticized for taking regulatory action on the basis of inadequate or incomplete scientific information.[8] The agencies respond that it is very time consuming and expensive to perform perfect studies. Once a study raises the possibility that humans or the environment may be harmed, the agency cannot avoid making a decision. A decision to allow the status quo to continue is still a decision, and it is a decision based upon the very same information as the decision to take regulatory action. Agencies can always await the completion of further studies before taking action, and the companies whose product and technologies are affected by regulatory action will predictably urge delay until the agency can be more certain that its action will reduce genuine, rather than hypothetical, risks. For example, cigarette manufacturers and tobacco growers even now maintain that government action limiting exposure to cigarettes would be overly precipitious in light of the uncertainies surrounding the question whether smoking causes cancer and heart disease.

The debate is played out in the same way under the gatekeeper statutes, but the roles are switched. Some consumer and environmental groups have urged gatekeeper agencies not to approve new technologies and products until more studies are performed to demonstrate that they are suitably safe. Since uncertainty always surrounds scientific data and since more studies can always potentially reduce this uncertainty, the argument that more studies are needed always has some plausibility. The practical effect, however, can be that society is indefinitely deprived of valuable products and technologies. For example, many pharmaceutical companies complain of a "drug lag" in the United States attributable to FDA's excessive demands for more information on drugs that are already in use in other countries. Consumer groups, on the other hand, point to thalidomide as an example of a product that did not harm Americans because of FDA's prudent concerns.

There must come a point at which the agency decides that it must act despite the uncertainties that attend the current state of knowledge about the risks posed by the product, by-product, or technology at issue. Discovering this "information threshold" in individual cases, however, can be an extraordinarily difficult task. Since scientific expertise is necessary in evaluating the quality of scientific studies, the agency must have the input of qualified scientists who are deserving of public trust. Yet the threshold determination is also strongly tinged with policy considerations. Scientists can inform the decisionmaker about the quality of the studies, but they cannot appropriately dictate whether or not the decisionmaker should act. Whether the agency acts on the basis of risk assessments that depend upon admittedly poor studies or waits until further study can reduce uncertainties depends to a large degree upon the directions that society, through Congress, has given the agency.

Hence, the information threshold for administrative action might be located at different points in different statutory programs. For example, Congress might dictate that one agency demand extremely well-conducted studies when it is performing a gate-keeping function for nuclear power plants while at the same time demanding that another agency act to take products off the market on the basis of studies that could never be accepted for publication in a major scientific journal.[9] Both commands are consistent with an overall policy of protecting health and the environment from risks. Whether the policy is wise or not is, of course, a matter of political debate, and the political debate depends greatly upon the trust that voters have in regulatory agencies and their advisors.

Conflicting Interpretations and Inferences. Even when well-conducted studies are available to a regulatory agency, the agency must attempt to interpret those studies, either alone or in combination with other studies, and draw inferences from the studies about real-world risks. This task, perhaps more than any other in the risk assessment effort, calls for the exercise of informed expert judgment. When the experts agree upon an interpretation of a study and the inferences that may be drawn from it, it is usually appropriate for the regulatory agency to defer to the expert consensus. Unfortunately, in many cases the experts cannot reach agreement and the radical dissensus that surrounds the interpretation of some scientific data is alarming to laypersons who expect scientists to provide definitive answers to interpretational questions.

For example, one might expect scientists to agree at least upon the proper diagnosis of the lesions produced by a chemical substance in animal tissue when that tissue is viewed under a microscope. Unfortunately, this is far from true. In one fascinating study, 43 instances of both spontaneous and induced liver cancers in laboratory animals were distributed to 15 experimental pathologists in Japan for histological diagnosis. The author concluded that "[o]ut of a total of 43 cases, identical diagnosis was returned by all of the pathologists in five cases, and their diagnoses varied with all of the others."[10] The disagreements among pathologists about how to interpret animal studies have dominated two important legal proceedings concerning the pesticides Heptachlor/Chlordane and mirex.[11] Varying scientific and engineering interpretation can also afflict attempts to use epidemiological data in worker health risk assessments and geological data in assessing the risks posed by deep well injection of hazardous substances and by the burial of high level radioactive wastes.

Scientists and engineers can objectively explain their interpretations of some kinds of data only to a point. Past that point subjective considerations weigh heavily in their conclusions. While this scientific and engineering judgment can be influenced by result-oriented policy considerations, it should have more to do with viewpoints, arising out of long years of study, on how the world works. As a result of different backgrounds and experiences, different scientists interpret the same data differently. The lay decisionmaker, having no criteria for choosing among the diverging opinions of the experts, is cast adrift. He cannot tell how much of an expert's opinion is shaped by legitimate scientific views about how the world works and how much is shaped by the expert's result-oriented policy preferences, which may be either pecuniary, political, or ideological in nature.

Similarly, experts draw inferences form studies on the basis of broad assumptions drawn from experience with the way that the world works. Most scientists, for example, will infer that a substance will be carcinogenic in man if it is carcinogenic in laboratory animals. The scientists who for years have been studying carcinogenesis mechanisms in laboratory animals have, after all, not devoted their lifetimes to protecting rodent species from cancer. Scientists frequently formalize a series of inferences about nature into a mathematical model in an attempt to infer from an observed set of data the answers to questions for which empirical data are not available. All such inferences and models must ultimately rely upon assumptions that are not easily verified. As with expert interpretation, expert inference drawing must depend upon expert judgment. Without a readily available mechanism for testing the assumptions underlying expert inferences, the lay decisionmaker is again at sea. He or she cannot know whether the inference is based upon an assumption about how the world works or an ideology about how the world ought to work.

The problem is exacerbated by the recent advent of "adversarial science." When an important public policy issue depends upon a risk assessment which in turn depends upon scientific or engineering judgment, the parties who have an interest in the outcome of the decision often shop around for scientists who are likely to express an expert opinion that will dictate the preferred policy result. Having found experts willing to testify on its behalf, a company might go even farther and place on retainer experts of the opposite persuasion to co-opt them. This is not to say that expert opinion can be bought and sold, although many of the experienced practitioners of this process have very cynical assessments of the system. The sharp relief in which the adversarial process casts the decision, however, does tend to erode away common ground and thereby force the decisionmaker to choose one side's experts over the other's.

There are obvious reasons why the views of scientists and engineers employed by the regulated firms should be treated with some skepticism. Even if their views have not been purchased, their services have usually been requested because they were expected to give the "right" answer to interpretational questions. The views of those employed by a regulated firm that do not coincide with the firm's views on the ultimate policy question are not likely to be revealed to the agency at all, absent some coercive mechanism such as a subpoena. It does not necessarily impugn the integrity of any scientist to suggest that his views should be less deserving of trust when compared with the views of another equally competent scientist whose views have not been solicited for pay.

The views of scientists and engineers employed by public interest groups might appear at first glance to be less suspect. While these experts, like all experts, work for pay, their pay is generally much lower than that of their contemporaries in industry, and many of them are capable of drawing much higher salaries elsewhere. Some have left the employ of industry precisely because their expert judgment continually played second fiddle to company policy. Although they could presumably be fired for reaching the "wrong" opinion on an interpretational question, the financial conflict of interest may not be as strong. Scientists working for public interest groups, however, may have their own axes to grind, and this may detract from the objectivity of their analyses. The area of the public spotlight is probably as attractive to the scientist as to anyone else, and it may sway his or her judgment to know that a position different from that taken by the agency and/or the regulated industry will likely receive the attention of the media. Moreover, the adversarial science and expert-shopping problem is still present. A public interest group like a regulated industry, will presumably look for experts who will exercise their expert judgment in a way that accords with its policy preferences. Hence, both sides to an adversarial science dispute must be viewed with a grain of salt.

Agency scientists offer the potential for objectivity. They presumably have no axes to grind, and their pay should not depend upon how they exercise their scientific judgment. Once again, however, neutrality and objectivity are not assured. While government scientists and engineers do not often lose their jobs for exercising good faith expert judgment, this phenomenon is not unheard of. In addition, experts can relatively easily be shifted to positions in the dark recesses of an agency if they persist in reaching conclusions that do not accord with the policy preferences of the politically appointed managers. (They can, of course, re-emerge when managers of a different policy persuasion are appointed.) While agencies rarely "shop" for staff scientists and engineers for individual projects, an agency with a particular policy that lasts through time may hire more experts who are likely to make the "right" interpretations and inferences. Finally, agencies cannot afford to pay enough to attract the most highly qualified experts in a particular field; nor do they offer the nonfinancial attractions of a position in academia. Unless the agency attracts scientists with some ideological commitment to its mission, in which case their judgment is thereby suspect, it will be unable to employ the kind of high quality scientists and engineers that are accorded respect among their peers and the public generally.

Time and work pressures can combine to cause agency experts to defer to the scientific judgment of others. When a study that is presented to an agency in support of a product or technology is accompanied by a concise summary by a competent industry or consulting scientist, there is a great temptation to take those interpretations and inferences at face value. Probing the tables of reported data and redoing questionable statistical analyses is difficult work. Reexamining the original raw data (for example, looking at the microscope slides from animal studies) is usually prohibitively time consuming. Yet public trust is undermined when the supposedly independent reports of agency employees consist of little more than cut-and-paste jobs with regulatee-submitted summary memoranda; nor is the public likely to place great faith in regulatory documents, such as some of EPA's "registration standards" for pesticides that have been compiled by teams consisting of EPA employees and regulatee scientists.

Dialogue between agency experts and outside experts can help the agency interpret data and draw appropriate inferences. It has been suggested that better decisions might result if experts were simply allowed to sit down together, discuss the scientific and engineering data, and reach a consensus on the interpretations and inferences that the data may properly support. The "adversarial science" process that typifies agency decisionmakers is, in this view, a perversion of the true scientific method.

The general tendency of groups of scientists to gloss over dissenting views in their efforts to reach consensus, however, may cast some doubt upon the validity of this approach. Moreover, the "decision conference" and "peer review" experiments of the Gorsuch EPA is not an appropriate model for this suggestion. The public can have little faith in interpretations and inferences that result from meetings between agency scientists and industry experts that exclude experts from public interest groups and academia;[12] nor can the public place much faith in agency reports that are made public only after they have been initially reviewed and "corrected" by scientists of the regulatees.[13] The scientific consensus-building process, if it is to be viable at all, must be open to all interested participants.[14] If it is not, it will earn the justifiable condemnation of the affected public.

Trans-scientific Questions. Many highly technical questions that are cast in technical terms cannot, given the current state of scientific knowledge, be answered by science. Dr. Alvin Weinberg has coined the term "trans-scientific" to describe this sort of issue. In Dr. Weinberg's words, trans-scientific questions "are, epistemologically speaking, questions of fact and can be stated in the language of science, [but] they are unanswerable by science; they transcend science."[15] A good example of a trans-scientific question is the shape of the dose–response curve for carcinogenic chemicals at the low-dose end. Scientists can phrase this question in scientific terms and even agree on an experiment that could resolve it. To demonstrate with 95 percent confidence that the carcinogenic effects response rate for a particular dose rate equal to the human exposure to the substance is less than one-in-a-million, the experimenter need only feed 3 million animals at the human exposure rate and compare the response with that of 3 million control animals. As a practical matter, however, this "mega-mouse" experiment cannot be performed. Scientists are therefore forced to test many fewer animals at much higher dose rates and to attempt to extrapolate that information to low dose rates through various assumptions and inferences.

As Weinberg suggests, trans-scientific questions are not really scientific questions at all—they are policy questions. To the extent that risk assessments require the answers to trans-scientific questions, therefore, they must rely upon result-oriented considerations of public policy. Experts *qua* experts have no role at all to play in this process, other than to aid the lay decisionmaker in separating true trans-scientific questions from questions that are not trans-scientific. Until the true carcinogenesis mechanism or mechanisms are known, the decisionmaker must, for example, choose from among the competing risk assessment models largely on the basis of his or her policy determination whether or not to "err on the side of safety."

This is a matter of no small importance, because the uncertainties inherent in carcinogenic risk assessment are enormous. The predictions of the number of cancers resulting from status-quo exposures to carcinogens can vary over ten orders of magnitude, depending upon which model is adopted.[16] Still there is no "scientific" way of choosing from among the available models. Indeed, if the administrator does attempt to couch the carcinogenic risk assessment question in scientific terms, and thereby avoids making explicit the policy judgments that motivate him to choose one model over another, he is simply deceiving the public—conduct not especially conducive to public trust.

THE ROLE OF THE UNIVERSITY IN REFORMING REGULATORY RISK ASSESSMENTS

The ordinary citizen cannot be blamed if he or she does not place much trust in regulatory agencies to make wise decisions concerning risks. Regulatory decisions are not always based upon valid data drawn from well-conducted studies. We cannot know whether an expert's interpretations and inferences are based upon scientific understanding or ideology and public policy preferences; nor can we be sure that the agency has resolved such questions in accordance with sound public policy articulated in a democratic setting rather than behind closed doors in a "decision conference" from which some interests are excluded. We do not usually know the extent to which the final output of a risk assessment depends upon scientific fact and the extent to which it depends upon the agency's policy-dominated answers to trans-scientific questions. There is obviously room for reform.

It seems clear that the quality of information can be improved. We need to ensure against fraud and bias in the studies that support risk assessments. EPA and the Food and Drug Administration have begun to implement a vigorous auditing program for company-owned and independent laboratories that produce studies for risk assessments. While this is an important first step, it has been suggested that more is needed. For example, the government could require that laboratories be certified through a renewable licensing process to ensure high quality data production. Both this solution and the laboratory audit program, however, share one major disadvantage. They are applicable only to information used by gatekeeper agencies. Auditing and certification do not ensure that the information that EPA relies upon in setting national standards for air and water pollutants is reliable.

One solution that would meet the needs of all risk assessment agencies is the creation of national toxicological laboratories financed by the federal government. Several such centers already exist for generating information to be used by EPA and OSHA in setting standards. The centers could be expanded to include product testing for gatekeeper agencies supported by fees charged to the manufacturers of the products.

The national laboratory solution, however, has several drawbacks. It would be very expensive to product manufacturers, and they would lose control over important timing and resource questions. It would also inevitably reveal confidential proprietary information to government scientists, thereby increasing the chances that the information would find its way to competitors. Moreover, national laboratories can produce high quality information only if they are funded at sufficient levels to attract high quality experts and to provide them with sophisticated equipment. In an age of shrinking budgets, it is not clear that this level of support will be forthcoming. If it is not, the quality of health and environmental information could deteriorate still further. Finally, even if national laboratories are adequately funded, the results that they produce may still reflect a bias toward the policy preferences of the regulatory administrators currently in power. While the scientists in a national laboratory would be independent from the regulated industry, it would probably not be entirely independent from the bureaucracy. Greater independence could be secured, however, by placing the laboratories beyond the reach of the agencies that they serve. The OSHA–NIOSH experience suggests that while this arrangement can have an adverse effect on administration priority setting, it can be very effective in ensuring the independence of the laboratory scientists and other risk assessment experts.

Can the university play a role in ensuring the integrity of scientific studies? The faculties of the universities of this country contain many highly credentialed scientists and engineers with expertise in evaluating the validity of scientific studies, and they can be retained on a consultancy basis or on a voluntary basis. There is usually no reason to believe that university faculty members and research associates are generally biased toward one policy or another. They can, however, be expected to be extremely critical and to have an imperfect appreciation of the difficulties encountered in some data-gathering efforts. This attitude, which characterizes scientists generally, may manifest itself in a "bias" toward gathering still more information. Even a very good study can be improved upon, and a brand new study can reduce uncertainties. The regulatory decision-maker, therefore, should call upon the university as a source of scientific expertise, but he should recognize that the advice may be that further study is desirable and be prepared to reject that advice if policy considerations call for action.

Should the university become a source of health and environmental information? The university is, of course, an abundant source of information about the effects of products, by-products and technologies on society, and it will continue to provide a constant flow of information to regulatory decisionmakers. But the university is not an appropriate institution for providing the routine information required for an agency's day-to-day decisions. For example, the proposed national laboratories should not be housed in the nation's universities along the Livermore and Los Alamos models. The kinds of studies that must routinely be performed to assess the risks of products, by-products, and technologies are not the stuff of basic scientific and engineering research. University research can provide the appropriate protocols for such studies and can suggest possible additional data that should be required. But the process of testing substances and technologies in accordance with standard protocols is mostly "cookbook" work that is not likely to earn the principal investigator much academic credit. To be sure, expertise is required, but the day-to-day testing is not really the sort of research science that should go on in universities.

There is also much room for improving the way that agencies are advised upon the interpretations to give to health and environmental information, the inferences to be drawn therefore, and the models to be used to predict future relationships. Closed door meetings with scientists and engineers employed in the regulated industries raises the suspicion of bias and conflict of interest. (Closed door meetings with public interest group experts would, of course, raise similar suspicions.) Yet these are precisely the experts that are most likely to be the most well-informed on the technical questions that the agency must attempt to resolve. The agency needs a source of neutral, disinterested advice.

The possible reform would be to create an elite corps of "certified public scientists" who would be licensed and overseen by a separate government agency and whose income would not depend upon the answers that they provided to interpretational and inferential questions. A profession of neutral experts, patterned after certified public accountants, might provide neutral advice to lay decisionmakers. This, however, would be an expensive and perhaps stultifying solution. It is not clear that this new profession would attract the highest caliber scientists. In any event, it is largely unnecessary to the extent that the university is available as a supplier of neutral, disinterested technical advice.

The agency can, for example, farm out important risk assessment decisions to august bodies like the National Academy of Sciences (NAS) whose membership is drawn principally from the university community. Since NAS review is often a deliberative and expensive process, it can be invoked for only a few of the most important interpretational and inferential questions that an agency faces. In addition, while the administrative process tends toward an overly adversarial mode, the NAS process may strive too mightily for consensus, burying or belittling minority views in the process. Moreover, the agency that addresses interpretational questions to such deliverative bodies carefully frames them in such a way as to minimize the external policy component of the required answer. Otherwise the agency is in essence delegating its decisionmaking duties to the nongovernmental entity. Institutions like the National Academy of Sciences have their own political and policy agendas, and they can be lobbied and vilified like any other public institution. It should, therefore, not be too readily assumed that the advice given by such bodies represents "pure" technical advice untinged by any result-oriented policy preferences. Still, our society is inclined to place great trust in prestigious scientific bodies, and they can play an extremely valuable role in policy formulation if they are used sparingly and if they are asked to answer the right questions.

Another solution is for the agency to select esteemed scientists and engineers from academia for advisory committees to review the efforts of agency experts and offer advice to them. The agency's own advisory committee should generally be more available than the NAS to help the agency with problems requiring rapid decisions. However, the agency will still have to take care to ask the advisory committee the right questions. An additional problem with agency-selected advisory comittees is that their members can be selected by result-oriented administrators with a view toward the kinds of interpretations and inferences that they are likely to draw in individual cases. The agency can, in other words, stack the committee in such a way as to assure that the advice will be consistent with the policy preferences of the person making the selections. The recent revelations of suggested hit lists for scientists on EPA's Scientific Advisory Board suggests that this a real possibility.[17]

Finally, the research arm of the university can perform a valuable function in a less direct way than participating in the actual decision-making process. University scientists and engineers can observe carefully the technical component of the regulatory risk assessment process and carry out a dialogue in quasi-popular scientific journals such as *Science, Nature,* the *New England Journal of Medicine,* and *Scientific American.* There is evidence of such dialogue already. A story in *Science* by a lay reporter about a particular regulatory development will occasionally trigger a response by an agency, industry, or public interest group scientist which leads to further commentary in the "Letters" section from the university community. This dialogue should be encouraged. It contributes to public understanding of the issues and to open debate and consensus-building among technical experts. Indeed, it might be wise for a periodical like *Science* to set aside a portion of every issue for dialogue on a current question of science/policy. In addition to providing a public forum for the agency and various interest groups, it would encourage the active participation of disinterested scientists from academia who might not otherwise contribute to the dialogue. It might also have the beneficial result of isolating extreme views that are inclined to acquire more credibility in a relatively closed debate.

There is little that university scientists and engineers can contribute to the resolution of trans-scientific questions other than continuing with the business of university research. The patient process of creating new theories about how nature works and testing them may ultimately lead to definitive answers to questions that science cannot

presently begin to answer. However, the political science, government, and economics departments and the public policy graduate
schools can contribute greatly to the debate over what the appropriate public policy should be. To some extent this debate can be
addressed to the regulator agency that must resolve individual trans-
scientific questions. But even more appropriately public policy
prescriptions should be addressed to the president, Congress, and to
the public in general.

An additional role that students of the public policy-making
process can fill is that of ensuring that agency decisionmakers do not
hide behind the facade of expertise when they are basing decisions
upon policy judgments. It is tempting for policymakers to attempt
this ruse, because it can provide shelter from uncomfortable political
heat. But it is deception just the same, and it should be ferreted out.
University-based observers of the policy-making process can point
out trans-scientific questions and the policy components of other interpretational and inferential science/policy questions, attempt to
discern the implicit policy judgments that underly those decisions,
and measure those judgments against articulated policy goals.

The foregoing discussion reveals that there is much that the
research arm of the university can do to aid the public policy risk assessment process, because the university can be a source of impartial expertise. Unfortunately, the impartiality of university researchers cannot
always be assumed. As the supply of research dollars has steadily
decreased over the last few years, more and more university scientists
and engineers have become increasingly dependent upon private enterprise for research dollars. When a scientist is paid by a company to
testify on a particular matter, his testimony may be viewed with skepticism because of the presumed "scientist shopping" that produced him
as a witness, but the impartiality of the scientist is not generally called
into question by the mere fact that he is being paid to testify in a single
proceeding. Unless he is in the business of testifying regularly in administrative proceedings, it can normally be assumed that the scientist's
concern for his reputation in the university and scientific community
will ensure that he will not let the regulatee call his tune.

When corporate funds, however, become part of the on-going
support for a scientist's research, and perhaps for much of the
research of his peers in other institutions, the threat of losing funds
for saying the wrong things or reaching for wrong results is higher,
and the scientist's impartiality might legitimately be questioned. I

know of few instances where the infusion of corporate funds into basic research is so thoroughgoing that scientific integrity can legitimately be called into question. One possibility is the pesticide research, in which pesticide manufacturers have funded much pesticide-related research in land grant colleges.[18] The recent highly publicized debate over the university–corporate relationship in genetic-engineering research is another area in which this issue will be played out, perhaps with regard to the risks posed by newly emerging genetic technologies.[19]

One principle that seems to be emerging from the genetic-engineering debate is that it is appropriate for a university researcher to consult occasionally for private corporations, but it is inappropriate for the researcher to allow the impact of corporate funding to affect substantially his or her research agenda. Another principle, about which there is less consensus, that may emerge from this debate is that university researchers should disclose to the public all of the significant sources of income that they receive from outside the university for research-related activities. Both of these principles would appear to be equally applicable in the risk assessment context. When a university researcher is appointed to a NAS or an agency advisory committee, he does not necessarily lose his objectivity or impartiality merely because he has done research for a party that might be adversely affected by the decisions for which his advice is solicited. Yet there is no reason why this fact should not be available to the decisionmaker and the public. More importantly, when the researcher's own studies may be at issue before the advisory body, the scientist's presence on the body may dampen criticism and otherwise have a stultifying impact, whether or not the research was supported by an affected corporation. Refusal would seem appropriate under the principle that no person should be the judge of his or her own case.

THE ROLE OF THE UNIVERSITY IN RISK EDUCATION

Thus far, this chapter has focused narrowly upon the nature of the risk assessment process in regulatory agencies. A larger question that bears directly upon the idea of public trust concerns the nature of the risks that we as a society are regulating. Are we regulating too many risks? Do the risks that we are regulating warrant regulatory attention? Are we, in the process, too rapidly applying the brakes to new technologies? The vociferous debate in the mid-1970s concerning public regulation of risks posed by recombinant DNA research raised many of these questions and answered few of them.

One lesson that emerged from the recombinant DNA experience is that while scientific and technical expertise have a large role to play in the risk assessment process, that kind of expertise is largely irrelevant to the question: "How much risk is too much?" The answer to this question, like the answer to trans-scientific questions, is entirely a matter of public policy. In our society this means that it should be a matter of public debate and democratic choice. Yet it would be vastly preferable that the acceptability of risk be a matter of *informed* public choice. And, unfortunately, there is evidence that members of the public are often uninformed or misinformed about the nature of risks and risk assessment.

It is possible that the everyday citizen is asking too much from the regulatory process. If "Joe Citizen" expects regulators to make the world risk-free, then he will inevitably be disappointed. Agencies can cause regulatees to reduce risks from products, by-products, and technologies to nearly zero, but only, in many cases, at enormous expense, (and, perhaps, change in lifestyle) that society is not likely to tolerate. On the other hand, if the everyday citizen asks that the regulatory decisionmaker assess the risks of products, by-products, and technologies, weigh them against their benefits to society, and set the standards at precisely the point at which benefits and risks are balanced, he is also asking too much of the regulator. As we have seen, the risk assessment is heavily freighted with uncertainties. For many, perhaps most, kinds of health and environmental risks it is simply impossible, given the current state of scientific knowledge, to predict with any precision at all, what the risks of products or technologies are, much less to balance them against precise estimates of their benefits.

For example, some time ago when I was an employee in the General Counsel's Office of EPA, I received a memorandum detailing the risks attributable to a fungicide that had caused cancer in one sex of laboratory mice at a marginal level of statistical significance. The risk estimators in the Office of Pesticide Programs had determined, according to the "log-probit" dose-response model, that over a 70-year period (the average lifetime of a human being) the fungicide would cause 27 cancers. This struck me as a very precise risk estimate indeed; so I asked the staff experts to provide confidence intervals with the assessment. Specifically, I asked that the staff specify the range within which the model predicted cancer incidence with 95 percent confidence. A few days later I received a memorandum that stated that with 95 percent confidence the log probit model predicted that the cancer incidence attributable to the fungicide would lie somewhere between 0 and 660,000 cancers. This latter accounting is illuminating, and it speaks volumes about the uncertainties that surround current risk assessment efforts. With this example in mind it is easy to view with a great deal of skepticism a statement by former EPA assistant administrator for Toxic Substances that the risks posed by the citrus fumigant EDB are approximately equal to that of smoking one cigarette over a lifetime.[20]

The public is understandably concerned about the risks that new and old products, by-products, and technologies pose. When they are told that there is dioxin in nearby soil or toxaphene in fish, they react negatively before inquiring into the exposure levels to humans that might result from those sources. When a communtiy learns that a hazardous waste facility or nuclear power plant is to be built nearby it often rallies to prevent it without asking whether the site is the most technologically and environmentally appropriate location for the facility. Yet many of the same people will continue to drive without seatbelts and smoke cigarettes.

All of this may indicate that Joe Citizen does not have an especially sophisticated conception of risk. A corollary to this proposition is that the public should be better educated about the nature of risk in society. The mass media, for example, does little sophisticated analysis of risk. The telecaster's announcement that dioxin is present in Lake Michigan fish is followed by a brief cut to a scientist who explains that dioxin is one of the most posionous substances known to man and another brief cut to an industry scientist or government bureaucrat explaining in a comforting fashion that there is no need for alarm, followed by a final cut to an environmental activist decrying the fact that the government allowed this to happen and proclaiming that he would certainly not eat the contaminated fish. Rarely does the public get a straightforward assessment of the risks posed by an environmental contaminant together with an honest evaluation of the confidence with which the risk statement is made.

This failure of the media to present studies about risk in a straightforward way may reflect a determination that esoteric risk assessments are not "newsworthy." Alternatively, newscasters may intuit that most of the viewing public would not really comprehend the output of a true risk assessment, even if it were presented to them in a straightforward way. If the latter is the case, the answer to greater public understanding of risk may lie in our educational system. And at this point the university can play a valuable role.

Most universities offer courses that discuss and explain risk assessment only in the business and professional schools. But this is simply a matter of training experts; it is not educating the public. Risk assessment ideas could play a public educational role if they were introduced into the undergraduate curriculum, perhaps in courses in environmental studies, political science, and even chemistry and physics. Perhaps the most appropriate place for teaching the importance of understanding the concept of risk assessment is in education courses where the concepts could be imported to the next generation of high school students. The nature of health and environmental risks is currently an important public policy question and its importance is not likely to diminish in the coming decades. Therefore risk assessment concepts might appropriately be made a part of the standard high school government course.

Providing better education to the general public, however, will not eliminate the need for regulatory agencies. Even a risk-sophisticated member of the public would find it extremely burdensome to educate himself as to all of the particular risks that he encounters on a day-to-day basis. Moreover, even if we are aware of risks and understand them, in many cases we will be powerless to do anything about them. We still need agencies to assess risks and regulate conduct that poses risks.

A risk-educated public, moreover, will not necessarily place more trust in bureaucratic risk assessors. To the contrary, a more sophisticated public may have less faith in the current system than a less educated public. Ignorance is often bliss.

An educated public will, however, be much better prepared to participate in the science/policy decision making that goes on in regulatory agencies. Since many of the questions that arise in the risk assessment process are policy-dominated, informed public input can offset the tendency of experts to dominate the risk assessment process. Often regulatory decisionmakers are inclined to dismiss the genuine views of everyday public citizens who testify at hearings concerning risks to the community, because the testimony is often viewed as hysterical and uninformed. The legitimate role of public input is thereby reduced. Perhaps better risk education would result in greater respect among bureaucrats for the views of nonexpert public representatives. Better education might therefore facilitate mutual trust and understanding.

Yet we are still a pluralistic society. Even when the participants in the political process are well-educated and even-tempered, they will still disagree. Since there are no "correct" answers to many science/policy questions, the decision-making process will almost always produce winners and losers. Interest groups that have a stake in the outcome can be expected to participate vigorously. Better education may well result in less overall consensus, but it should precipitate a better policy debate.

CONCLUSION

A free enterprise economy cannot function without public trust in the public and private institutions that make up that social arrangement. For many reasons, regulatory agencies must intervene in the marketplace to protect citizens. These agencies legitimate the burdens that the marketplace places on humans and the environment. If the public cannot trust these agencies to assess the risks that products, by-products, and technologies impose upon society, then the legitimizing function is lost and the marketplace itself is vulnerable to attack. The research arm of the universities can play an important role in the risk assessments that agencies rely upon in determining the appropriate extent of regulatory intervention. Perhaps an even more important role can be played by the education arm of the universities through risk education. In the end, it is in the best interests of companies as well as workers and consumers that risk assessment be an open and well-informed process in which genuine policy disputes can be aired, uncertainties probed, and debates resolved.

REFERENCES

1. This proposition was expressed as an algebraic equation by Judge Learned Hand in the case *United States* v. *Carroll Towing Co.,* 159 F.2d 169 (2d Cir. 1947) "[I]f the probability be called P; the injury L; and the burden, B; liability depends upon whether B is less than L multiplied by P; i.e., whether B < PL. . . . " See also, Posner, R., *Tort Law, Cases and Economic Analysis* (Little, Brown and Company, 1982) for an economic application of this equation. "B, the burden of precautions, is the cost of avoiding the accident, while L, the loss if the accident occurs, is the cost of the accident itself." Ibid., at 1.

2. There is some question whether EPA can cancel a pesticide on the basis of evidence of misuse. See, *Stearns Electric Paste* v. *EPA,* 461 F.2d 293 (7th Cir. 1972) (fact that phosphorous past rodenticide was subject to misuse was not sufficient reason for administrator of EPA to cancel its registration under the Federal Insecticide, Fungicide, Rodenticide Act §§2(Z) (2), 4(c), 7 U.S.C.A. §§135(Z) (2), 135b(c).

3. The 1977 Amendments to the Clean Air Act established two permit schemes for nonattainment areas and for clean air areas that place the burden on the person seeking the permit. See, Clean Air Act Parts C and D, 42 U.S.C.A. §§7470-7491; and 42 U.S.C.A. §§7501-7508 (Supp. 1982).

4. See Emshwiller, J.R., "Nuclear Safety—Sabotage by Insiders," *The Wall Street Journal,* (September 3, 1980) p. 1, col. 6; Malcolm, "100 Agents Hunt for Killer in 7 Tylenol Deaths," New York *Times* (October 3, 1982) p. 1, col. 2; Borowitz, "Packaged Death: Forerunners of the Tylenol Poisonings," 69 *ABA Jour.* 282 (March 1983); Bass and Wiesen, "Tylenol's Aftermath: Product Liability Implications," 69 *ABA Jour.* 287 (March 1983).

5. See Staff Report to the Senate Subcommittee on Administrative Practices and Procedure of the Committee on the Judiciary, 94th Cong., 2d Sess., "The Environmental Protection Agency and the Regulation of Pesticides," 15 (Comm. Print 1976); "Federal Pesticide Registration Program: Is It Protecting the Public and the Environment Adequately from Pesticide Hazards?" GAO Report to Congress, December 4, 1975, RED-76-42, p. 3.

6. Picciano, D., "Pilot Cytogenetic Study of Love Canal, New York," prepared by the Biogenics Corporation for the EPA, May 14, 1980. Picciano, D., "Love Canal Chromosome Study," *Science* 209: 754-56 (1980).

7. Epstein, S., Brown, L., and Pope, C., *Hazardous Waste in America* (Sierra Club Books, 1982), pp. 117-118.
A similar dispute arose which resulted in the cancellation of the pesticide 2,4,5-T. See, Scientific Advisory Panel Defers Recommendation on Cancellation Hearings," Environ. Rep. 833 (August 17, 1970); "2,4,5-T—Miscarriage Investigation Planned Actions Noted," *Pest. and Toxic Chem. News* (December 27, 1978); "Alsea II Report on 2,4,5-T Abortion Effects Said to Be Flawed," *Pest. and Toxic Chem. News* 25 (March 29, 1979); "EPA's Alsea 2,4,5-T Study Had No Scientific Validity, Professor Says," *Pest. and Toxic Chem. News* 21 (April 14, 1979); "EPA's Alsea II 2,4,5—T Study Defended and Attacked Again," *Pest. and Toxic Chem. News* 7 (April 11, 1979).

8. Crandall, R. and Lave L. (eds.) *The Scientific Basis of Health and Safety Regulation* (The Brookings Institution, 1981), p. 13. "The underlying scientific basis

for each regulation [studied] was far from complete in each case: anyone asserting that scientific evidence determined the regulation simply did not have the correct information."

9. Green, H., "The Risk Benefit Calculus in Safety Determinations," 43 *Geo. Wash. L. Rev.* 791, 796 (1975) "Two thirds of the so-called 'scientific evidence' that I read could not have found acceptance by the editorial board of a reputable scientific journal."

10. Takayana, S., "Variation of Histolingual Diagnosis of Mouse Liver Tumors by Pathologists," in *Mouse Hepatic Neoplasia*, App. 1, Burler and Newberne, eds. (1975).

11. See, McGarity, T., "Substantive and Procedural Discussion in Administrative Resolution of Science Policy Questions: Regulating Carcinogens in EPA and OSHA," 67 *Geo. L. J.* 729, 740–43 (1979).

12. EPA announced that the agency will seek to reach voluntary agreements with registrants whenever possible. *Pest. and Toxic Chem. News* 9 (January 6, 1982); Ibid., (March 24, 1982) at 7.

13. "Three Top EPA Holdover Officials Are Expected to Resign Posts Today," Washington *Post* (March 25, 1983), p. 1, col. 2.

14. Wessel, M., *Science and Conscience* (New York: Columbia University Press, 1979).

15. Weinberg, A., "Science and Trans-Science," 10 *Minerva* 209 (1972).

16. Comment, 33 *Stanford L. Rev.* 551–556 (1981).

17. "Compiler of EPA 'Hit Lists' Resigns," Washington *Post* (March 16, 1983), p. 1, col. 1.

18. See, "Potential Conflicts of Interest Among University of California Academic Personnel," Comments by California Rural Legal Assistance to the Fair Political Practices Commission, August 1981; Noble, D., "Academia, Incorporated," *Science for the People* 7 (January/February 1983); Meyerhoff, A., "Campus Research," *Tribune* (March 26, 1982) p. A-11; Meyerhoff, "UC Research Ties: A Secret Needing a Dose of Sunshine," Los Angeles *Times* (February 14, 1982).

19. See generally, McGarity, T. and Bayer, K., "Federal Regulation of Emerging Genetic Technologies," 36 *Vand. L. Rev.* 461–540 (April 1983).

20. *Pesticide and Toxic Chem. News* (September 2, 1981) 14; Ibid., (August 26, 1981) at 19–20.

4

THE USES OF RISK ASSESSMENT
IN REGULATION AND SELF-REGULATION

Edwin L. Zebroski

Some kinds of risks are associated with all human activities, including activities which produce and use necessities such as food, clothing, shelter, and related amenities including health care and education. For any area of government regulation, as well as for the running of an enterprise, a principal guide for intelligent management by regulation or self-management is the proper ordering of the risks involved.

From the regulator's viewpoint, proper ordering is important so that the regulatory body devotes its attention to the elements of its territory in proportion to their relative importance. Otherwise, it will sooner or later be perceived as having concerned itself with minutiae to the neglect of more important matters. From the standpoint of management of a given enterprise, ordering of risks (as well as opportunities to develop added benefits or "goods") is essential for prudent allocation of resources. For example, insurance coverage is normally taken in proportion to the value of an asset at risk (given equivalent risk exposures). It is also not uncommon in industry to insure against loss of productivity—as for example, key facilities or employees—in proportion to the impact of the potential for loss of productivity and its likelihood. At a personal level, people generally keep insurance coverage on property in proportion to its value. It would be generally recognized as imprudent to keep insurance coverage only at the purchase price of a home that was bought 20 years ago.

At the level of business operations, "insurance" can also take the form of investment in backup capability. For example, backup computers and training in backup procedures are now recognized as prudent for shops, banks, and airline ticketing services and aircraft computers.

In complex and highly interdependent societies, direct relationships between productive actions or inactions, and the consequences to human welfare, are subtle and often indirect. For example, the effects of a recession on a generally affluent society, for some people, can be equated to little more than a minor amount of belt-tightening or dispensing with some luxuries. However, for many others the belt-tightening can be much more fundamental. At the margin, a decline in disposable income, both individual and national, has direct effects on nutrition, health care, education, and social services. Even without gross signs of mass malnutrition there will be subtle increases in malaise, incidence of diseases and injuries, crimes, and eventually increases in infant, juvenile, and adult death rates. Even where some of these do not actually worsen, it becomes less possible to implement and reap the benefits of available opportunities to improve conditions.

For small enterprises, or the regulation of small sectors of the public well-being, misrankings of risks, and the associated misallocation of resources, from over-response to minor issues, is not of great public concern. If a small enterprise underinsures and succumbs to a loss—the consequences are localized. The resources available by small diversions from other sectors of the economy are perceived to be effectively unlimited. (For example, a firm producing the most-prized sourdough French bread in San Francisco succumbed when a truck accident resulted in a judgement of several million dollars in excesss of insurance coverage. Other firms now fill the resulting void with only subtle and intangible social costs.)

RANKING OF RISKS TO AVOID MISALLOCATION OF RESOURCES

When the area regulated, or the enterprises involved, comprises a substantial fraction of the total national resources, improper ordering of risk perceptions and risk response allocations has much more serious consequences. For example, providing a continued secure energy supply has required the largest single segment of annual capital investment for the United States (and for many other countries). For a large segment of the economy, the available resources are in a proportionate sense more finite than for small enterprises—contrary to the common perception.

For a small segment, increase in costs can be accommodated by barely perceptible shifts in many discretionary expenditures. For a large segment of the economy (and for goods which are regarded as essential and already represent a substantial fraction of many families' incomes) increased costs of some essentials can be greater than can be accommodated by small changes in discretionary spending. Other essentials must suffer.

A Proposed First Law of Regulation of Risks

For the sector of regulation (and self-regulation) which deals with the management of risks to the public, to the environment, as well as to particular enterprises, the following might be considered as the "First Law of Regulation of Risks":

> For the management of risk in any public sector or enterprise for which the resources available are finite and bounded, the proper ranking of risks, and the proportionate allocation of resources to limit risks, is essential. Actual overall risk is often increased if more than proportionate resources are allocated to less important risks, detracting from the resources available to limit more important risks.

This is particularly true in the case of regulatory decision making with respect to health, safety, and environment in the energy sector, and also in respect to the regulation of other industry.

As we shall discuss later, ranking of risks *within* a given sphere of endeavor is reasonably feasible. It can often be made "scrutable," which is to say understandable, by the informed layman as well as the specialists.

THE AGE OF AFFLUENCE AND THE CONCEPT OF ZERO RISK

Many Western societies have experienced an "Age of Affluence" —nearly two decades of an unprecendented rate of increase of material affluence—until the mid-to-late 1970s. In the United States especially, people with only marginal skills and productive capabilities could enjoy many material and nonmaterial amenities equivalent to those available only to top sectors of most societies in the world only a few years earlier. The growth in social services also led to an unprecedented increase and rate of increase of amenities for the segments of the population with submarginal marketable skills. For a whole generation, the natural order of things seemed to be the continuing fulfillment of ever-rising expectations. The concept of entitlements of many kinds has become nearly universal.

Perhaps, in historical perspective, this period will be seen as another of many historical boom periods. For example, in an area experiencing a gold rush, or new oil discoveries, or the sudden exploitation of a generally wanted item, it seems for a time that almost everyone can become relatively rich. Then the bubble bursts and the unusual income ceases. Most of the momentary riches are swept away since it is harder to curtail spending on perceived necessities, as well as on luxuries, than it is to increase it.

One of the dubious luxuries left over from the age of affluence is the concept that a risk-free society or a zero-risk ideal for some activities is a desirable and attainable social good, *regardless of cost*. This has led us into some strange if not bizzare situations in the pattern of social decision making in respect to risks.

We have the situation in which our willingness to make balanced expenditures to avoid or take care of the consequences of risk range widely. The range is from almost nothing per life saved, to almost infinte expenditure. To informed minds this situation must seem abhorrent from several different viewpoints. For example there are situations, such as traffic intersections, where expenditures are not made (community or state) of a few thousand dollars per life saved and a few hundred dollars per disabling injury expected. The losses are not hypothetical; they accumulate year after year. At the other extreme, by regulation, in some areas society is taxed for expenditures and lifetime costs well into nine digits per life saved. In some cases the hazard avoided is hypothetical, involving a compounding of worst-case expectations so that the hazard may ultimately prove to be not only extremely improbable, but unreal.

The extreme risk-aversion posture is practiced so far only in a few areas which acquired great visibility and became social movements and regulatory hobbies during the Age of Affluence. This is fortunate since the application of similar reasoning (the compounded worst-case) would almost preclude most human activities. For example, on this reasoning, industrial life is to be abhorred since dangerous materials and machinery must often be handled. Transportation is to be abhorred since airplanes sometimes fall—and sometimes in populated areas—ships sink, trains derail, and automobiles and trucks crash. Energy and energy production is to be abhorred, especially in cost-effective concentrated forms. Production of energy produces pollution, contamination, industrial accidents, and is generally unaesthetic, even from a distance. Nuclear energy is abhorrent since it poses unknown and presumably unprecedented hypothetical risks, contaminates the environment—and anyway is not as cheap as it was once thought to be. Overall, this line of reasoning leads to the view by some that a deindustrialized society is an unmitigated good heedless of the broader social costs and consequences.

If the worst-case viewpoint were applied consistently, even the Rousseauvian ideal of a primitive life in a park-like environment, would be perceived as intolerantly hazardous from both the known and the hypothetical hazards.

INCENTIVES FOR BALANCED ALLOCATION OF RESOURCES

The present period of selective and unbalanced response to real hazards (not to mention the hypothetical ones) is a serious aberration of our society. Correcting this aberration seems, in my judgment, worthy of the greatest and most distinguished efforts we can muster —philosophical, economic, governmental, and in public leadership.

The basic proposition is that in a finite world the excessive allocation of resources to some risks starves the resources available to control other risks and to take advantage of beneficial opportunities. If continued, it directly contributes to an increase in human wretchedness and death.

This situation is unattractive from many viewpoints. At the base level, it is a terrible misuse of natural and human resources even if crudely measured only as so many dollars per life saved or per health effect avoided. At the philosophical level it raises the question of values and social "goods." Democracy is a form of government that is capable of implementing an implicit philosophy—that social policies and practices should strive for the greatest good for the greatest number. In the sense of this system, and perhaps many other moral-ethical frameworks as well, a continued misallocation of resources for risk aversion and control must be questioned on fundamental, moral–ethical–philosophical grounds. From the standpoint of the average citizen, the serious misallocation of resources tend to deprive him or her of some essentials and other desired amenities by making them more expensive and less available. To the extent to which such increased costs consume a larger and larger portion of the citizen's discretionary income, they reduce the latitudes he or she has in freedom to travel, to educate, to maintain health, and generally to run his or her own life.

From the viewpoint of the regulator, continuing serious misallocation of resources by regulation should be regarded as a fundamental betrayal of public trust. The temptation to be resisted by regulators is to knowingly accept an exaggerated view (worst-case only reasoning) of a given risk with consequent misallocation of resources by regulation *and the consequent eventual increase in real risks and damage to people and to society.*

As noted earlier, the ranking of relative risks within a given sphere of activity is to a large degree a manageable and developed discipline. By discipline is meant not only the esoterica of technical risk analysis. Such analysis has its place as one of the inputs for risk decisions. It is subject to the obvious limitation that no abstract model is ever completely realistic to the real world, and the data put into the model are ever-changing and slippery. Classical statistical risk analysis is in many cases a worthwhile input to regulatory decision making, but it must be tempered by a deep and intimate qualitative knowledge and understanding of the field being regulated, and overlaid by commonsense notions of reality based on intensive study of past experience. Given this approach, the *relative* ranking can be made reasonably well. Resources to be allocated accordingly and a cutoff for a *de minimus* level of some concerns which can be regarded as trivial, can be reasonably defined and adhered to. This permits—at least within a given sphere—the responsible regulator, (as well as the responsible manager) to allocate remedial resources in an effective manner. Ideally, this situation is parallel to that of insurance actuaries who set the prices of each coverage in proportion to the best available measures of loss experience. The buyer of insurance further refines this by taking various types of coverage in amounts proportional to the relative size of exposure for his or her particular situation.

RESOURCE ALLOCATION FOR RISK LIMITATION BETWEEN FIELDS OF ENDEAVOR

A Proposed Second Law of Regulation of Risk

Given that a number of spheres of activities and of regulation can attain reasonable balance of risk control efforts in proportion to the hazards considered, this begs the more difficult and broader question of the allocation of resources between different fields of endeavor and regulation. To a large extent, the relative allocation between fields of endeavors is done inadvertently, which is to say as a by-product of legislation. A constituency can be found for many specific issues of protection ranging from the possibility of airplane crashes in crowded cities, to protection of endangered species such as the snail-darter. However, it is difficult to define, let alone find, a constituency for attainment of a reasonable balance in efforts warranted *between* different fields. Occasionally, courageous leadership at national, state, and regional levels will appear which will provide insights and effective guidance to the public. All too often, however, such issues are influenced, if not decided, at the level of the most prevalent folklore and media sensationalism, since this is usually the "safest" route politically. The following might be offered as the "Second Law of Regulation of Risk":

> For the management of several sectors of public risks for which the resources are finite and bounded, the total relative resources allocated to risk control in each sector should be generally in proportion to the ratio of the total measurable public risks and benefits involved. Actual overall risk to the public will be increased if more than proportionate resources are allocated to less important risks, detracting from resources available to limit the more important risks, or to develop more important benefits.

The proposed Second Law is fraught with considerably more practical and conceptual difficulty than the proposed First Law. The questions of relative social values of the benefits and the present worth of future social values or risks are more difficult to measure. It is also increasingly difficult to define and find credible schools of thought, practical disciplines for evaluations, and supporting constituencies for such comparisons.

A legislative amendment offered in 1980 (by Congressman Ritter of Pennsylvania) called for *comparative* risks assessment between fields of regulation. The development of a practical and credible intellectual–political discipline for such comparisons is a vital need for society. However, one may expect that the attempts to make such comparisons broadly will take the best efforts of schools of philosophy, public policy, environmental studies, law, and the sciences. For this reason, the proposed Second Law was formulated to suggest that a necessary—and possibly sufficient—condition is to develop the ability to make a credible *relative* ranking between any two fields of endeavor. One can formulate both the question and the campaign in relatively tangible terms if one defines the task of ranking as follows:

> Relate the total public and occupational risks of hazards, health effects, and other losses for field A and field B, and relate these to the size and distribution of the benefits for field A and field B.

One can speculate on ways around some of the conceptual difficulties of such a comparisons. Inhaber's work[1] is important in highlighting one of these issues. He assumes that a death or health effect is equally important regardless of whether it is any citizen, or someone engaged in one of the production or support occupations required for the particular endeavor. Until recently, social practice has often been to view occupational hazards with relative composure compared with public hazards. Society has also tended to view public hazards in some locations or sectors of society with considerably more composure than in other locations or other sectors of society. Such discrepancies may be politically expedient, but they are morally and ethically impoverished.

Another conceptual challenge is the relative weighting of hypothetical risks, or risks of major accidents which have never occurred, versus the actual year-by-year experience of numbers of people hurt or killed. A byproduct of the Age of Affluence is that in some fields, especially heavy industry generally and energy particularly, hypothetical accidents have tended to dominate the efforts on risk control in regulation. The tendency tô over-reaction to hypothetical, and possibly unreal, hazards on one hand, against a real, tangible "body count" of actual ongoing, year-by-year damage to identifiable individuals is a strange and unattractive legacy of the Age of Affluence.

THE VALUE OF DIVERSITY AND ADAPTABILITY

Inhaber's work leads to the conclusion that nearly all real energy sources exact considerable tolls in both occupational and public health effects. This conclusion is less surprising when one considers that essentially all energy sources are now costly. With one or two useful but limited exceptions, newer sources are more costly than older ones. High costs reflect the requirement for high content of materials, energy, and labor. These in turn have their associated human and environmental costs. From this work, one may conclude that the differences in risks usually are not large enough to dominate choices. A dimunition of risks or health effects can be achieved locally by restriction in one or another source of energy. The diminution is misleading however, since it is offset by the increased use of alternate energy sources—each with their own risk, sometimes larger than the risk avoided. A diverse mix of energy sources provides the best economic and social insurance against forseeable disturbances in, or depletion of, the supply of some sources, notably oil.

In recent testimony[2] on the U.S. Magnetic Fusion Program before a House Science Subcommittee, Herbert H. Woodson (director of the University of Texas Center for Energy Studies and chairman of the National Research Council's Committee on Magnetic Fusion), commented on the need for flexibility in that program, saying:

> There are few things as irretrievable as the right answers to the wrong questions. We must guard against becoming prisoners of preconceived answers.

This statement has broader implications for many human endeavors which involve decision making in the face of uncertainty. In the case of health and safety regulation, decisions taken in response to a particular challenge must always consider a "no change" alternative lest resources be diverted from some more significant challenge or lest risk be increased because of the change itself. The temptation to be resisted is to "do something" to show the regulator is in charge, even when the worth of "something" is dubious.

Lester Lave[3] has proposed a four step process to improve regulatory decisions as follows:

1. Clarify the agency's goals;
2. Improve scientific information relevant to the decision;
3. Structure the decision process so that data area interpreted correctly and their degree of accuracy is neither underestimated nor overestimated as they are incorporated into decisions; and
4. Carefully examine the implications of alternative decisions and methods of implementing a decision.

Keep this process in mind as we review briefly an area of regulation, and self-regulation for nuclear power.

REGULATORY DECISION MAKING PERSPECTIVES

A November 1982 report[4] by the Council of Independent Regulatory Agencies entitled "Regulatory Relief at the Independent Regulatory Agencies" noted that the decade of the 1970s witnessed a virtual explosion in federal regulatory activity. "Between 1970 and 1979 the number of pages in the *Code of Federal Regulations* nearly doubled, the number of pages published each year in the *Federal Register* tripled, and the expenditures of the major regulatory agencies more than quadrupled. No one knows the exact magnitude of the burden of the massive body of regulations that resulted, but by the end of the decade, estimates of the cost to the economy imposed by these regulations ranged as high as over \$100 billion per year."

An area of regulation which has grown—in terms of volume of regulation—more than 1,000 percent in the last decade is concerned with civilian nuclear energy production for electricity supply. Since 1979, this field has also been subject to intensive philosophical review and relatively high rates of change in regulatory approaches and in regulations issued. The need for some changes from the pattern which prevailed prior to 1979 was highlighted in an authoritative presidential commission headed by George Kemeny, president of Dartmouth College. This commission concluded, in effect, that the pattern of increasingly prescriptive regulation was not necessarily productive to increased safety, and under evident circumstances could be counterproductive to safety. The high rate of change of regulations has contributed to the collapse of 40 percent of the construction projects still underway in the mid-1970s. Unpredictable delays in completion, or in obtaining the permission to operate have created unpredictable and unmanagable increases in the preoperational costs of many projects. Several important new initiatives have occurred in this area which attempt to limit the trend to increasing unpredictability of regulation. Discussion of some of these trends and techniques may be of interest.

Currently NRC regulations provide adequate protection of public health and safety by requiring conservatism in design, construction, testing, operation, and maintenance of nuclear power plants. A defense-in-depth approach is mandated in order to prevent accidents from happening and to mitigate their consequences. Siting in less populated areas is emphasized for new projects and emergency response capability is mandated to protect the surrounding population. This body of regulations and guidelines has evolved over the last 30 years against a backdrop of changing political and economic conditions. Centralized congressional oversight via the Joint Committee on Atomic Energy has given way to more diffuse and competitive oversight responsibilities of several congressional committees. Growing environmental concerns, including key judicial decisions (in the case of Calvert Cliffs and the Uranium Fuel Cycle) led to the development of detailed environmental impact assessments and the emergence of the "As Low as Reasonably Achievable" concept. Institutionally, the Nuclear Regulatory Commission was formed by extracting the regulatory function from the Atomic Energy Commission which also had equally important functions related to nuclear research and development.

RECENT TRENDS IN THE ENERGY INDUSTRY TOWARD GREATER SELF-REGULATION

A new phase of interactions of industry with the NRC started on the last days of March 1979. Utility leaders and EPRI rallied to the calls for help from GPU,* at first providing round-the-clock technical

---

*EPRI = Electric Power Research Institute
 GPU = General Public Utilities, owner of Three Mile Island

support, and later, administrative and logistical support in the trying days and weeks immediately after the accident.

Out of this experience came a perception of the need to organize new and stronger institutional arrangements in both industry and in government. The perceptions of the lessons learned were documented extensively in the Kemeny Commission Report,[5] The Rogovin Report,[6] several congressional and GAO studies, and the report[7] of the Nuclear Safety Oversight Commission chaired by Governor Babbitt. Even before these studies were done, industry leaders perceived many of the needs highlighted in these studies, and proceeded to form NSAC, the Nuclear Safety Analysis Center, then INPO, the Institute of Nuclear Power Operations, then NEIL, Nuclear Energy Insurance Limited. NSAC represented a recognition that the analysis of generic safety issues needed to be done at the best scientific and engineering level attainable, without the constraints of the legalistic trappings which have made the licensing process overly legalistic, procedure bound, and often irrelevant and diversionary to the substance of any safety issues involved.

NSAC, provides greater continuity and consistency of approach on some topics than had been evident in either industry or government previously. INPO was organized partly in recognition of the evident differences in the effectiveness of plant operation and frequencies of events or accidents that could not be attributed primarily to plant design. The human factors were the key element in the degree to which known aspects of engineering science were used in disciplined plant operation and maintenance. Some design features may make plants harder or easier to run or maintain. But, even among plants with less than ideal design features, some organizations manage the technical and managerial insights to cope with such difficulties much better than others. It was also evident that some organizations were able to take better account of lessons learned from cumulative operating experience than others. Accordingly, INPO was formed with a charter of supporting continued improvements in the human and technical factors of plant operation and management, including the technical support, training, and emergency response functions. These were also areas of need highlighted by the Kemeny Commission Report.

LEARNING FROM EXPERIENCE

In order to ensure that industry effort is focused on meaningful safety questions, a rigorous and comprehensive method for screening and analysis of all plant operating experience was established and has been in operation in the United States for over three years.[8] The process is able to discern the risks associated with events which may have been benign in terms of consequences as they actually happened, but which carry a potential of severe consequences if they were to continue to occur 1,000, 10,000 or even 100,000 times without any remedial measures being taken. INPO provides a three level measure of importance on the Significant Operating Experience Reports, which also contain functional recommendations for remedies. The remedies usually cover a set of options in procedure, maintenance, control adjustments, and occasionally, design changes. These may address either reducing the likelihood of repeating similar events (reliability improvement) or changes in operation or hardware which minimize the likelihood of damaging consequences, given that the initiating faults may sometimes occur.

Events which bring with them a possibility of severe consequences if they were to reoccur 1,000 or fewer times, are generally regarded as "red tab significant events." A system for the analysis of and for the prompt dissemination of information about such events is in operation. Recommendations for means to prevent or minimize the consequences of such events, are also developed and disseminated. A follow-up process to observe the implementation of the recommendations has been in place for two and one-half years. A review and screening of operating experience for the ten year period (1969–1979) shows great similarities relative to the period 1980–82 in the types of operating events which would warrant remedial action. The process of recognizing, analyzing, and comprehensively disseminating remedial actions recommended was not in place prior to 1980. Certain types of events occurred repeatedly during the 1969–1979 period. Similar events continued to occur in 1980 and 1981, generally showing the same range of types of events that were observed in the prior decade. The process of analyzing, recommending, and implementing remedies (which either reduce the likelihood, or consequences, of such events or both) is now coming into widespread operation and use. Some degree of remedial actions were also being taken prior to 1979, but the technique for discrimination of the relative importance of events was not generally available or not systematically used.

Reasonable expectations of the effects of the process of recognizing, analyzing, disseminating, and implementing necessary remedies for observed operating events can be estimated (but not proven) as follows:

1. The likelihood of severe events which result in extended plant outages can be decreased by a factor of about three. There have been 54 plant years of outages in excess of three months in the United States (through February 1983). This is somewhat more than 7 percent of the total plant availability since 1960.
2. For plants which systematically implement recommendations based on operating experience in a timely fashion, the likelihood of severely damaging events, leading to extended plant outages of several years, or major releases of radioactivity such as at TMI-2, should be reduced to a frequency of less than one in five thousand unit years. (This is to be compared with the TMI-2 accident which occurred after about 430 unit years at the time of its occurrence, or one in somewhat over 1,000 unit years taking a total world experience to that time.)

This means that for plants which participate in this process on a continuing basis, there is a likelihood of at most one severely damaging event during the lifetime of all reactors operating or under construction in the United States. This indicates at most one such event through most of the first quarter of the next century. The continued operation and refinement of the improvement process should further reduce even this small probability.

A remaining concern is that a small percentage of operating units may not be able to mobilize sufficient quality or amount of technical, managerial, and operating resources to apply the lessons learned from operating experience in a timely, systematic, and rigorous fashion. A principal motivation for both government regulation and industry self-regulation is the recognition and correction of such situations.

RECENT GOVERNMENT INITIATIVES
IN NUCLEAR REGULATION

In January 1982 the NRC took a major step in clarifying the agency's goals and providing increased structure for the decision making process by issuing NUREG-0885, Issue 1, "NRC Policy and Planning Guidance 1982." The stated purpose of the document is "to provide guidance to the staff for establishing priorities and for improving the regulatory process—starting immediately." Issues 2 and 3 for 1983 and 1984 follow through on this theme.[9]

The section entitled, "Coordinating Regulatory Requirements" contains policy statements indicating sensitivity to the volume of requirements, evaluation of a cost-benefit basis, and prioritization for implementation based on analysis of the relative significance of issues. Planning guidance calls for continued single point control of proposed generic requirements by the Committee for Review of Generic Requirements, prioritization of new requirements based on expected risk-reduction potential, a mechanism for control of specific backfits, and establishment by the licensees of specific implementation schedules for new and existing requirements, based on the safety significance and the best use of the licensees' resources. The section entitled, "Improving the Licensing Process" calls for a more effective and efficient licensing process based primarily on standardization, early site approvals, and one-step licensing.

James R. Tourtellottee, chairman of the NRC's Nuclear Regulatory Reform Task Force, has said that regulatory reform is "a quest for certainty", that is, a quest for more predictable regulatory requirements and procedures.[10,11] His task force has made several constructive recommendations regarding the licensing and hearing processes as well as backfitting policies. The NRC addressed some of these recommendations by submitting legislative proposals for licensing reform to Congress in 1982 and by considering administrative remedies which can be effected without changes in legislation.

A START AT DEFINING SAFETY GOALS

The section entitled, "Improving Related Regulatory Tools" contains policy statements indicating a decision to develop safety goals to address the question, "How safe is safe enough?" and to make cautious use of quantitative risk assessment techniques. The NRC is currently seeking comments on its two year plan for evaluating safety goals published March 14, 1983.[12] The Commission has decided to adopt qualitative safety goals, supported by design objectives, for use during a two year evaluation period. The former provide that no individual should bear significant additional risk to life and health and that societal risks should be comparable to or less than the risk from other viable electric generating technologies and not a significant addition to other societal risks. The quantitative design objectives address risk to an individual and the population in the vicinity of a nuclear power plant as well as a plant performance objective related to the likelihood of large-scale core melting accidents.

During the evaluation period, implementation is "limited to uses such as examining proposed and existing regulatory requirements, establishing research priorities, resolving generic issues, and defining the relative importance of issues as they arise." By policy, the goals and objectives are not to be used as such in the licensing process nor are they meant to be subject to litigation.

PERSPECTIVE ON JUDGMENT, INTUITION, AND FORMAL RISK ASSESSMENT

The importance of checking analysis-based risk assessments, prioritizations, and the resultant decisions against experience and intuition cannot be overstated. Risk assessment has been utilized by society in decision making for a long time, ranging from simply intuitive judgments to decisions based on complex models and statistical data. Techniques for data gathering and analysis, modeling, calculation, and consequence assessment have evolved considerably since 1975. Risk assessment models now cover a broad range including; intuitive perceptions, simple projections, deterministic analyses, specific probabilistic analyses based on particular logic models, generic analyses, and "pure" analyses. It often seems that broad unqualified pronouncements and seemingly absolute statements are operating more toward either end of the spectrum—either mostly intuition or the pure analytical end of the spectrum. In reality, the closer one gets to a specific decision, especially in the face of uncertainty, the more one senses the need to make full use of qualified judgment as well as realistic deterministic analyses, and to question simplified analytical models and assumptions. To be effective, the decision-making process must be open at all times to new information.

This is an area in which industry and regulation should have near-identical interests—to recognize important issues and events and to get the best possible fix on the true relative importance of plant events and the implied safety issues.

A possible mechanism for improving the attainment of this result is to have a systematic process of review whenever a new or revised perception of a safety issue or presumed hazard is proposed. The review must include the physical models for the problem, the function-failure rates assumed and evaluation of the human factors of operation, maintenance, technical support, perception, and management. The mutual reviews by industry and NRC can be fact-finding and nonadversarial. They can be objective and confirmable by direct observation for most items. By keeping this fact-finding phase separate from conclusions to be drawn or remedies to be considered by NRC, the roles of industry and regulation can be kept distinct, yet largely cooperative.

Such an approach is already working on some occasions. For example, INPO, EPRI, and utilities' owner's groups are sometimes asked to comment on draft material. Comments are limited to the factual analysis of the problem (models of the concern and its probabilities).

The comments provide the opportunity for getting the most factual physical, analytical, and circumstantial information into the system. It is useful to take account of actual details of plant design and modes of operation—and the variations from one unit to another. The use of typical or generic information that is not directly representative of any given specific reactor unit, is now recognized as an unreliable basis for regulatory judgments. More specific information helps to provide the best attainable basis for deciding what should have priority for attention by regulators and by industry.

The continued working of a systematic and rigorous process for setting valid priorities for implementing remedies (for perceived significant safety issues and operating problems), I believe, will lead to some interesting results on future risk assessments. Since we do not yet have this situation fully implemented, the size of the benefits in reduced risk and in reduced occurrence of severe events cannot yet be measured directly. A distinct trend to reduction in the frequency of defined levels of troublesome events is now evident when one compares 1982, 1983, and 1984 to prior years. I will venture that it will yield highly welcome results in actual and perceived levels of safety in future years, approximately the potential gains mentioned in the previous section.

IMPRACTICAL AND PRACTICAL USES OF SAFETY GOALS AND RISK ASSESSMENT

A safety goal using a probabilistic risk envelope as its benchmark is useful as a broadly limiting guide, but seems unlikely to become a practical tool for licensing and regulation.[13] The uncertainties in the analysis of the overall risk envelope can involve a span of a factor of ten to 100, or more. A large portion of the uncertainties—measured by health effects in the environment—is in the consequence part of the analysis. There is a further large element of uncertainty due to the tradition of using "worst case" scenarios. This kind of assumption has traditionally been necessary if one is to answer the question that is traditional in this field: "What is the worst that can conceivably happen?" While this question will continue to be asked, it should no longer displace the more realistic questions of how to improve practical responses to the kinds of malfunctions which actually happen.

A major practical use of probabilistic discipline in the aerospace industry and in the space program has been to model the different sources of malfunction and hazard, and to *estimate the relative importance of different sources of hazard. The estimates of relative importance have been used to define the relative effort placed on providing remedies, improved reliability, testing, inspection, or added redundancy in design features.* This process establishes a common set of goals and priorities for the "regulator" (NASA) and the operators (NASA contractors and operating facilities). In any regulatory agency, the same method can be used as a test for consistency of new or more prescriptive regulations, codes, or standards, and to attain a common set of goals and priorities with the operators.

ASSESSMENT OF REGULATIONS

A possible procedure for use of relative hazard assessment to structure regulation is relatively straightforward. One asks of a new or changed regulation the following questions:

1. What dominant hazards sequences does the proposed change influence?
2. For a proposed change, what is the expected likelihood of success (degree of improvement and probability of achievement) in reducing the risk from the dominant sequence?
3. Can the proposed change have the effect of increasing the probability or consequences of *other* risk sequences?
4. What is the measure of regulatory manpower and enforcement effort, and industry implementation effort, including direct costs and outage costs?

5. Assuming effective implementation, what is the net decrease in the product of time and risk exposures, considering the whole population of reactors which are in operation and expected to operate?
6. What is the ratio of the risk reduction achievable to the regulatory and industrial effort required? *This ratio can be regarded as a figure of merit for the proposed activity.* (This risk reduction benefit should be discounted by the estimated effect of possible increase in alternate risks, as in [3.] above.)
7. Each proposed regulation or change in regulation can be ranked on this relative scale of merit. The use of a safety goal to establish target values for relative figures of merit for proposed actions would be a powerful management tool for regulation.

The steps listed above, if used consistently, would avoid the present situation in which actions which have a relatively small—and sometimes even potentially negative—impact on risk improvement are allocated larger resources in both NRC staff and in industry requirements than other items with a greater potential risk-reduction value. The problem of misallocation of staff and industry resources is not limited to the NRC—it occurs in virtually all regulatory agencies.

ASSESSMENT OF RATE OF RESPONSE NEEDED

A practical and immediately usable aspect of a safety goal that is important to the management of safety regulations is the determination of the required *rate of response* to a perceived deficiency. For example, the guidelines discussed on page 3 of NUREG-0735 [14] suggest response in days if a likelihood of 0.1 percent per year; in years if the likelihood is .01 percent per year; and to only "consider taking action"—presumably in a time frame of the order of several years or more—if the probability of core damage is lower than .01 percent per year. Below .01 percent, if relatively cost effective means are available to improve probabilities, they could still be taken as measures of prudence, but not as regulatory requirements.

A further refinement would take account of the duration of the perceived hazard (the product of time and risk exposure, more precisely the time integral of the increment of risk involved.) For example, a risk of .02 percent per year which would be remedied in one year would rank equivalent to a risk of .01 percent which would persist for two years. For the more general case of several units, the relative percentages are multiplied by the number of units which share the same problem.

The explicit adoption of such principles of timeliness can be used in the near-term to prevent or minimize the misallocation of priorities for timely response in both NRC and in the industry.

Possibly the most important aspect of a safety goal formulation is its use to *determine the relative priority and the timing of response required* by regulation for perceived departures from the licensed conditions, which are relevant to and consistent with the overall goal targets. This also makes use of *relative* risk assessments, which are more readily available and which can have smaller ranges of uncertainty than absolute risk assessments.

PUBLIC PERCEPTIONS AND THE PUBLIC INTEREST IN BALANCE

Ultimately, an informed public should favor the allocation of resources in both regulation and enterprise which provides a balance in two dimensions. In the first case, the expenditure of effort by regulation and enterprise on risk aversion should be in proportion to the size of risk reduction achievable in a given hazard. Secondly, the public should prefer a balance between the cost of risk aversion activities and the likely negative impacts on productive activities, which is to say loss in the availability of some of the benefits of the productive activity. The public also ultimately determines to a large extent the allocation of resources between risk aversion options on a given issue and the balance between overall efforts in risk aversion in this field. The degree to which risk aversion efforts represent a diversion from efforts required for productive activities needed by the public has had relatively little attention. This reflects the common assumption that resources are unlimited. Public perceptions of risk aversion needs appear to be formed by a combination of personal experience, influence of public leadership figures, and media presentations and interpretations. To the degree that public perceptions of risks are sometimes considerably at variance with experience and informed analysis, these perceptions may be regarded as folklore or mythology, but nevertheless powerful forces in shaping public policy.

The literary and entertainment genre of exaggerating fears and hazards is well developed. It works especially on the gullible segments of the public which have difficulty in discriminating fact from mythology. (We note more than two decades of declines—sometimes to near-zero—of general education in the natural sciences.)

The concerns of civilian nuclear energy are not insignificant but the confusions of real issues versus unfounded perceptions are widespread. The risks of individual harm are historically lower than several dozen other inadvertent sources of risk to society which show tangible damage each year, including those from most alternate energy sources.[15]

Unlike virtually any other human activity, intensive scholarly and technical efforts to prevent or contain accidents which might pose public hazards (as well as to reduce occupational exposures) have been the sine qua non of the industry. These efforts have been redoubled since the accident to the reactor at Three Mile Island, even though public radiation exposures were very small relative to exposures from nature, and small *even relative to the local variations in natural radiation backgrounds!*

Another obstacle of balanced perception and regulation is the search for "the perfect solution." The prolonged debates on ideal systems for disposing of wastes is an example. Of the various practical candidates, it is unlikely that any single one (the waste form, or the location of deep underground disposal) will be provably "the best." But many of the options are likely to be more than adequate. Most of the horses can finish in this race and it is unimportant to pick the exact winner since the differences between the finishers are likely to be small.

SOME ROLES OF THE UNIVERSITY COMMUNITY

The university community of scholars has several different roles in respect to regulation and self-regulation. Nearly all of the various roles which can be identified involve some degree of intuitive and implicit as well as explicit risk and benefit assessments. At the broadest level, the university community—regardless of the particular discipline—plays a role in the general public perception of risk simply by virtue of being informed, educated, and respected members of the public. In this role, the university is torn between the role as "keeper of the culture" which includes whatever mythology of risk perception is current in the general public, versus the role of the university as "seeker for truth" which tends to demand healthy skepticism of any generally accepted mythology. If one is to judge by polls which give some measures of risk perception, there is a greater tendency to reject exaggerated perceptions of risk with increasing level of education.

In the area of specific scholarly disciplines, various university departments participate in various aspects of regulatory (and sometimes self-regulatory) processes as their particular specialties are involved. These activities involve both fact-finding research, and sometimes opportunity for creative syntheses of institutional, social, legal, and technical approaches to perceived risks.

Possibly the most frequently involved specialty is the application of economics, or more generally stated, economic reasoning, to cost-benefit analysis. The economic reasoning is more widespread than the work which might be done principally in an economics department. In a generallly utilitarian society, a great many decisions, both social and individual, are made on the basis of known, projected, or intuitive guesses of costs of desired benefits, the costs of desired risk aversion actions, and sometimes the indirect costs which affect viability of productive enterprise. Other fact-finding research activities of the university can include study or development of technical options for attaining a given benefit. In the field of energy, major efforts in science and engineering departments are devoted to finding and developing methods for increased efficiencies of utilization. Similarly in departments of government, law, and philosophy, some contributions to regulations are made which amount to fine-scale tinkering with existing regulations or legislation. The synthesis of more basic reassessment of institutional roles and of the relative roles of incentives versus penalties, or prescriptive versus functional regulation are also possible areas for contributions. Technical departments in science and engineering can contribute to specific technique developments and to orderly and authoritative organization of information, and to the development of needed data.

SOME SPECIFIC CHALLENGES TO THE UNIVERSITY

In respect to the output role of the university, there remain many intellectual and practical challenges in the arena of regulation and self-regulation. Some of these are as follows:

- How to resolve the perceived biases among the different sectors in estimating risks, benefits, and consequence of loss of benefits. (Sectors such as regulators vs. enterprises vs. media vs. the public are of interest.) Can the university be a catalyst for consensus and cost-effective actions on some specific topics?
- Regulatory issues are now heavily overlaid with actual or threatened litigation, sometimes by special interest groups claiming to be in the public interest. Should the judicial process continue to neglect the social and economic effects of the delays induced by litigation, whether or not the issue proves to be meritorious?
- Should there be limits on the power of denial by delay through litigation, such as requirements for timely resolution, or requirements for considering and assigning responsibility for the cost and social impacts of delay?
- With respect to Lave's four step process, universities have a specific role in improving scientific information relevant to the decision. Is research designed and prioritized to add precision to previous results, that is, to reduce uncertainty, or to raise new doubts without providing data relevant to the decision?
- The risks to society from benefits avoided or lost are often neglected in cost/benefit comparisons. Avoided or delayed benefits can have substantial social and economic costs and risks. How can these factors be brought into the analysis and decision process more effectively?
- There are developing major evident social costs of unemployment, deprivation, and decline in social services (possibly due in part to a trend to deindustrialization, which is an inadvertent byproduct of regulation which has made some industries noncompetitive in world markets). This has led to a regulatory climate in which the social costs of reduced competitiveness or dissolution of some domestic industry has often been neglected as a social and economic cost factor in legislation, regulation, and in judicial decisions. Such damaging side effects are typically neglected—even if recognized as likely—due to reasoning along the lines of "that's not in my department—or scope." Can acceptable means be found for systematically taking account of the hazards from such benefits delayed or lost? Can they be recovered?
- Creative synthesis of better approaches are needed to the institutions of regulation, and where applicable, the relationships to self-regulation.
- The institutions of regulation have numerous known difficulties, for example overlap and competition within and between agencies. Mixing of legislative, policing, judicial, and penalizing functions is also common. (Legislator, judge, jury, and executioner roles are often combined in some agencies without the traditional patterns of checks and balances provided for other functions of government. The delineation

of roles between the state and federal judiciary, and regulatory judicial functions is not well defined in some areas, leading to virtually unlimited duplication and growth of due process.

- In many highly developed countries, regulation which monitors the accomplishment of nonprescriptive general objectives and guidelines has been successful. Considerable latitude is allowed in how general objectives are met. Extensive reliance is placed on industry to develop detailed criteria and specific means for their implementation. Joint efforts in specific problem solving and in means to improve performance, are jointly funded. (This is in contrast to the option of a prescriptive and punitive style, which places extreme reliance on the perfection of technical and managerial judgments of the regulatory staff and its contractors.) Developing and defining roles and processes for institutional patterns for less prescriptive regulation may be a worthy intellectual endeavor.

Most of the challenges listed above involve some elements of risk assessments, either explicit and analytic, or implicit and intuitive. Explicit comparisons of relative risk exposures are now often practical with relevant experience as a basis. The development of more "scrutable" and widely understood explicit risk analyses, and their prudent use along with more broadly based judgments, may be an important tool for progress on most of these challenges.

REFERENCES

1. Inhaber, H., *Energy and Risk Assessment*, (New York: Gordon and Breach, 1982).

2. Woodson, H. H., Testimony before the Subcommittee on Energy Research and Production of the House Committee on Science and Technology, March 16–17, 1983.

3. Lave, Lester B., *Quantitative Risk Assessment in Regulation*, (Washington, D.C.: The Brookings Institution, 1982).

4. "Regulatory Relief at the Independent Regulatory Agencies," A Report by the Council of Independent Regulatory Agencies, Office of the Chairman, Administrative Conference of the United States, Washington, D.C., November 1982.

5. Kemeny, J.G. (chairman), *Report of the President's Commission on the Accident at Three Mile Island,* (New York: Pergamon Press, 1979).

6. Rogovin, M. (director), Three Mile Island, A Report to the Commissioners and to the Public, Nuclear Regulatory Commission Special Inquiry Group, January 1980.

7. Babbitt, B. (chairman), Nuclear Safety Oversight Commission, Report to the President, (Washington, D.C.: U.S. Government Printing Office, 1980).

8. Zebroski, E.L. "The Dynamics of Institutional Changes Following the Accident at Three Mile Island," *Progress in Nuclear Energy 10*, (Oxford: Pergamon Press, 1982), pp. 249–57.

9. U.S. Nuclear Regulatory Commission Policy and Planning Guidance 1983, NUREG-0885, Issue 2, Washington, D.C., January 1983.

10. Tourtellotte, J.R. (chairman), NRC Nuclear Regulatory Reform Task Force, "Enlightened Cost Consciousness in Nuclear Regulation," November 1982.

11. Tourtellotte, J.R. (chairman), NRC Nuclear Regulatory Reform Task Force, "Nuclear Regulatory Reform: Common Sense Revisited," December 1982.

12. Nuclear Regulatory Commission Policy Statement on Safety Goals, Federal Register Volume 48, Issue 50, pp. 10772–83, March 14, 1983.

13. Zebroski, E. L., "Utilization of Safety Goals in Regulation," Comments at the Brookhaven National Laboratory Conference on Safety Goals, April 1981.

14. Plan for Developing a Safety Goal, NUREG-0735, Washington D.C.

15. Inhaber, op. cit.

Part III

New Policies
for Regulatory Reform

5

A DEMOCRATIC CAPITALIST APPROACH
TO REGULATION

Robert Benne

The climate in our country is conducive to fresh public policy thinking. We have experienced enough stagflation in the last decade to convince almost everyone that increased *efficiency* and growth are necessary. Romanticism about stationary economies has diminished. There are few Robert Theobalds around, wondering what we can and should do with uncontrolled abundance.[1] People want to get the tide rising again so that all boats may be lifted. Further, our people seem to have an increasing distaste for large, centralized structures of power whether public or private. Americans are finding their social and psychological distance from big government and big business disturbing. They are open to calls for cutting back the power of both big government and big business. They find *decentralization* an appealing value. On the other hand, however, there is no great surge to roll back the agenda of *justice* that has been set and pursued for the past 50 years. We are still jealous of our private and public liberties; we stand for equality of opportunity; and we are committed to a floor of dignity for all persons. There is genuine disagreement about how high or low that floor should be and how it should be established, but it seems evident to me that we as a people affirm basic access to primary social goods—adequate shelter, health care, sustenance, security from inordinately dangerous environments, or a minimal income that can assure such goods.

Thus, I see three values coming to the fore: efficiency, decentralization, and justice. It is certainly not the case that these values have not been prized in the past, but it is my contention that they have not been brought together with sufficient coherence and creativity.

Conservatives have always been concerned about efficiency and

159

growth. They have argued that the sources of American well-being are in a healthy and growing economy. An efficient economy will provide jobs in a noninflationary context. Conservatives have also been for a diffusion of power, if that is taken to mean a limitation on the power of government for intervention into the private sector. They have been less concerned about concentrations of private power. But it would be hard to argue that in recent times conservatives have been passionate about the extension of justice to more disadvantaged segments of American society.

Liberal democrats have focused more vigorously on the agenda of justice. Extending equality of opportunity and providing a decent floor of living for the disadvantaged have been important elements in that agenda. But many of their interventions on behalf of justice have seemed to lead to a burgeoning of the apparatus of the state. Large, inefficient bureaucracies drink up the water from the proverbial leaky bucket as it is passed by various transfer programs from the well-off to the not-so-well-off. There has been an exponential growth in the human services and welfare budgets of local, state, and federal agencies, and yet dependency and misery continue to grow among the worst cases. Concentration of state power and function do not seem to have the effect intended. And heavy programs of taxation on the productive sector are often accompanied by a hostility toward it that leads to the most punitive and inefficient kinds of regulatory intervention. So, if the conservatives prize productivity and the limitations of state power and neglect the agenda of justice, the liberals prize justice but pursue it in ways that are statist and inefficient.

This state of affairs opens the door for centrists of various sorts, who sense that a healthier combination of efficiency, decentralization, and justice is called for. All too often these centrists do not have a coherent and consistent approach, but rather respond willy-nilly to the various challenges and interests that confront them. Then we get, as we got with Carter, a frightening sense of instability and rudderlessness. Or, we get independents like Anderson, who appear to be putting these values together in appealing ways, but who as outsiders would have no effective access to the levers of political power even if, by some miraculous occurrence, they were elected.

What we need, then, is a resurgence of creative political thought and policy making from centrist groups—neo-liberals and neo-conservatives. They have the best chance of putting together these values in creative new ways, persuading others of their merits, and then, most necessary of all, winning.

It is the intent of this chapter to contribute to such centrist thought. I believe a *democratic capitalist* approach can provide a fresh, coherent, and persuasive strategy toward public policy, especially, for the purposes of this conference, with reference to regulation. I will pursue my thesis in three steps. First, I will analyze two other models—that of the commercial republicans and that of the social democrats. In examining those models, I will make explicit their implicit moral theories, which are the bedrock upon which their respective edifices are built. Second, I will propose a democratic capitalist approach and outline examples of regulation in that mode. Finally, I will offer some suggestions about how universities might contribute helpfully to the conversation about regulation.

H. Richard Niebuhr, in laying out the tasks and uses of ethical reflection, insisted that before ethics could speak in a prescriptive way, it had to engage in careful analysis of an ethos, to lay bare the roots and character of its moral presumptions. If such critical inquiry is done properly, Niebuhr held, several advances are made. We come to clearer self-knowledge about who we are and what we believe; we have a chance at greater integrity through that self-knowledge; and through both we may arrive at more accuracy of action.[2] In the following I can only try to do such ethical inquiry properly, leaving it to the reader to assess whether it helped to enhance self-knowledge, integrity and accuracy of action.

COMPETING MODELS

There are three main models of *political economy* competing for public assent today. They are not coterminous with any extant political party in the United States, but do find their way into the thinking of particular political figures. These three models are theoretical constructs that provide the conceptual framework for our current options. We might call them: the commercial republican, the democratic capitalist, and the social democratic.

Commercial republicanism has a long history well documented by Ralph Lerner and Alan Bloom in two recent articles.[3] Drawing from resources as diverse as Montesquieu and John Adams, Adam Smith and Benjamin Franklin, David Hume and Benjamin Rush, the proponents of the new order of commercial republicanism were united in this: "they saw in this new possibility a more sensible and realizable alternative to the theological–political regime that had so long ruled Europe and its colonial periphery."[4] Rather than base the emerging civilization on the vainglorious imagination and pretension of aristocratic and religious tradition, which constantly led to fanaticism, intolerance, and economic stagnation or disaster, the commercial republicans proceeded from the ordinary passions of free, ordinary people.

> Indeed, where the ancient polity, Christianity, and the feudal aristocracy, each in its own fashion, sought to conceal, deny, or thwart most of the common passion for private gratification and physical comfort, the commercial republic built on those passions.[5]

The mechanism for satisfying and harnessing those passions was the market. While the market was certainly not the instrument for realizing the grand dreams of priests and kings, it was the perfect vehicle for realizing the mild ambitions of middling men. The ethos created by such an arrangement led to a limited and pragmatic polity, which widened the chances for freedom and prosperity for more people. As de Tocqueville put it: "violent political passions have little hold on men whose whole thoughts are bent on the pursuit of well-being. Their excitement about small matters makes them calm about great ones."[6]

Alan Bloom argues a similar line, but emphasizes the revolutionary break from traditional philosophy taken by the proponents of commercial republicanism. In building on low but solid ground, the emerging bourgeois civilization defused the dynamite lurking in the older perfectionist ideals. In its resplendent utilitarianism, politics and economics come to focus on those milder ambitions and passions. It is not as though there was no room for virtue, truth, and perfection in the commercial republic; they were just edged off the main stage and become peripheral to economics and politics. The market took over center stage and has remained there ever since, at least in their normative thinking.[7]

A good number of American conservatives and libertarians are in the lineage of the commercial republicans. They agree with their progenitors on the centrality of the market as the organizing center for much of life, in their animus toward perfectionist politics, and their enthusiasm to extend marginal utility theory into family life, law, and politics. But, above all, they believe that the market is a great preserver of liberty.

While von Hayek, von Mises, Aron, and Nozick may be more sophisticated philosophical proponents of commercial republicanism, Milton Friedman is no doubt the most influential spokesman for the tradition. His *Capitalism and Freedom* and *Free to Choose* lay out the agenda of this school. In fact, I think it safe to say that the seminal ideas of *Capitalism and Freedom* have made more impact on modern American reflection on political economy than those of any other living theorist.

The social democrat school cherishes the long struggle in Western society for political democracy. That long struggle needs no detailed chronicle here. But a current in that broad democratic stream can be identified as democratic socialist or social democratic. While Europe and many other countries in the world have had identifiable political parties shaped by this perspective, the United States has had no persisting and/or successful embodiment of the social democratic ideal. But many theorists have such a perspective, and they have important effects on public discussion and policy. Many names come to mind—Lindblom, Lekachman, MacPherson, Heilbroner, Harrington, Hook—but the most influential light among them is John Kenneth Galbraith. His *American Capitalism, The Affluent Society, The New Industrial State, Annals of an Abiding Liberal*, and his many occasional writings make him a weighty presence in public discussion.

Incidentally, it is almost impossible to find adherents of commercial republicanism among religious social ethicists. A few can be found among the democratic capitalists. But a large number move toward the social democratic model, which they believe has the most possibility for achieving distributive justice and a greater modicum of the common good. Because of their influence in the churches and ecumenical agencies, those bodies often espouse the social democratic agenda.

Many of these religious social ethicists accept the basic Marxist critique of capitalism and are using it to press further questions about Western society. There is, in fact, a veritable explosion of Marxist writings, as a visit to any major bookstore will attest. This is not to say of course that those using Marxist approaches to various subject matters are communist or anti-democratic. But it is to say that per-vasively hostile analyses to market economic systems will be coming on strong in future years. Few areas of academic inquiry will be able to escape the questions raised by neo-Marxist perspectives. By and large, these analyses strengthen the hand of the social democratic ap-proach as well as the notions of regulation implicit in it.

Thus, we have two strongly competing models; one—the com-mercial republican—is presently in the ascendancy, particularly in view of the number of its adherents in the present administration. But the other has wide currency in the intellectual world, and will have much stronger appeal if the economic recovery long anticipated fails to appear. Let us look more closely at these two models and their views of regulation.

Each proceed from different organizing metaphors. The com-mercial republicans opt for an economic metaphor—the market. To them the free market is a marvelous mechanism. It increases well-being through mutually beneficial exchange while it ensures freedom of choice, both on the production and consumption sides of the ledger. Its competitive dynamics encourage creative exploration for better means of production. As it approaches perfect competition, it allocates resources precisely where they ought to go and rewards con-tributions to the process in a fitting way. Given these benefits of the market, the commercial republicans aim to extend the market into areas of life that have heretofore been characterized by public or private monopoly—education, medicine, natural resources, postal services, pension funds, and so on. They see the main enemy of well-being and freedom as bungling and rapacious government interven-tion. They recognize that private enterprise also covets monopoly, but they tend to believe that such monopolies could not be held without strong government collusion. Government ought to be limited to bedrock necessity; it ought not have room to press forward an expanded notion of the public good since that will no doubt be both coercive and inefficient. The market will do a much better job of enhancing the general good—defined as the sum of goods of in-dividuals and families—and it will do so with due regard for liberty.

The commercial republicans operate with the empirical judg-ment that the economy is competitive and it could be much more so if government would intervene less. In fact, when commercial republicans prescribe public policy, they assume a highly competitive world.

Social democrats make quite a different empirical judgment about the extent of competition in our society. (You would think that economists could settle the empirical question among themselves, but apparently ideological blinders or imperfect information prevent them from reaching consensus . This failure in their own field of inquiry should make them reluctant to charge their opponents with "doing theology" when disagreements arise. Compared to economics, theology may be an empirical science.) They argue that the economy is monopolistic or oligopolistic. Michael Harrington calls it "corporate collectivist."[8] Whatever it is called, the market economy doesn't do the nice things the commercial republicans think it does. On the contrary, because it is seriously distorted, it misallocates resources, distributes poorly, generates inequality, spins out destructive neighborhood effects. The beneficiaries of this skewed market are the large private corporations, many of them multinational in scope. They administer prices, dictate tastes, move capital with impunity and have undue influence in the political arena. They are the true sovereigns of the modern world, to the detriment of ordinary people.

Moreover, even if competition could be assured, there are many areas of life where the market should not apply. Social democrats have an expanded notion of the common good which should be shared and shaped by all, not opened to the vagaries of the competitive market place. The very list given above, plus many other goods like the arts and education, ought to be taken out of determination by the market which, according to them, is not a very good producer and distributor of public goods.

Since a free, competitive market is a fiction, and since it should not apply to many areas of life even if it were competitive, the social democrats adopt a political metaphor as the organizing center of their agenda. Democracy is their touchstone. The agenda of the social democrats is to overthrow the dominance of the economic model, which according to them is the main enemy of equality and well-being, by democratizing economic life. This extension of democracy into economic life can take two basic forms. One is an expansion of the regulatory apparatus so basic economic decisions are heavily hedged in and conditioned by governmental decision. What is to be produced, where, how, in what quantities, and in what technological manner—all these are shaped politically. Price and wage controls are also part of this scenario. Another tack recognizes the heavy costs of such pervasive regulation, and would rather extend the model of participatory democracy into the heart of economic decisionmaking itself. All those affected by the productive process itself ought to be legitimate participants in decisionmaking about that process. This would overcome the contradiction involved in highly socialized modes of production coupled with privatized decisionmaking.

Currently, the latter tack lies far on the political horizon so the former is taken. Social democrats like Galbraith and Lekachman repeatedly call for government regulation of prices, wages, and rents. They press for further elaboration of rules governing the treatment of persons in their productive and consuming roles. Anti-discrimination laws, often entailing quota systems, are encouraged. Consumer protections are expanded with the intent of wiping out all serious—and many not so serious—risks. Access to productive or service roles are regulated by accreditation and licensure in order to maintain standards and protect the consumer. Regulations monitoring and stipulating the whole productive process are applied to those industries whose externalities have serious environmental repercussions. Finally, in recent social democratic analyses of the alleged "deindustrialization of America," there is a call for increased government regulation and control of investment capital so that we might have a rational and effective "industrial policy."

The commercial republicans, operating with far different empirical judgments and assessments of the possibilities of free markets, have a diametrically opposed philosophy of regulation. Regulation of prices, wages, and rents is always a mistake, for it will lead to future shortages and misallocations. According to Friedman, even technical monopolies are best left unregulated. If their prices become too high, substitutes will quickly appear.[9] We should try to persuade business to be racially and sexually nondiscriminatory, but it should not be coerced by law to adopt such policies. Access to productive and service roles should not be impeded by licensure or accreditation; these are simply devices to perpetuate monopoly. In the area of externalities, commercial republicans like Friedman do recognize limits of the market, and they propose such things like "selling pollution rights" in order to include the cost of such neighborhood effects in the accounting of the enterprise.[10] They are dead against control or regulation of the flow of capital since that will aim investments at politically-favored targets, not at what is economically viable.

The crux of the commercial republican argument goes something like this: The absence of encumbering regulation will allow free individuals and firms operating in a competitive market to engage in mutually beneficial productive and consumption exchanges. This will expand the aggregate good while protecting liberty and encouraging individual autonomy and responsibility. The social focus of this approach is on the *long-run, incremental gains* for the *general* population. Conversely, regulatory intervention leads to long-run, incremental losses spread widely. The cumulative effect of the former is positive, while the cumulative effect of regulation is a serious loss in efficiency and liberty. Unfortunately, neither of these effects—the positive or the negative—is dramatically visible. The political order, more responsive to dramatic short-run turns of events, will move in quite a different direction.

The social democratic perspective applauds that different direction. For it focuses on the *short-run, dramatic gains* or *losses* that happen to *specific segments* of the population. The political community, proceeding democratically can prevent those large losses to vulnerable people in the short run. It can be governed by a deontological principle in which the right is prior to the good. It can intentionally distribute burdens and benefits according to canons of *fairness*. The community can bear the long-run small losses of efficiency and liberty that are spead widely because that is what it means to be a community. Social solidarity means precisely that fair sharing of burdens and opportunities.

So, according to the commercial republican, the rational free individual can have both liberty and generalized well-being if he or she is willing to take the responsibility and bear the risks of the competitive market place. The market transmutes self-interested freedom into an expanding general good. But it does so with real risks of short-run, large gains and losses to specific people. The commercial republicans are willing to put up with the latter for the sake of the former.

The social democrats are unwilling to make that trade-off. Through various sorts of regulation, the political community can express its moral principles in a fairer way. It can even out the short-run, dramatic gains or losses for specific persons by distributing burdens and opportunities into the whole community. In so doing, it may diminish long-run efficiency and liberty by intentionally lowering risk, but it is willing to make that bargain. In this way, the political model can tame the economic. This is not a great source of worry because the social democrat believes that markets have worked poorly or not at all. It's time to be done with them as a major vehicle of economic choice.

A DEMOCRATIC CAPITALIST APPROACH

It seems to me that in most cases—not all, by any means—we need not be forced to make the kind of trade-offs made by the commercial republicans and the social democrats. The democratic capitalist wants the long-run, generalized, incremental gains that the operation of a workably competitive market can offer. Moreover, the support for freedom and responsibility given by the market are prized by the democratic capitalist. But there is a blindness in the commercial republican perspective. There are large numbers of people who are made to absorb heavy burdens by the creative destruction of the market. There are many who are overwhelmed when the market signals appropriately higher prices. There are exploiters who enter the market place and take advantage of people who do not have a lot of choices and who are not well-informed. Arguments that in the long run things will work out for most people do not carry much weight with specific people who are hurting a lot in the present.

The social democrats are responsive to the distributive principle that demands fairness for those specific persons suffering badly now. The democratic capitalist wants to be sensitive to them too. But the social democrats want to intervene too quickly into particular markets, and they want to do so in ways that are least efficient. They want to control prices, wages, and rents. They suggest command and control strategies of protective regulation. They do not use the incentives of the market to encourage acceptable behavior. In short, they impede the market; they try to call a halt to its creative destruction. By being too conservative they will block the long-run incremental gains that the market will bring. By such interventions they will also diminish liberty, autonomy, and the capacities for self-help and risk taking.

Each perspective is wanting because it relies too much on one organizing model—the market in the case of the commercial republican and political democracy in the case of the social democrat. The democratic capitalist distrusts this reliance on one metaphor. There are many needs in our life together on earth and there are many excellences that are called upon to meet those needs. There are spheres where the tentative sovereignty of various excellences must be respected. The economic sphere is one. There, economic rationality is appropriate. Individuals and firms must economize; they must be able to put the factors of production together in efficient ways. Being able to do so is an excellence. Further, it appears that markets ensure the efficient working out of that economic rationality better than any other kind of mechanism. Not that there are no moral or political issues involved in economizing. There certainly are. But in most cases in the normal world, they must coexist with economic rationality, not smother it, or everyone will pay dearly in the long run.

So, the democratic capitalist appreciates economic rationality as it works itself out in a competitive market setting. But he or she respects them as servants of the human enterprise, not as masters. The economic model—the market—is limited. It must be complemented by other models, one of which is political democracy. Democracy—limited by constitutionalism—can be the expression of the will of the whole community in a way that the market cannot. It can express principles of justice that simply are not intrinsic elements in the life of the market. Moreover, because it has legitimate monopoly on coercion, the political sphere can embody those principles of justice into fixed rules and laws that move them beyond voluntary assent. It can be the vehicle through which the whole community does justice to those specific segments of the population which are threatened seriously in the short run. The political sphere has an excellence beyond that granted to it by the commercial republicans, and the democratic capitalist affirms that.

Further, the democratic capitalist finds the eternal tension between the political and economic spheres necessary, and often creative. Both spheres have imperialistic tendencies that aim at dominance, both practically and theoretically. To place them into a countervailing situation is one way a wise society prevents undue concentrations of power. This countervalence can lead to stalemate and paralysis, but both poles in the mix have capacities for dynamic change that generally undermine a static situation. Most of all, however, the democratic capitalist sees the possibility of creative complementarity. The market economy produces a rising standard of living that benefits all strata of society. It does this without centralized coordination. The state need not be omnicompetent. The workings of the market support the liberty and autonomy of individuals, families, and social groups. An efficient, growing economy distributes opportunity profusely and arranges a rough reward-for-contribution. In terms of moral theory, the market economy expands the aggregate good.

However, there must be a distributive principle that complements the utilitarian thrust of the market economy. That is embodied in democratic justice. Thus, the democratic capitalist adopts a mixed theory of moral obligation, assigning the expansion of the aggregate good to the economy and the distribution of the right to the democratic polity. The polity must make sure that public and private liberties are equally distributed, that fair equality of opportunity is pursued, and that a minimal floor of dignity, security, and order is approximated. Working together, the economy and the polity can achieve a creative combination of the good and the right. Without the expanding good created by the market economy, the right has little to distribute. Without the right-making interventions of the polity, the good is poorly distributed.

The democratic capitalist approach, then, has more respect for the gifts and possibilities of the political order than the commercial republican, and more respect for the gifts and possibilities of the market economy than the social democrat. But what does all this mean for regulation? It means several specific things:

1. A democratic capitalist approach is very reluctant to regulate specific markets. It distinguishes questions of efficiency from those of distribution, assigning the market the former and the government the latter.
2. It will aim at reforming direct, protection regulation in ways that work with the market rather than against it.
3. It will encourage as many private sector alternatives to public regulation as possible.

Before I develop illustrations of the preceding principles, I should mention that I find a number of economists writing in what I would call the democratic capitalist mode. Among those that I find most helpful are Richard Lipsey, Charles L. Schultze, and Alfred Kahn. My illustrations are either directly or indirectly indebted to their writing.

Let us take the current controversy over the regulation or deregulation of natural gas prices as an occasion to discuss the first principle, that is, we should not regulate specific markets for the sake of distribution, but rather distinguish between the two issues. I would and do support the deregulation of natural gas pricing. I make this judgment with the assumption that the lifting of regulation would lead to vigorous competition in the supply of natural gas. Indeed, a good argument can be made that the sharply increasing prices we are experiencing today is the result of government intervention, setting the price of old gas too low and new gas too high. At any rate, we have been shielded from paying the full cost of natural gas; up until last year we paid only about half its worth. These interventions, based partly on moral considerations but mostly on the self-interest of middle class consumers, have had and will have unfortunate effects if they are continued. They have been based on the analysis that price is the problem, when in fact it is part of the solution.

A true market price set under competitive conditions will do four important things. First, it will encourage conservation by no longer subsidizing consumption. Already the higher prices are leading to conservation. People are dialing down. Utility companies report a slackening of demand. Second, higher prices will encourage exploration and further development of supply. Higher prices will signal that a profit is to be made, which will be a great incentive to find and market more gas. Third, as true costs are reflected in higher prices, other forms of energy become competitive with gas. Oil is again competitive and if prices rise further, solar energy may become viable as an alternative. However, if prices are held down there will be little economic incentive to find substitute forms of energy. Fourth, true prices will encourage technological changes that will make the heating of homes, factories, and public buildings more efficient. Waste in heating has been immense because natural gas has been subsidized.

Prices set in a competitive context will reflect the true cost of production and the future cost of replacement. This will lead to more economic efficiency by moving resources in the proper direction. The market can do this far better than government.

However, there are serious justice issues having to do with distribution, that is, how natural gas is divided out among its citizens. As prices have risen, there are specific groups of people who presently endure serious hardship. The poor or economically marginal elderly come immediately to mind. They have become visible to us; too many have to choose between heating and eating.

As these hardship cases are dramatized, there is a great temptation to adopt social democratic strategies of relief, even though the proponents of price control may not ideologically be in that camp. There are calls to intervene in the market itself and thereby create long-run inefficiencies and shortages,.

There is a better way. If we wish to redistribute income to the elderly poor by making energy cheaper for them, let us do so by tax or direct subsidy. We can, through energy vouchers or tax credits, support those who need help directly, not indirectly through intervention in the market whereby the whole society will lose in the long run. Such a strategy is politically difficult, though, because we middle-class folks would rather pursue our interest in subsidizing energy use by market controls than by direct help to those in need.

There are effects of the productive process, however, which entail direct, protective regulation. Air and water pollution are cases in point. Here our second principle comes into play. Direct regulation should be done in ways that work with the market rather than against it. In my opinion, Charles Schultze has made the most persuasive case for this kind of strategy in his aptly titled book *The Public Use of Private Interest.*[11] In it he grants the need for rather extensive government intervention, but goes on to support a particular kind. He believes, with many mainstream economists, that we have relied almost exclusively on the most expensive and bureaucratic kind of intervention. But there is another way.

> Society can go about dealing with market failure in two quite different ways. It can try to isolate the causes of failure and restore, as nearly as possible, an efficient market process. Or it can take matters completely into its own hands, supplant the market process, and directly determine the outputs it wants. In other words, social intervention can be process-oriented, seeking to correct the faulty process, or output oriented, seeking to bypass the process and determine outputs directly by regulation or other device.[12]

Schultze goes on to argue that social intervention has usually been output oriented, and this has been a costly bias. It taxes the ability of the government to make complex output decisions, and it stretches thin the delicate fabric of political consensus by unnecessarily widening the scope of activities it must cover.[13]

It would be more effective to use the incentive structure of market arrangements to get the desired outcome rather than to try to regulate the outcome directly. Thus, in the cases of air and water pollution, the government could institute pollution charges rather than try to make thousands of decisions based on detailed considerations it cannot possibly know or keep up with over time. Speaking of water pollution, Schultze suggests:

> If the polluting side effects of industrial activity were priced, several consequences would follow. Depending on the size of the effluent charge, firms would have incentives to reduce pollution in order to increase their own profits, or to avoid losses. The higher the charge, the greater the reduction; hence, the fee could be adjusted to achieve any desired set of water-quality standards. Firms with low costs of reducing pollution would reduce their waste discharges by more than firms with high costs of production, which is precisely what is needed to achieve any given environmental standard at the lowest national cost. Even when the standards were met, firms would still have incentives to look for ways of reducing pollution still further because they would be paying a fee on whatever residual pollutants remained. And again, more important, there would be strong incentives throughout industry for the continuing development of new technology of a pollution-reducing character.[14]

Such an approach is by no means the sole answer. It would have to be introduced gradually to supplement the direct regulation of outcomes.

Later it could replace many of such regulations. But certainly some highly dangerous effluents and pollutants will always have to be controlled by output regulation rather than incentive. The same can be said about some efforts to provide safe conditions of work. Even with these qualifications, however, the potential role for an incentive-oriented approach is considerable, and its absence very costly.

Finally, in order briefly to illustrate the third principle, I would call attention to private sector alternatives to public regulation. Unions can bargain with management to achieve many of the same objectives of public safety regulation. Information strategies can provide regulatory surrogates for government command and control interventions. Liability law provides another possibility. Insurance arrangements are another avenue. These, and attempts at self-regulation, are listed and examined by Bardach and Kagan in the book they edited entitled *Social Regulation—Strategies for Reform.*[15] They provide instances in which regulation can be achieved through private sector efforts.

In concluding this section, I would like to return to my starting point. As I argued in the introduction, there is a climate in our nation that is inviting fresh public-policy thought. Americans are concerned about getting our economy going in more productive and efficient paths; they appreciate decentralized, less statist approaches to our problems; and yet they do not want to relinquish the gains that have been made in extending and refining justice.

As a nation we await creative combinations of those values—efficiency, decentralization, and justice. Commercial republicans and social democrats provide theoretical constructs for combining the three. But my contention has been that a third, centrist way is more fruitful and persuasive. If articulated well, it could grasp the imagination of many Americans who are now aware that those three values are crucial for the future. Regulatory approaches can be found that embrace all three.

THE TASK OF THE UNIVERSITY

Everyone is aware that the university is really not "uni"; it is a *multiversity*. Fields, schools, departments, and areas of inquiry go in different directions, rarely engaging one another seriously, if at all. At least this is my judgment after spending many years around a major graduate university. The professors in the economics department and business schools are honed in on their own specialized areas of research. They are so well rewarded for their specialized expertise that there are few incentives to engage in a broader conversation. Further, their writing is often so arcane and unintelligible to other educated persons that they are not heard publicly even if they have good and important things to say. Political scientists and sociologists, who are often attracted to the social democratic paradigm, are sometimes too envious of the power and status of the economists to carry on a civilized conversation. They generally do not understand an economic way of thinking and therefore do not appreciate its gifts. They prefer to take potshots from the periphery.

Ethicists, whether philosophical or religious, have by and large not been engaged with specific public policy issues; when they have, they tend to be moralistic, that is, they exaggerate the moral factor in highly complex situations. This makes them unattractive to the economists, who habitually underestimate the moral factor in human actions. Ethicists are more drawn to political science and sociology where value questions are more visible.

Besides these attitudinal and ideological obstacles, there are genuine dilemmas concerning the use of time and energy. Too much expended in interdisciplinary pursuits detaches one from the cutting edge of one's own area of inquiry.

In spite of all this, our task is to become more of a university, to bring people together from many disciplines to look at issues common to us all.

A wise person once said that the most knowledge is gained in conversations among friendly critics. I think that gives us something of a hint about how we might proceed. If what I say is true, there are several distinct models of political economy among us. The distance between the center and either pole is not impossibly great, but perhaps the distance between the poles is too much for fruitful exchange to take place. Those who share enough common ground to be friendly critics need to come together for mutual edification and criticism. Economists, political scientists, experts in public policy, lawyers, and ethicists need to sit down together to view a common issue, but it will be helpful to the conversation if they share enough commitment to a model of political economy to be friendly critics. The outcome of their investigations will then most likely have sufficient coherence to be persuasive.

The university, of course, should have no commitment to any model of political economy. But it can encourage coherent interdisciplinary proposals to surface from several models. The public discourse of the nation can then be enriched by more foundational and coherent thinking.

REFERENCES

1. Robert Theobald, *The Challenge of Abundance* (New York: Mentor Books, 1961). It is fascinating to notice the shift from the notion of abundance in the 1960s to scarcity in the 1970s and 1980s. Analysts of both eras often operated with assumptions of permanence for their respective notions. Such assumptions lead to embarrassment when conditions change, as they no doubt will continue to do.

2. H. Richard Niebuhr, *The Responsible Self* (New York: Harper & Row, 1963), pp. 12-16.

3. Ralph Lerner, "Commerce and Character: The Anglo-American as New Model Man" in *Liberation South, Liberation North* (Washington: American Enterprise Institute, 1981), and Alan Bloom, "Commerce and Culture" in *This World,* Fall 1982.

4. Lerner, op. cit., p. 24.

5. Ibid, p. 30.

6. Ibid, p. 38.

7. Bloom, op. cit., p. 11.

8. Michael Harrington, "Corporate Collectivism: A System of Social Injustice" in *Ethics, Free Enterprise and Public Policy* (New York: Oxford University Press, 1978), pp. 43-56.

9. Milton Friedman, *Capitalism and Freedom* (Chicago: University of Chicago Press, 1962) p. 128.

10. Ibid, p. 30.

11. Charles L. Schultze, *The Public Use of Private Interest* (Washington, D.C.: The Brookings Institution, 1977).

12. Ibid, pp. 28-29.

13. Ibid.

14. Ibid, p. 20.

15. Eugene Bardach and Robert Kagan (eds.), *Social Regulation—Strategies for Reform* (New Brunswick: Transaction Books, 1982) pp. 201-315.

6

ENVIRONMENTALISM:
DOES IT REQUIRE REGULATION?

William G. Tucker

THE PROBLEM

The question of private effort versus government regulation is perhaps the most important issue facing current society. It is important not simply because it presents a struggling private sector trying to produce ongoing prosperity in the face of a growing burden of regulation. Rather, it is important because it cuts right to the heart of the future agenda for our society.

Are we going to be a society where individuals look to themselves and feel they can make headway through their own efforts? Or are we going to be a society in which everyone looks to the government for help in the most common, everyday matters?

This is an absolutely critical choice because it is not really a choice at all. It is more a matter of whether we are going to pursue a reality or an illusion. As far as private effort is concerned, there should be no doubt in anyone's mind that the world in which we live today is the result of the efforts of private individuals trying to better themselves. The enormous prosperity and the wide latitude of choices of the consumer economy that we enjoy today are entirely the work of private enterprise. Almost everywhere in the world where the private economy has been allowed to flourish—from the industrial growth of England in the early nineteenth century to the offshore outposts of free enterprise in the Far East today—the same results have occurred.

Conversely, in almost all instances where the state has wiped out private effort and tried to direct economic growth through a centralized system, the results have ranged from depressing to miserable. Sure enough, there may be a kind of slow, cumbersome growth in the economic statistics, but most of it is in the area of heavy industry, national monuments, and ultimately, those handiest of all public works projects—armaments.

There should be no illusions, then. The state cannot cause growth. Progress and the general amelioration of life are almost entirely the work of private individuals and private instititions trying to better their own lot, mainly by providing goods and services that other people will want to buy. This is the essence of the private enterprise system—the "invisible hand" mechanism that Adam Smith described when he noted that we do not depend on the humanitarian impulses of the butcher and the baker for our meat and bread, but on their own pursuit of efforts to improve their own lot.

The reasons why govenment attempts to take the place of free enterprise always end in failure are too numerous to mention, but I will try briefly to list a few. Economic planning is too centralized and does not take into account either the desires or the potential contributions of the great mass of people. Decision making is based on access to power, rather than on economic performance, and therefore the people most skilled or most ruthless in playing the game of politics rise to the top. The state usually absorbs all the profits in the system—the profits made both by the enterprises and by individuals through their private efforts—and therefore no one has any incentive to work. Everybody takes it easy and tries to live off the efforts of someone else. In fact, the only time that government-directed economics ever show any trace of success is when they imitate or duplicate the free market. Witness the recent case of Hungary, which has not long ago made an independent "discovery" of private ownership and free enterprise and is now beginning to prosper.

All this seems fairly clear. America was built on free enterprise. The American economy was the freest of all from government interference during the nineteenth century, and we prospered as no other country has ever done before in history. Look around the world today, and on every continent you will find that those countries that practice free enterprise and allow private and individual effort to be rewarded are moving ahead, while those trapped in the collectivist dream of mass progress through absolute equality and centrally orchestrated effort are wallowing in stagnation.

It would seem remarkable that any American could be brought to doubt the fundamental virtue of private effort, considering our long history of success. Yet you would never know this from watching television. Turn on any network newscast at night and you will soon find yourself watching an "in-depth" report from some provincial hamlet telling us private effort is failing, while the federal government is trying to stem the tide by "bringing funds into the community." The federal grants usually turn out to be the local ballet company or subsidizing some ill-begotten progam where people are being taught handicrafts under the cruel illusion that they are training for jobs—but no matter. The important thing is that the government is "doing something." All the banks, the factories, the shopping centers, the private training schools, and the employment agencies that the television crews drove by in search of the local CETA office—they are only there as part of the natural landscape.

Then after you have watched the network news and heard the latest report of what the government is doing to solve the problems of the world, you can flip the dial to the MacNeil-Lehrer Newshour and watch the whole thing in embryonic form. Night after night a parade of fusty college professors will tell you how they could solve all the problems of the world in a few weeks if only the government would give them a couple billion dollars to get started.

There is no question, then, that a large portion of the American populace has become hypnotized with the idea that nothing can be done about a problem until the government takes action. The idea that private, voluntary efforts can have similar and more efficient effects is simply seen as a veil behind which sinister private interests hide. The idea that people themselves might be able to exercise a little influence over their future is simply out of the question. This, of course, is the exact opposite of the principles on which the prosperity of this country was founded. It is not uncommon in history, however. It forms a typical set of symptoms of an aging, geriatric society that is beginning to become encrusted in layers of lawyers and unproductive bureaucracy. It is a sign of a culture that is beginning to lose its vitality. The case, however, may not be terminal, and so I am going to pass over any morbid prophecies and try to analyze just how we got this way.

THE CAUSES

The principal wedge that has brought the hand of government into the everyday workings of the economy has been the principle that there are things that the free market cannot do—thus requiring the intervening hand of the government. These are the so-called "market externalities."

The principal market externality that has persisted throughout history—and throughout each permutation of political and economic systems—is inequality. I am not going to attempt to deal with this broad and vast subject, except perhaps to note Winston Churchill's observation that when socialist and communist countries do succeed in creating perfect equality in society they invariably do it by making everybody equally poor. As George Gilder argues effectively in *Wealth and Poverty*,[1] inequality is in many ways necessary to any society that is going to advance technologically and materially. In a freely operating economy, the odds that everyone is going to come out equal are approximately the same as the chances that, in a fairly uniform population, every child that is born in a given year is going to come out looking the same. The odds are virtually impossible.

In this kind of situation, then, all the government can do to promote equality is to take from people who are more successful and give to people who are less successful. This, of course, does not create any new wealth, but simply redistributes whatever wealth has been created by private effort. It is probably justified in certain extreme cases and may even win widespread approval for a long time, if the majority of people sense that they have a better chance of being on the receiving rather than the giving end. But sooner or later this effort creates its own problems. It encourages people to look at the government activity as a *source* of wealth—*discourages* people—particularly entrepreneurially active and creative people—from working to *create* new wealth, since they know it is only going to be taken away from them and redistributed anyway. Thus, the goose that lays the golden egg suffers a slow strangulation. If you think that this mechanism has anything to do with the economic doldrums in which we currently find ourselves, you are probably right.

The real "externalities" that I would like to take hold of, however, are of a different variety. They are the common occurrences of our society that we have been led to believe cannot be solved by economic or market mechanisms and necessarily require the interventions of an active and benevolent government. Among these are problems with the environment, pollution, the deterioration of landscapes, the exhaustion of resources, occupational health and safety, the risks of new technologies—all the social issues that have led to the new brand of post-1960s regulation. This new regulation does not attempt to regulate competition the way various New Deal and other regulatory authorities have been trying to do for the greater part of this century. Rather, it argues that there are certain "higher values" that cannot be considered in economic terms at all.

What are these considerations? They are such a familiar litany that they probably do not need to be elaborated to any great extent. But let me mention a few. It is argued that the economy cannot adequately take care of the environment. It is argued that our resource base deteriorates under the capitalist system. It is argued that businesses emphasize present consumption without taking the needs of future generations into account. It is argued that the market cannot preserve resources for the future. It is argued that the market cannot prevent pollution. It is argued that economic calculus cannot take into account scenic and aesthetic values or the spiritual virtues of wild areas or endangered species or the general beauties of nature. It is argued that the market cannot preserve health and safety in the workplace or prevent damage by long-term toxic chemicals. In short, "environmentalism," with all the implications and side-issues that this term has become freighted with over the last 15 years, is argued to be a "market externality" that requires the intervention of an active, aggressive, regulation-minded, lawyer-dominated government, operating under the aegis of something with a title like "The Environmental Protection Agency."

I wish to argue a rather startling proposition. I am going to try to make the case that things are almost exactly the opposite. I am going to argue that it is not a *lack* of government interference in the marketplace that has led to environmental problems. Rather, government intervention in the marketplace has *caused* most of the environmental problems we have today. In addition, solving some of our newest and most intractable environmental problems is really nothing more than a matter of extending the workings of the marketplace into areas from which it is now excluded. The free market protects the environment. Or, to put it more bluntly, the search for profit *protects* the environment. It is only the government's interference in the private pursuit of economic gain that has led directly to the "environmental crisis" of our contemporary era.

Since this is a rather broad and bold proposition to be making, let me try to begin by looking at this issue in a long historical perspective. The environmental crisis seems to have hit us rather suddenly in the twentieth century. In the very first years of this era, a group of political leaders around Theodore Roosevelt became acutely concerned that the workings of American enterprise were destroying the nation's resources. They formed what is called the Conservation Movement and made strenuous efforts to protect our resources "for the greatest good of the greatest number in the long run."

Almost 50 years later, these concerns were revived and extended to encompass worries about pollution of the air and water, the fate of endangered species, the preservation of wilderness, and a host of new environmental issues. Thus, we have the contemporary environmental movement.

Now if we are to understand the roots of this crisis, it is worth asking the questions, Why did it emerge at this particular moment in history? Why didn't it happen sooner or later? Who protected the environment before there was a conservation era and an environmental movement?

The common answer is that our technology has improved too well and that we never before posed a threat to the environment. But this is plainly wrong. Human beings have always had technology. We are the tool-making animal. This argument is also undercut by the long record of environmental destruction that environmentalists often cite in trying to make the argument that human nature is incompatible with the conservation of resources and the preservation of natural surroundings.

But in fact, there is ample evidence that conservation issues and worry about depleting resources have been a constant concern of almost every known civilization. In an article in *Natural History*[2] magazine in May, 1981, Canadian biologist Robert M. Alison traced a long history of conservation movements from the Egyptian, Akkadian, and Indian civilizations of the second millenium, B.C. through the age of Queen Victoria in England. Edicts have been going out since the dawn of history protecting trees, watersheds, game birds, and animals. The authors of one of the first Sumerian legal codes in 1900 B.C. specified a penalty of "one-half mina of silver" for cutting down a tree without authorization.

What is most notable about this long history, however, is that these restrictions have almost inevitably sprung from the crown itself.

By far the most common edicts have concerned the protection of wild animals and game birds, so that even Alison himself is forced to admit that "many limitations . . . had the effect of affording wild animals better treatment than that enjoyed by human residents."

Now, the question presents itself, Why did the royalty of almost every country work so hard to protect game animals? There is a very simple answer. They wanted to preserve these species for their own pleasure. The crown early laid claim to all the beasts of the forest and field, with the specific idea that they would be reserved for sport hunting. The king's gamekeeper was the principal enforcer of these laws, and poachers were the main problem. Thus, it was decided under George IV that anyone caught taking one of the king's birds would be sentenced to either "three years of hard labor or, alternately, fourteen years in North America."

Why did the king then protect the wild herds and flocks of the realm? Because he had a private interest in doing so. How did he do it? By exercising ownership over them. It is as simple as that.

Of course, someone will jump to a conclusion and say, "That's all the government is doing today. The government lays claim to ownership over the air, water, resources, and general property use of all the land and natural resources within its domain and does not allow them to be destroyed. That is why we have a conservation movement and an Environmental Protection Agency."

This would be fair enough—if we were still living in the fifteenth century, when the crown could lay claim to just about anything it wanted. But a lot of water has passed over the dam since then. We have had several historical occurrences, variously titled the Industrial Revolution, the rise of representative government, the democratization of society, and several odd reforms and revolutions that have carried us beyond the highly centralized monarchical systems of the Middle Ages. Is it necessary that, at the first sight of a denuded forest or a whiff of air pollution, we must immediately go running back to the archaic and autocratic systems of royal governments in order to deal with them?

The answer can be perceived in recognizing that it wasn't simply the benevolence of the medieval kings that caused them to put a price on the heads of poachers. It was in their *private* interests. The kings probably had no more aesthetic appreciation for natural landscapes than does the average senator or congressman today. The royal crown simply wanted its private game herds preserved for its own enjoyment.

When John Locke inaugurated the era of modern Western society with his essay, "Two Treatises on Government," he posited that the rights to "Life, Liberty, and Property" that were previously assumed to belong only to the crown—and to be extended to others by royal permission—belonged to all individuals.[3] He posited the principle of "Natural Law," which said, roughly, that what was good for the king was good for everybody else. Individuals had just as much right to private property as did the crown. Both laid the same claim to their land in the idea that they had "mixed their efforts" with it in wresting it from its original condition.

This system of private property has turned out to be an enormous benefit to Western society. Many commentators argue that it was precisely the system that allowed individual ownership and the right to the fruits of one's labor that is responsible for the uninterrupted era of progress that has ensued. Many civilizations have experimented with technology, but none have ever seen so many private individuals willing to put so much time and effort into inventing so many new ways of doing things and improving their lot. It has been the principles of private property and relatively low taxation that have set off this explosion.

So the question remains, does the evidence of environmental damage mean that we have to repeal the private-property institutions of the last 300 to 400 years and go back to a centralized government authority that is, presumably, the only responsible agent who has it in its heart to protect nature?

The answer is no. By following through the logic of the situation, we can see why this is so. Why did the king protect the game herds of the Middle Ages? Because he was more benevolent than anyone else? Hardly. It was simply in the *private* interest of the crown to do so. This protection, naturally, did not extend to animals that did not pique the personal interest of the crown. At the same time that Henry VIII was executing people for killing partridges and deer, he was also carrying on a campaign to reward people for killing rooks and crows, for which he had a peculiar personal dislike.

The key point is this. What happened when property ownership became much more widespread? Did the stewardship ethic of the crown disappear? Absolutely not. It was simply widened to include other people—the new property owners.

Anyone on earth feels a particular imperative for preserving nature and conserving resources when they are his or her *private* property. We do not depend on the benevolence of the king or the Environmental Protection Agency to preserve nature any more than, as Adam Smith said, we depend on the benevolence of the butcher and the baker for our meat and bread. *Landlords always have a private interest in protecting their own property.* No sane landlord will ever allow his animal herds to be slaughtered, his forests to be destroyed without regeneration, his pasture to be overgrazed, or his livestock to become an endangered species. The conservation ethic is an occupational disease that comes with the job of owning property.

The "environmental crisis," on the other hand, has been the result of a steady encroachment on the part of popular governments acting against the rights of landlords. In general, this has been a reflection of the declining economic position of landlords in relation to the rise of business and labor—plus the political overkill that often accompanies such long-term economic trends.

In this country, the problem has been compounded by an excessive government ownership of resources. The fatal flaw of most conservation and environmental reasoning has been that resources will be much safer in government hands. In fact, the opposite is true. Once government retains the ownership of resources, it inevitably uses its political powers to override the forces of the market and to subsidize their use far beyond the point of economic efficiency. This is why, in today's environmental battles, we find the constant paradox that the huge government agencies—the Tennessee Valley Authority, the Bureau of Reclamation, the Bureau of Land Management—that were orginally set up as *conservation* efforts have inevitably ended up *overutilizing* resources and causing much environmental havoc.

Let us go into a little more historical detail once again before tackling the contemporary environmental scene. In 1968, another Canadian economist named J. H. Dales was writing a book about pollution.[4] While lamenting the worsening conditions of Ontario's trout streams, he received a letter from a fellow economist, who registered his surprise about how similar problems did not exist in England. The letter, which Dales included in his book, *Pollution, Property, and Prices,* reads in part as follows:

> It is not because they (the British) do not have to watch out for pollution. There is an organization called the Anglers' Cooperative Association which has been in existence nineteen years.

> . . . These anglers have behind them a simple fact. Every fishery
> in Britain, except for those in public reservoirs, belongs to some
> private owner. Many of them have changed hands at high prices,
> and action is always entered on behalf of somebody who has suf-
> fered real damages. . . .⁵

After explaining how the Anglers' Cooperative has dogged various
utility plants and manufacturers and made them clean up their pollution through private lawsuits, the writer went on to explain their success in this way:

> Part of the explanation may be social. The A.C.A. has the
> Duke of Edinburgh for Patron. Apparently it is quite all right for
> him to be honorary keeper of a watch dog that has sunk its teeth
> into government corporations such as British Electric and the
> Coal Board, municipalities big and small, industries and private
> individuals, without fear or favor. I notice that His Grace the
> Duke of Devonshire is President, and there are two more dukes
> among the vice-presidents (that is over ten percent of the total
> number of non-royal dukes), as well as two additional peers, [and]
> a couple of knights, . . . [and here Dales left off].⁶

What is going on here is very simple. What these two writers were in
the process of discovering was that the British aristocracy, in exercising its *private* ownership of much of the English countryside, was
protecting the environment long before the government or popular
environmentalism came along. There was no need for the intervention of either—no popular passions to be aroused, no need for
elaborate regulatory procedures, no government agencies. Private interest took care of everything.

Why, then, does such private interest not work all the time?
There are a multitude of answers and explanations. None of them,
however, contradict the central premise that the exercise of private
interest—the natural conservation ethic of the landlord—is the chief
source of energy we have in any society for protecting the environment.

One of the problems that has emerged is this. It is conceivable
that trout streams in the British countryside can be privately owned
and protected from pollution by their landlords. But what do we do
about Lake Superior or the Atlantic Ocean? Who owns these and
who is to protect them? Likewise, it is possible that the crown (or the

Department of Interior) can lay claim to ownership of elk herds or wild forest game. But who owns the whales which spend most of their time wandering beyond all recognized national boundaries, and thus have become the world's most endangered species?

REMEDIES

The first problem we have to deal with in contemporary environmental difficulties is that, in many instances, property rights have been disputable or difficult to apply to the resources in question. Small streams can probably be privately owned and protected. But large lakes, rivers, or oceans cannot. And what about the vast expanses of air that surround us and are regularly used as a garbage dump to the detriment of all? None of these resources can easily be divided up and sold in one-acre parcels.

Here it is obvious that the government must take constructive action. Most easily, it must claim the resource as its own and act the part of a protective landlord.

To an extent, this has happended, of course. But to a much greater extent, the state has used its rights to claim ownership to a resource like the air in order to impose a wide variety of arbitrary and needless restrictions on the rights of individual property owners. It is the same principle by which the government interprets its "ownership" of the airwaves, not simply to define individual bandwaves and license them to radio and television stations, but to impose all manner of restrictions on what those stations can and cannot broadcast. Governments are a bit like in-laws—they will use any handle they can to pry into your business.

Controlling air pollution, for example, should be a very simple matter. All it requires is licensing certain minimal allowances for pollution—to meet with generally accepted public health standards—and then putting these licensed rights on the market. Pollution industries would then vie with each other to buy these "rights to pollute." They would bid up the price—until some industries would find it was cheaper to clean up their pollution than to pay for government permission. Through the unregulated activities of a free market in these "pollution rights," we would have all the environmental protection we wanted. What's more, we would achieve it in the *cheapest possible way* to society as a whole.

There are also several other nice implications. Suppose, once the minimal standards were achieved, the public decided it wanted the air still cleaner. It could do this simply by passing a bond issue to buy up ever more pollution "rights," and then retiring them. Industries would not be forced into impossible standards since they would not *sell* the rights until it became more profitable to clean up. Instead of a haggling bureaucracy and clever environmental groups slipping powerful little clauses into seemingly innocuous legislation, the public would have a full, clear, and open choice of how much pollution it was willing to bear.

"Marketable rights to pollute," then, are a simple and effective way of dealing with pollution that does not violate anybody's property rights or put them under the Draconic charge of arbitrary government agencies. Nearly every economist who has studied the matter (including Mr. Dales of Canada) has decided that it is the cheapest and most efficient solution to pollution problems.

But do we use it? No. Instead, we have a clumsy "command and control" system where state and federal authorities make it their business, not just to give people incentives to clean up, but to go around telling them exactly when, where, and how every smokestack is to be modified and every sewer line constructed in order to achieve the same ends. One of the key elements of the situation is that the bureaucracy is *mandated* by Congress *not to pay attention to costs.* Instead, industries are instructed that they must install the "best practical technology" and the "best available technology" (and occasionally even "better than the best available technology"), no matter what the expense. The regulators are not paying the bill so why should they be concerned? It is only "evil polluting businesses" that bear the burden. (Among other things, this serves as a positive *dis*incentive for industries to invent new clean-up methods, since they are only raising the standards to which they have to conform, regardless of the cost.) All this does not produce a cleaner environment. It simply raises public antagonisms and makes huge amounts of work for lawyers.

For example, look what has happened in the steel industry with water pollution over the past decade. The 1972 Federal Water Pollution Control Act required that the nation's waters be cleaned up according to all kinds of legal gibberish, which included "best practicable control technology currently available," "best available technology economically achievable," plus "best available demonstrated technology" for "new source performance standards." ("New source performance standards," as far as anyone can tell, are laws that mean that new plants have to install equipment better than anyone has put on the old plants, which of course discourages anyone from building new plants at all.)

What this meant in practice was that state and federal authorities came around and told the steel companies what they had to do. The EPA put all its new attorneys and environmental technicians to work and decided, for some reason, that steel making involved eight discrete steps. The government officials then decreed that the law required that the steel companies install the "best available technology" at each and every one of the eight arbitrarily defined steps.

The steel companies looked at it a different way. They wanted to meet the standards at the cheapest possible cost. "Wouldn't it be easier," they proposed, "if we took all the wastes from the entire operation and routed them all into one big treatment facility where we can deal with them in one single operation?"

No, the EPA decided. Although the results might be the same or even better, this method still would not mean that the "best available technology" was being employed at each of the eight EPA-defined steps.

And so the two parties went to court and fought it out for ten years. The decision, only settled upon on February 24, 1983, was that the steel industry will be allowed to treat its effluents as a single pool—which is what it wanted to do in the first place. Thus, the cleanup may now begin—unless some environmental group or other party intervenes to try to drag the decision back through the courts again. In the intermittent ten years, the water has not gotten any cleaner. But a lot of lawyers have gotten richer.

The government, then, has been woefully unperceptive in recognizing the power that property rights and the automatic efficiencies of the market can bring to the battle for pollution control. They are actually far more efficient than any of the bureaucratic rigamarole that we have been dragged through for the last ten years.

But what about those instances where the government remains the principal owner of resources that could easily be put into private hands? What has the record been here in "protecting resources for the future"—"for the greatest good of the greatest number in the long run?" It is here, I think, that environmental groups have been most delinquent in overlooking the vast benefits private ownership brings—and the vast problems that government ownership creates — in the matter of environmental protection.

Let us start with a simple example. You may remember the famous episode of the mid-1960s when someone was trying to build the Marble Canyon Dam which would back water into the end of Grand Canyon. Here, as never before, was an example of how the "profit motive" and the free market failed to account for scenic, aesthetic, and environmental values—isn't that right?

Well, test your memory for a few seconds and try to recall which cold-hearted minion of capitalism was trying to build the dam. Was it Pacific Gas and Electric? Was it Southern California Edison, or the Anaconda Mining Company?

The answer is none of these. The entity that was trying to build the dam was the Federal Bureau of Reclamation, one of the most notorious "conservation" agencies created in the early part of the century. Was the Bureau of Reclamation going to make money on the project? Hardly. It was going to *lose* money—plenty of it—in its ongoing "mandate" to dam every bit of running water that it could find west of the Mississippi.

The same scenario has occurred in almost every one of the "conservation agencies" set up to manage the development of resources around the turn of the century and afterwards. In almost every instance, federal ownership has become a way of cutting corners around the dictates of the marketplace in developing resources. Ideally, the government—as landlord—would collect a proper rent for the use of these resources. Lacking the proper monetary reward, it would hold these resources off the market and wait for their commercial value to increase. Thus, by the automatic efforts of landlords to collect their rents, resources are conserved for future use in an optimizing fashion.

But the government has not played the role of an intelligent landlord. Instead, once resources are held in government hands, they become the prey of special-interest groups—and of the bureaucratic entrepreneurs who make it their business to build and cultivate these constituencies in order to maximize their own power and responsibility.

In his recent book, *Locking Up the Range*,[7] Professor Gary D. Lidecap has shown how the Bureau of Land Management has consistently shifted its policies on its 170 million acres of range land in order to aggrandize its own power. In the early days, the Interior

Department fought against fencing on range lands—not because it would help limit the number of cattle on them, but because it would create a confusion among private owners and leasors that only a powerful Interior Department could solve.

When grazing practices were reformed in the 1930s, the Department of Interior offered ranchers unrealistically low grazing fees in order to create a constituency that would prevent these federal lands from being consolidated with the Forest Service's holdings in the Department of Agriculture. Finally, in the late 1950s, the newly created Bureau of Land Management started critiquing its own policies in order to create pressure to increase its staff and policing power. Riding the growing wave of environmental strength in the 1970s, the BLM has now become an advocate of *under*utilizing these resources and turning much of the nation's grazing land back to habitats for wild game.

The one thing that has been consistent in this long-standing policy has been the *mismanagement* of resources in the hands of the Department of Interior. Private ranchers in the West have had no trouble keeping their lands from being overgrazed and preventing ecological deterioration. It is only the federal lands that have been consistently abused. This is because the Department of Interior is in an extremely poor position to play the role of a landlord. It is under constant pressure to shift its policies this way and that in order to satisfy large pressure groups.

Government agencies are almost congenitally incapable of charging the proper rents and severance costs for their resources. The flaw of all the government-run "conservation" agencies is that they are given the difficult task of telling people that they must *pay the proper price* for a resource in order to have enough of it left for tomorrow. Governments have a very difficult time playing this authority figure role. Instead, they want to be "on the side of the people" and give their resources away as cheaply as they can. Private landlords do not have any easier role to play in charging people the proper price for resources (witness the problems of the oil industry in the 1970s, the natural gas industry over the last 40 years, or the owner of any apartment building in New York City). Playing the role of the landlord was never an easy one.

But the private landlord *has no choice* except to charge a market rent for the use of a resource. The landlord cannot endlessly subsidize the use of his own resources out of other revenue sources—taxes, for example. He must make the resource pay for itself. With renewable resources, this means charging prices that will modulate their use in order to give them time to regenerate, as forests or grazing land will. With nonrenewable resources, he must charge the highest possible price today in order to make the resource's availability stretch as far as possible into the future. The role of the landlord has never been a popular one, but it is essential in preserving the value of natural resources. Not surprisingly, the era of the "environmental crisis," which has really been upon us since the early part of this century, has also been the era of spectacular decline of landlords.

By limiting the ability of landlords to exercise their economic rights, governments limit the landlords' ability to protect the natural resources in their charge. The accelerating restrictions placed on landlords by popular governments over the last century have certainly won great favor from the mass of voters. But they have also removed the market protections from natural resources and, in the end, created the environmental crisis.

How did it come about? The situation becomes more understandable if we think of the original division that Adam Smith set up in the way people make their livings.[8] Smith posited that there were three players in the economic game—laborers, capitalists, and landlords. Each makes his contribution to the "wealth of nations" in a different way, and each is rewarded through a different mechanism. Laborers contribute their work efforts and are paid through wages. Capitalists contribute their capital (which they own) and their entrepreneurial decisions and receive their reward through profits. Landlords, finally, contribute the natural resources in their possession and are reimbursed through rents.

Smith is often remembered as an apologist for business, but anyone who has ever leafed through *The Wealth of Nations* realizes that Smith had very few nice things to say about business people. His main criticisms were against the untiring efforts of businessmen to restrict trade by getting the government to grant them exclusive monopolies. But Smith's enduring contribution was that he accepted the *legitimacy* of market rents and profits and argued that they were necessary in assigning both capital and resources to their most efficient uses.

Subsequent economists have always tended to become advocates for one of these three groups—labor, capital, or landlords—and to argue that the wages, rents, or profits of the other groups are illegitimate. An alternate argument is that the market system is permanently skewed and that either capitalists, landlords, or laborers will eventually end up owning all the resources in the society, completely eliminating the influence of the other groups.

Experience has shown, however, that the system is really quite well balanced. The overwhelming historical trend has not been the complete elimination of landlords or capitalists, but rather the diffusion of the ownership of capital and resources into the broad reaches of the population. One of the reasons why capitalism is so successful in America is because ownership of industries is so widely diffused through stocks, pension plans, and other forms of investments. The definitions in the rigid, tripartite "class system" have long since become blurred. It is difficult today for large masses of working people to rage against the "evils of capitalism" because so many of them own a small piece of the economy.

What has happened, though, is that the natural shifts in the balance of power among these three parties has often been exaggerated and punctuated by efforts by any group to use legal means to strengthen their economic positions. This, of course, is just what Adam Smith was criticizing. For many decades in the nineteenth century, capitalists used the legal system to try to limit the wages of laborers. If this had gone on long enough, it might have led to the impoverishment and last-ditch revolt of labor that Karl Marx confidently predicted would be the outcome of normal market operations.

In our own time, the trend has been much more against the capitalist. Various regulations and restrictions have been placed on entrepreneurial efforts and the workings of free enterprise so that their efforts have been generally hamstrung. The result is the "stagflation" that we have experienced in recent years. Anyone who has watched the news clips of Midwestern factory workers complaining that they are nothing but "mill hunks," and really do not have any other way of making a living besides taking their place on a factory assembly line, will realize that capitalists really create our economy when they come up with new ideas about organizing labor and making it more productive.

Overlooked, however, has been the role of that third player in the old economic game—the landlord and his modern reincarnation, the environmentalist. It is often forgotten that they were always resented by both labor and capital. Both saw the landlord's "conservation" in limiting the use of resources as a selfishness that obstructed their ambition for further economic growth. Throughout the nineteenth century, in most European countries, there was a constant jostling for position between landlords and capitalists for the favor of the great mass of workers. The capitalist usually advertised the virtues of cities and the rewards of industrial enterprise. The landed aristocracy emphasized the beauties of country living, the pleasures of nature, and the grime and pollution that were generally associated with industrial effort.

American environmentalism slips comfortably into their general pattern. Environmentalists are, in a sense, "landlords without an estate." Or rather, their estate, they argue, is the public lands, plus the air, water, and other general resources that belong to everyone, but that everyone has been particularly neglectful about preserving.

What is wrong then, it might be asked, with simply letting environmentalists have sway in their self-appointed role as stewards over publicly owned resources, plus the common resources like air and water that are so difficult to police?

This is an important point. Environmentalists are indeed playing a critical role in American society. Whether they realize it or not, they have rediscovered the role of the landlord in modern economics and are desperately trying to reinstitute the kind of safety mechanisms that protected resources at a time when more resources were in private ownership—and before we started such serious invasions of common resources like the air and water. Thus, there is nothing inherently wrong with environmental efforts. I think it is one of the most important realizations awaiting both organized labor and large businesses that environmental concerns are a permanent factor in the American economy and are not just a passing fad that will eventually go away.

IMPLEMENTATION

But once again, we are faced with a choice of methods. Do we implement environmental concerns through economic or political methods?

The answer, I think, must be that we must find ways of instituting environmental reforms through economic means. There are many reasons. First, there is the question of efficiency. It benefits the entire society when environmental protection is instituted in the most efficient manner possible. Otherwise, money is wasted and we all lose out through squandered effort. Second, there is the matter of the stability of institutions. If government regulators are given the continuing choice of how much environmental protection the public shall have, then we will be at the constant mercy of whoever is in power. We have witnessed this over the last two presidential administrations. The Carter term was replete with environmental fanatics, who wrote such strict standards and made such demands on industry that it had serious adverse effects on the American economy. Now the Reagan administration has arrived and, instead of trying to introduce more public choice into the procedure, has simply tried to unravel programs to the low standards of protection that it thinks businesses want. The result has been a yo-yoing of environmental issues that produces much controversy but very little public benefit.

If the public were given the choice of how much environmental protection it wanted, however—through such mechanisms as a marketable-rights system—these fluctuations would not occur. Pollution standards, instead of being a function of what a lobbyist could persuade a congressional staff member to put into obscure bills, would be a matter on which the public at large could make intelligent and responsible choices, with the costs as well as the benefits made as clear and visible as possible.

In addition, in the last analysis, it must be admitted that there is one more key reason for making economic rather than political decision making the means of choice for environmental protection. This can be understood that all three players in the game—landlords, capital, laborers—hold only part of the truth on how the system should function. The economy is one of those functioning organisms —often described in biology as ecosystems—where the key to survival is in maintaining an equilibrium among the competing forces, rather than allowing anyone to dominate.

While there is no danger in any of the three players acting out their economic role to the hilt, there is a problem if any of them should be successful in using the political system and the monopoly power of the state to obtain complete domination. Each, of course, would only pursue its own wisdom to a dangerous extreme. If labor were to run the economic system completely to its own advantage, for example, both capitalists and landlords would be driven out of the system. Entrepreneurial effort and resource protection would disappear, such as has been happening in France recently.

If capitalists were to override the market for their own benefit, on the other hand, both labor and landlords would lose. Resources would be pillaged and labor would be driven to the point of revolution. We had a small whiff of this after the unchecked business activities of the 1920s.

Finally, if landlords—or their modern equivalent, the environmentalists—are allowed to manipulate the political system to their advantage, the results will go badly against both capital and labor. Economic stagnation will be the result. Landlords, after all, like all historical aristocracies, are a bit prejudiced in favor of the status quo and against further growth among both capital and labor. They tend to like to let things stand the way they are economically. As the owners of the most permanent resources, they tend to be wary of invention and progress and worried that greater productivity among capital and labor will further undermine their economic power—which, in fact, it usually does. Aristocracies tend to have a stand-pat attitude and prefer to romanticize the rural past rather than to glorify the industrial future.

Once again, however, it must be emphasized that these inborn attitudes among landlords and environmentalists are not inherently disruptive to the economic system. Rather, they perform a critical modulating role against heedless development and the overutilization of resources. Certainly, landlords would like to keep their estates "forever wild" and preserve them permanently. But it is economic pressures that constantly force them to lop off a few lots for condominiums and to put their resources into the general economy. Preservation and no-growth attitudes are only dangerous when they are wed to the political power of the state. When sublimated into the whole of society through economic means they become a strong moderating force that ensures that we use our resources wisely.

THE KEY

The key, then, is to find economic expressions for these political attitudes. This is not an argument against the role of government. Far from it. It is an argument that government must set the rules of the game so that all these inherently competing forces can express themselves in something that roughly approximates the best interests of all.

The task in reforming environmental regulatory efforts—and all forms of regulation, in fact—is to let economic choice substitute for political coercion. The government must not play the game. It should be the umpire and inventor of the game all at once, setting the rules and making sure everyone competes fairly. It is only by this rough but uninhibited expression of the individual desires of the millions of people involved that we will arrive at a true representation of the "public interest."

A CASE IN POINT: AN "INTRACTABLE" ENVIRONMENTAL PROBLEM

One of the most difficult environmental problems we face is how to deal with toxic wastes, both chemical wastes and high-level radioactive material from nuclear plants.

Can the market deal with these problems? It certainly can. Once again, it is only a matter of defining the property involved—a task that has always fallen to governments—and then setting market forces in motion.

There is general agreement among scientists that most of the technical aspects of recycling or storing toxic wastes can be handled. The real problem is getting a state, county, or local community to become the site of these disposal facilities.

For example, the Department of Energy is currently looking for two places to put national "repositories" for high-level radioactive wastes. It is using the usual carrot-and-stick approach, handing out all sorts of "research funds," but holding back the right to impose the site on some state if the situation becomes desperate enough.

As usual, a round of political thrust and counterthrust has begun. The DOE has chosen about 17 "possible" sites in as many states. These states are being asked to consider the possibility of accepting the facility. Predictably, each state has set up "action boards" that are busily producing a blizzard of reasons why their state is *not* the site that ought to be chosen.

And in fact, there are many reasons for opposing such a site right in your backyard and few for accepting it. The economic benefits, no matter how many incentives are poured into the process, are going to be few. The responsibilities are many, and the risks are not undetectable. Therefore, it is very much in everyone's interest to push the problem off into some other political jurisdiction and encourage the DOE to put it somewhere else.

What can the government do to alleviate this situation? The answer is simple. It should set up a procedure where the right, privilege, or burden—whatever you want to call it—of accepting such a facility is *auctioned off* in a manner that reflects both the disadvantages of bearing the brunt of the risks and the advantages of letting someone else deal with the problem.

The DOE should divide the country in two halves and then have all the states east and west of the Mississippi draw up a plan of how they would site one of the country's two "repositories" within their borders. They should have about three to five years to make all their studies and solve all their environmental problems.

Then, at the end of the allotted time, all the states in the western region, for example, would be brought together for an auction. The bidding would start, say, at $1 million a year. This would represent the amount that each state that *does not* accept the facility is going to pay to the one state that *does* accept the job. In this instance, it would mean that 25 western states would each be paying $1 million a year, and the "winning" state would be collecting $24 million a year.

If no one bids, then we raise the price to $2 million. This means that each state is now going to be shelling out $2 million annually, and the winning state is going to be collecting $48 million a year. The bidding may have to go as high as $10 million, with a "pot" of $240 million, but at some point, somebody is going to find it in their interest to bid.

There are many advantages in this "freedom of choice" approach. First, nobody *has* to take the facility if they don't want to. But second, states don't escape the responsibility simply by passing laws or putting up a big fuss about not taking them. Letting someone else deal with the problem costs money, which will cause everyone to take a very hard look at exactly how difficult it is to deal with the problem.

The most common objection that is usually raised to this idea is that it will "discriminate against the poor." Since the poor will want the money and will be less able to pay the costs of avoiding the problem, it is argued they will end up having all the undesirable facilities dumped on them.

This is one of these extraordinary bits of logical flim-flam that are so common in our society today. Even the most cursory inspection of the landscape will reveal that communities of poor people are already having undesirable facilities dumped on them at a steady pace. Garbage dumps, sewer treatment plants, jails, drug rehabilitation centers, power plants, and toxic waste dumps are a rare sight in affluent suburbia. These facilities are almost inevitably imposed on the communities that are least capable of resisting them politically. Witness, for example, North Carolina's recent decision to dispose of illegally dumped PCMs in a "technically favorable site" that just happened to be located in one of the poorest counties with one of the highest black populations in the state.

The poor have nothing to fear from such an auction system. The people who must worry are the most affluent communities who will no longer be able to shrug off these undesirable facilities without paying someone else to take them. The kind of equity produced by the market would far surpass the equity produced by political decision making, where clout is the currency that replaces dollars and cents.

REFERENCES

1. George Gilder, *Wealth and Poverty* (New York: Bantam Books, 1982).

2. Robert M. Alison, "The Earliest Traces of a Conservation Conscience," *Natural History*, May 1981, p. 72.

3. John Locke, *Two Treatises on Government* (New York: New American Library, 1965).

4. J. H. Dales, *Pollution, Property, and Prices* (Toronto: University of Toronto Press, 1968).

5. Ibid., p. 68.

6. Ibid., p. 70.

7. Gary D. Lidecap, *Locking Up the Range* (San Francisco/Cambridge: Pacific Institute for Public Policy Research/Ballinger Publishing Company, 1981).

8. Adam Smith, *The Wealth of Nations* (New York: Modern Library, 1937).

7

TRIAL WITHOUT ERROR:
ANTICIPATION VERSUS RESILIENCE
AS STRATEGIES FOR RISK REDUCTION

Aaron Wildavsky

In a different era, John von Neumann postulated that for any whole to endure it would need to be more reliable than its parts. Though my particular part might fail, a sufficient number and variety of alternatives would give the system as a whole a higher probability of performing than any of its constituent elements.[1] Redundancy would improve reliability. Western society appears to be moving in the opposite direction by seeking to insure each part against failure. Would society be safer under non-von Neumann conditions where each part is stronger than the whole?

NO TRIALS WITHOUT PRIOR
GUARANTEES AGAINST ERROR

The model of risk aversion I will discuss (nothing new should be done unless there is evidence it will do no damage) may be called the rule of "trial without error." If required to give a guarantee that future generations will be better off in regard to every individual action or that no harm will come of it, the scientist (or the businessman, or the politician, or the citizen) cannot so certify. Without trial there can be no error, but without error there is no learning. Science, its historians say, is more about rejecting than accepting hypotheses. Knowledge grows by criticizing the failure of existing theory to explain or predict events in its domain of applicability. Rules for democracy say little about what one does in office, but much more about getting officials out of office. "Throwing the rascals out" is the essence of democracy. Similarly, in social life it is not the ability to avoid error (even Goncharov's *Oblomov*, who spends his life in bed, cannot do that), but learning how to overcome it that is precious.

This mode of learning has seeped so far into collective consciousness that it has become a stock phrase—by trial and error. The debate on risk proposes a radical revision of this practice. If we have to assure against error before we start, then we cannot start at all.

How can consensus be achieved, David W. Pearce asks, when damage may be cumulative and when technologies are "introduced without first having solved the problems they create. This 'reverse solution' phenomenon characterizes the use of nuclear power, where waste disposal problems remain to be solved even though the source of the waste, the power stations themselves, forms part of whole energy programs."[2] One could well ask whether any technology, including the most benign, could have been established if it first had to demonstrate that it did no harm?

In 1865, to take but a single instance, a million cubic feet of gas exploded at the London Gas-Works, killing ten people and burning 20. The newspapers were full of claims that the metropolis faced a disaster.

> If half London would be blown to pieces by the explosion of the comparatively small quantity of gas stored at Blackfriars, it might be feared that if all the gas-holders in the metropolis were to 'go off,' half the towns in the kingdom would suffer, and to be perfectly secure, the source of danger must be removed to the Land's End.[3]

Could anyone who introduced gas heating or lighting have guaranteed the public there would be no explosions or that these would not cumulate to blow up the city? I think not.

In order to guard against the potential for harm from technology whose adverse consequences are not yet under control, Pearce suggests the active provision of information with experts on both sides and attention being paid to the possibility of not going ahead with a particular technology. By funding the opposition and by bringing in wider publics, Pearce hopes to ensure that "surveillance of new technology is carried out in such a way that no new venture is embarked upon without the means of control being 'reasonably' assured in advance.''[4] This is not trial and error but a new doctrine: no trials without prior guarantees against error.

The best argument against learning by trial and error is that it should not be used unless errors are small enough to permit new trials. If errors lead to irreversible damage to large populations, there may be no one around to take on the next trial. A strong statement of this view comes from the philosopher Robert E. Goodin:

> Trial and error and learning by doing are appropriate, either for the epistemic task of discovering what the risks are or for the adaptive task of overcoming them, only under very special conditions. These are conspicuously lacking in the case of nuclear power. First, we must have good reasons for believing that the errors, if they occur, will be small. Otherwise the lessons may be far too costly. Some nuclear mishaps will no doubt be modest. But for the same reasons small accidents are possible so too are large ones and some of the errors resulting in failure of nuclear reactor safeguards may be very costly indeed. This makes trial and error inappropriate in that setting. Second, errors must be immediately recognizable and correctable. The impact of radioactive emissions from operating plants or of leaks of radioactive waste products from storage sites upon human populations or the natural environment may well be a 'sleeper' effect that does not appear in time for us to revise our original policy accordingly.[5]

There must be zero probability of error, in this view, before any trials can take place.

Has there, then, been no useful learning about nuclear energy? Yes, there has, Goodwin writes, but he draws a pessimistic conclusion:

> Sometimes, once we have found out what is going wrong and why, we can even arrange to prevent it from recurring. Precisely this sort of learning by doing has been shown to be responsible for dramatic improvements in the operating efficiency of nuclear reactors. That finding, however, is as much a cause for concern as for hope. It is shocking that there is any room at all left for learning in an operational nuclear reactor, given the magnitude of the disaster that might result from ignorance or error in that setting.[6]

Doing badly is forbidden and doing well is worse.

In an effort to bolster his position, Goodin argues that nuclear power plants are different because "we would be living not merely with risk but also with *irresolvable* uncertainties."[7] Others, like the author of this chapter, claim that "irresolvable uncertainty" is a condition of human life.

Aware of counter-arguments to his position, Goodin cites economists who contend that while it is all right for individuals to be risk averse, there is no reason for society to follow suit. Their reason is that while some projects turn out badly, others do well, so that over time society can select the good ones, thus ending up better off. In response, Goodin argues:

> This argument crucially presupposes that the venture is symmetrical in its payoff structure, admitting of both the possibility of worse-than-expected and better-than-expected payoffs. This seems to be missing in the case of nuclear power: what unexpected windfall might we imagine that would balance out the giant costs associated with a meltdown breaching containment walls. It is of course difficult to say for certain, but it seems extraordinarily likely that all the good that can ever come from nuclear power we can anticipate ahead of time, leaving only the evil to surprise us. Thus society should, contrary to economic advice, display the same aversion to large and uncertain risks of nuclear power as to individuals.[8]

Let us try to help Goddin think of symmetrical payoffs. He rejects, wrongly I think, the suggestion that a partial switch to nuclear energy will decrease the cost of conventional fuels, thus improving living standards for poorer people. Many more people might be better off by mitigating malnutrition or reducing starvation through lower energy prices than would be lost in nuclear accidents.

If the trouble with the economic argument is that it lacks an apocalyptic vision, I can supply that too. Goodin has left political hazards out of his balance sheet. During the crisis surrounding the fall of the Shah of Iran, the United States government, under President Jimmy Carter, warned that it would use nuclear weapons to prevent a loss of Persian Gulf oil. Is it too much to suggest that enhanced use of nuclear power might mitigate the danger of nuclear war over oil supplies?

The implication for seeking safety in energy policy would be not to rely exclusively on any single source or mode of generation so that, whatever happened to supplies or technology, we would be able to respond effectively. Solar energy, with its small size and independence of central coordination, is desirable to develop; it is less likely to be knocked out all at once with one blow. Yet it might prove vulnerable to climatic change or an unforeseen demand for continuous high bursts, capacities contained by nuclear power. Some scientists claim, for instance, that burning fossil fuels will increase carbon dioxide in the atmosphere, thereby warming the earth so that polar ice will melt. If and when this became apparent, we might wish we had nuclear power to substitute for fossil fuels so as to ward off what had become a greater danger. When the one sure thing is that we won't be able to predict important difficulties that the nation will face in the future, developing diversity and flexibility, I shall argue, not sticking with what we have, are the best defenses.

My intent is not to take sides on the nuclear power issue. If this were the only or the main issue of risk in our time, I would not have become interested in applying risk analysis. Rather it is the across-the-board character of the complaints about risk that have claimed my attention. The risk-averse position which requires trials to give guarantees against error has spread over the whole spectrum of daily life. What is involved, we may ask, in adopting a criterion of choice that would restrict new technologies to those that meet Goodin's risk-averse criteria?

CONSEQUENCES OF RISK AVERSION

The direct implication of trial without error is obvious: if you do nothing without knowing first how it will turn out, you cannot do anything at all. Risking and living are inseparable. Almost any act may stand convicted when judged by the rule of no trial without prior guarantees against error. The indirect implication is not at all intuitive: if trying new things is made more costly, there will be fewer departures from past practice, and this very lack of change may increase risk.

Recent environmental impact statements in America may be read as saying that all the values being protected should remain constant. The environment is to remain inviolable in all its parts. No problem, at least not much: but when one adds health, safety, employment, inflation, urban, rural, and other impact statements, the world of public policy is then comprised of nothing but constants, with no variables.

Safety depends on learning and learning depends on error. Safety features found effective in one area may be adopted in others to their mutual betterment. Reliability is enhanced when, as in a submarine, there are numerous systems capable of replacing those that break down.[9] This duplication depends on having sufficient resources to add additional units and sufficient diversity to create new approaches. Imposing innumerable uniform safeguards on all the parts, by contrast, inhibits them from either accumulating resources or trying out alternatives. When none is to be allowed to suffer a first-order effect, none takes on the task of accommodation to changing circumstance. The worst case is when the whole contributes uniformity and the parts rigidity. Then the scope for passing learning on to others or for discovering new configurations or for responding to the unforeseen is diminished.

Relative safety is not a static but rather a dynamic product of learning from error over time. Pioneers pay the costs of premature development. First models are rarely reliable; as experience accumulates, bugs are eliminated and incompatibilities alleviated. Were history halted, development deterred, so to speak, risks for innovators would be markedly increased. The fewer the trials (so there are less mistakes to learn from), the more error remains uncorrected. As development continues into the second and succeeding generations, moreover, the costs of error detection and correction are shared to some extent with future practitioners, and the benefits passed back down to the originators. Forced to follow rules that tell us there will be no tomorrow, few would be willing to start up something new today. Needless to say, the second generation cannot learn from the first if there isn't one. Who, then, will want to be the first to face risks?

A risk of guarding against all conceivable risks is that the costs are raised to such a high level that the ability of small scale units to compete declines and with it the rate of innovation. Rules and regulations designed to provide protection also increase the cost and hence the size necessary to carry on the activity in question. Thus is it possible to rail against risk and large scale organization without realizing that the one reinforces the other.

A preoccupation with rejecting risk leads to large scale organization and centralization of power in order to mobilize massive resources against possible evils. The probability that any known danger will occur declines because of risk-averse measures; but the probability that if the unexpected happens it will prove catastrophic increases, because resources required for response have been used up in advance.

By devaluing experience, the doctrine of "trial without error" simultaneously increases the importance of theory and of theorists. Given the desire to avoid experience, the only way to know what to avoid, other than prohibiting all new developments, is to theorize about possible effects of proposed new technology. (Come to think of it, since it is often not clear what is new or not, hence conflict over patent rights, extensions of old technology may also be interdicted.) Theorizing is a highly specialized activity, even more so when its purpose is precisely to avoid empirical tests. Not only would government grow larger in an effort to ward off danger, but there would be larger organizations in the private sector to meet the riskless criteria, and all of these organizations would have to have large numbers of theorists to argue their cases. This new breed of intellectuals-cum-scientists-cum-lawyers might not exactly be a modern form of Dostoevsky's Grand Inquisitor but they would be in a strong position to issue compelling commands. For this safety directorate could claim to make authoritative pronouncements on doing this or forbidding that to protect our lives. If society asks who ought to allocate safety, the only answer can be the experts on risk aversion. To the traditional unanswerable imperatives—there is no money, no time, God is opposed, and it is unnatural[10]—there would be added no trial without prior guarantee against error.

On the one hand, risk aversion increases the demands for coordination among organizations; in order to prevent evils from occurring, coordinated action across a wide front of possibilities is necessary. Otherwise, what is done in one area—say replacing a suspected chemical carcinogen—will hurt another—say spoiling meat. Yet the growing size of organizations is bound to reduce their flexibility. The larger they are, the more they operate by rule, the less quickly they can move. The spur to change, of course, is error, which comes in the form of feedback, that is, differences between what is desired and what occurs. Without tolerance of error, feedback must be reduced or eliminated. It is, after all, a uniformity of condition that is desired ("feed forward," so to speak, rather than "feedback"), so as to avoid danger to people and to the physical environment. To uniformity, therefore, the principle of "trial without error" adds inflexibility. How, then, will these large and inflexible organizations deal with the change (or the challenges) that must occur despite their best efforts?

A policy of "no trial without prior guarantees against error" decreases safety by increasing vulnerability. The loss of wealth used up in guarding against the possibility of error, that is, in defensive moves, decreases the surplus available for innovation. The decline in innovativeness reduces variety, which in turn exposes society to surprise. It is not that variety decreases the likelihood of surprise but rather that it enhances the prospects of being able to counter the unexpected when it occurs.

The consequences of removing the risks from all the parts are bad for the whole and bad for the parts. Recall the dilemma that faced Consolidated Edison before the New York City blackout of 1977. There were not one but two potential problems: reducing the risk that the entire city would be blacked out compared to the risk of a blackout for a single neighborhood. The greater the willingness to "dump" loads by blacking out a neighborhood, the less the likelihood the entire city would be overloaded and all neighborhoods break down. The safety of the whole is a function of the willingness to sacrifice a part, the particular part being unknown, and the occasion unforeseen. If there is unwillingness to risk a shutdown in any specific site, as events proved, the city system itself may be at stake, and all the parts suffer.

Thus it is wise to ask what will happen if a risk is not taken. It is known, for example, that early innoculation against mild diseases, such as German measles, may lead to susceptibility to much more serious illness later in life. And, if substitutes for risky substances are deemed essential, no one knows what their risks will be compared to the risks of substances given up.[11] If the consumer demands red foods, red dye number two, long in use as a food additive but now recognized as a potential carcinogen, may be forbidden only to be replaced by numerous other dyes about which much less is known. If some degree of risk is inevitable, suppressing it one place may merely move it to another.

It would make sense to anticipate and so avoid global catastrophic risks. But talking about catastrophic risks is not the same as identifying or knowing what to do about them.

Consider the costs of prediction associated with what Bertrand de Jouvenal calls "the railroad track": a pattern has always obtained in the past; therefore projecting it is reasonable, but it can lead to absurd consequences because, somewhere along the track, it sets off a systematic reaction which had never occurred before (for whatever reasons that may be specific to the subject being examined). For example, suppose that the pattern that has always obtained in the past was the function of a social given (as in population dynamics). When something changes in the society, the pattern changes too. So far the relationship between wealth and safety has been linear, the more of one, the more of the other. Is it impossible that the cumulative result of radical environmental changes (some of which we will not see for 50 or 100 years) amounts to a vector which will bend the curve?

Suppose it is so: something we have neglected turns out to be important and dangerous. Suppose government seeks to protect the people against this possibility. Even so, anticipation is not necessarily the best policy. If we are working in the dark, we might choose a few potential disasters to try to avoid, even at high cost. But when the expectation of catastrophe becomes common, priorities among the potentially preventable have to be established or else there will be few resources left to respond to the unexpected. Knowing so little about whether the risk will materialize, we are in as much danger of harming as helping. How would government know which of an infinity of evils will be manifest? Many, which now appear dangerous, may actually turn out to be benign. Others may actually be a little dangerous but the consequences of trying to anticipate them may be much worse than letting them run their course. The most likely eventuality by far is that whatever happens will be unexpected. We might be better off, then, increasing our strength in efforts to ward off we know-not-what.

ANTICIPATION VERSUS RESILIENCE

Anticipation is a mode of control by central cognition; potential dangers are averted before damage is done. Resilience is the capacity to use change so as to better cope with the unknown; it is learning to bounce back. Are risks better balanced, we may ask, by attempting to anticipate them before they occur or by trying to mitigate their effects after they have manifested themselves?

Ecologist C. S. Holling compares control by anticipation with the capacity to cope resiliently:

Resilience determines the persistence of relationships within a system. . . .Stability, on the other hand, is the ability of a system to return to an equilibrium state after a temporary disturbance. . . .With these definitions in mind a system can be very resilient and still fluctuate greatly, i.e., have low stability. I have touched above on examples like the spruce budworm forest community in which the very fact of low stability seems to introduce high resilience. Nor are such cases isolated ones, as Watt has shown in his analysis of thirty years of data collected for every major forest insect throughout Canada by the Insect Survey Program of the Canada Department of the Environment. This statistical analysis shows that in those areas subjected to extreme climatic conditions populations fluctuate widely but have a high capability of absorbing periodic extremes of fluctuation. . . .In more benign, less variable climatic regions the populations are much less able to absorb chance climatic extremes even though the populations tend to be more constant.[12]

To repeat: "low stability seems to introduce high resilience."

Though the language of Holling's theory is abstract, its policy implications can be made quite concrete: the experience of overcoming danger increases safety, whereas continuous safety is extremely dangerous to the survival of living species. Keeping "out of harm's way" (something Don Quixote preached but never practiced, hence his longevity) is harmful. I stress the counter-intuitive implications of the superiority of resilience over anticipation as strategies for securing safety because they should guard us (and policymakers as well) against the facile conclusion that the best way to protect people is to reduce the risks they face rather than enabling them to overcome dangers.

The debate over regulation of risk reveals a strategic conflict between anticipation and resilience. J. C. Smith's elegant essay on "The Process of Adjudication and Regulation, A Comparison"[13] is about anticipation versus resilience under other names—regulation versus adjudication or the criminal versus the tort law. He is concerned, as I am, to compare mechanisms of social control, which he also calls "institutional paradigms. . . as methods of protecting people from the harmful consequences of action." Tort law enforces obligation by awarding damages as compensation in order to protect personal and property rights. Far from settling conflicting claims over rights, the criminal law establishes certain behavior as so harmful that it incurs penalties stipulated in advance. Functioning after the alleged harm has already occurred, civil or tort law is essentially a mode of resilience; the criminal law is anticipatory. According to Smith,

> The distinctive feature of criminal law is that it prohibits certain kinds of harmful acts . . . because the harmful effects can be taken for granted, while the civil law tends to concentrate on the results or effects of actions . . . .The distinguishing feature of the process of regulation is that . . . it prohibits a wide variety of acts by providing for fines, imprisonment, or both, irrespective of whether harm will in fact result.

Regulation is a form of anticipation. Consequently, because regulation cannot wait for evidence from actual events, it does not fit well with many particular circumstances within a general class. As Smith says,

> When standards are established by regulations in general terms, they will inevitably be too high for some of the situations to which the regulations apply, and too low for others. Particularity is just not possible through regulation. Often where an adequate standard in general is too low for a particular situation, and a tragic accident takes place, the ensuing adverse publicity leads to the standard then being raised substantially higher than need be for most of the situations to which the regulations apply, in order to prevent a similar accident from again happening. In an unregulated situation where a serious accident has occurred, each individual actor or enterprise or industry will examine itself in the light of the particular circumstances, and in only those cases of a similar nature will corrective action need to be taken.[14]

Where anticipation requires bureaucracy to enforce standards, resilience is based on self-regulation by the people who are closest to the scene and who, therefore, have the best information about what is happening.

It is hard to remember now, so harsh and vindictive has been the attack, that until the 1930s there was a doctrine of substantive due process protecting property rights. Under this doctrine, the courts assumed that regulations affecting property rights produced initial harmful consequences so that the government, acting through the legislature and executive, had to accept the burden of proof in showing that the property rights of individuals have been turned aside for good reason. Today, all this is taken for granted in regard to the due process requirements that have to be met whenever interference with freedom of speech or assembly is contemplated. This protection, however, has been taken away from property rights, which have been given an inferior place. Thus, regulation itself, based on the legislative police power, has become the embodiment of due process to be challenged only if there was some flaw in the way in which the public will was manifested, whereas restraints on expression became subject to the same criteria of substantive due process that had heretofore protected property.

Observers of the American political scene will note that interest group activity flourishes as never before; by contrast, the economy, based on property rights, languishes. Once we understand that political participation has been allowed to become resilient by applying due process against governmental intervention, whereas property rights have been subject to anticipatory regulation, the reason for the anomaly becomes evident: resilience outperforms anticipation.

Anticipation emphasizes uniformity: the less fluctuation, the better. Resilience stresses variability; one does not do so well in good times but learns to persist in the bad. As Holling sums up,

> The very approach, therefore, that assures a stable maximum sustained yield of a renewable resource might so change these deterministic conditions that the resilience is lost or reduced so that a change and rare event that previously could be absorbed can trigger a sudden dramatic change and loss of structural integrity of the system.[15]

Resilience relies on variety. Instead of attempting to guard against every evil, only the most likely or most dangerous would be covered, fully expecting that whatever was missed would be countered as and after it occurred.

Of course, everyone would like to pick out the eyes from the potatoes of life, choosing to regulate only those that we have reason to believe will do considerable harm. Is it true, then that governmental activity is geared towards using the knowledge of modern science to create priorities among possible dangers, choosing to eliminate or control those that promise to do the most harm? Since expenditures per accident or fatality averted vary from a few thousand to several hundred million, this claim can hardly be substantiated.[16] Moreover, advocates of regulation via anticipation to reduce harm to people and nature face a disconcerting anomaly: in the past, with a minimum of regulation, morbidity and mortality have shown dramatic improvement. Obviously, allowing things to go on as they were is far from deadly, "We are fully free," Hayek warns, "to pick and choose whatever combination of features we wish our society to possess, or to ... build a desirable social order like a mosaic by selecting whatever particular parts we like best. ..."[17] The good and the bad are inextricably mixed; all we can do is choose a strategy that over time will leave us better rather than worse off. How shall we come down, then, for a preponderance of anticipation or of resilience?

Assessing a variety of efforts to manage resources, ecologist William Clark concludes that

> In each case, uncertainty or variablitiy in the natural system was initially viewed as a source of risk/hazard. Without exception, it was assumed that removal of the variability would be an unmitigated good, resulting in reduced risk and improved performance of the resource sytem .... With that variability removed, [however,] relationships shifted to accommodate the new reality: people settled the unflooded floodplain, budworms spread through the undefoliated forest, brush accumulated on the unburned understory, and so on. As a result, *the decreased frequency of variation in the system was accompanied by increased vulnerability* to and cost of varitation when it finally broke loose from managerial controls.[18]

Again, loss of variability leads to decline of resilience.

Three Mile Island (I am aware it is used to "prove" everything) is a case in point. It occurred after (not before) large numbers of safety measures were retrofitted onto existing reactors. The idea was that by strengthening every part—pipes, valves, containment, alarms, and so on—the plants would be safer than ever. There was no effort to link the parts to the whole, that is, to ask whether the relationship among parts was optimal in view of the hundreds of changes made. The point was to prevent failure. Training to respond to failure was minimal because that would have meant admitting that things could go wrong. When the some hundred warning lights and whistles went off, the staff became confused. The system lacked resilience because the staff had been taught to rely on anticipation.[19]

There are also more subtle ways in which the belief that it is possible (because it is desirable) to control all dangers, by creating a false sense of security, compromises coping ability. The dependence of Bay Area Rapid Transit on a computerized scheduling system that would make no errors, for example, led to a disregard for coping with breakdowns that were never supposed to occur.[20] There was no fail-safe. "The classic example here," Clark says, "is the ship Titanic, where the new ability to control most kinds of leaks led to the understocking of lifeboats, the abandonment of saftety drills, and the disregard of reasonable caution in navigation."[21]

A more restricted interpretation might be that unless risk is reduced across-the-board, in all elements of a system, due to a common increase in capability, holding it down here just makes it pop up there. "Managment efforts had changed the kinds of risks encountered," Clark writes, "but not the fact of risk. More often than not, management shifted the risk structure from a sort people were accustomed to dealing with to one they had never before experienced."[22] Shifting risks may be more dangerous than tolerating them both because those who face new risks may be unaccustomed to them and those who no longer face old ones may become more vulnerable when conditions change.

Left to their own devices, each element or part of society will seek its safety at the expense of others. So may individual entrepreneurs. Linked together by markets, however, capitalist firms cannot avoid the danger of loss. If they attempt to safeguard their subsystem, that is, to prevent loss without risk, others will undersell and outproduce them. Only when the reduction of risk is widely shared will it become feasible for any one firm to put "safety first." Instead of shifting dangers to others through sub-optimization, there is a general advance. Were this not so, it would be impossible to explain why wealthier societies are safer[23] or why encouraging risk taking by some over time increases safety for others.

If there is merit in this line of argument—markets increase safety over time precisely because they need not respond to every subunit's demand for protection—the implications for decisions about risk are profound. Except where persuasive evidence and remedies exist, direct decisions should not be made about risk per se. Focusing on risk in itself is dangerous. It leads to suboptimization.

Risk aversion by anticipation will do one thing it is supposed to, namely reduce variability and increase uniformity. In the field of evolution, this sort of suboptimization by protecting the parts has a name of its own:

> All evolutionary textbooks grant a paragraph or two to a phenomenon called "overspecialization," usually dimissing it as a peculiar and peripheral phenomenon. It records the irony that many creatures, by evolving highly complex and ecologically constraining features for their immediate Darwinian advantage, virtually guarantee the short duration of their species by restricting its capacity for subsequent adaptation. Will a peacock or an Irish elk survive when the environment alters radically? Yet fancy tails and big antlers do lead to more copulations in the short run of a life-time. Overspecialization is, I believe, a central evolutionary phenomenon that has failed to gain the attention it deserves because we have lacked a vocabulary to express what is really happening: the negative interaction of species-level disadvantage and individual-level advantage .... The general phenomenon must also regulate much of human society, with many higher-level institutions compromised or destroyed by the legitimate demands of individuals ....[24]

"Individual-level advantage" is sub-system optimization. Risk aversion is specialization by anticipation. The best way to reduce risk of morbidity and mortality, for most people most of the time, is to enhance overall economic performance, that is, "species-level" advantage.

Given two processes—markets and bureaucracies—one of which tends to "over" and the other to "under" select dangers, which one would leave people better off? Ruling out Goldilock's strategy of getting things just right as beyond cognitive and collective capacities, my last reformulation goes, Would people be better off having their porridge too hot (that is, too much risk)? Which horn of the dilemma of risk taking—anticipation or resilience—do we wish to grasp?

If the risks are being undertaken via private markets rather than public agencies, my view is that more people will be healthier by taking a larger rather than a smaller number and extent of risk. I come to this conclusion without believing that private industry is more competent, not to say altruistic, than public agencies. The advantages I believe inherent in private enterprise are several but above all is the possibility of failure. Companies, divisions, managers, and products may ultimately be (and frequently are) rejected. It is in high rates of failure, in the errors which result from innumerable trials, that advantages of markets reside.

The trade-offs between anticipation and resilience may come into clearer focus if we shift the field from technological dangers to crime and defense. There is considerable evidence that much if not most strong-arm crime is committed by "career criminals." By their late thirties, when there are enough convictions to put them away for a long time, they are likely to be burned out. If they could be gotten early, say in their teens, and put away for 20 years or so, society would be a lot safer and less fearful. So much for the advantages of a policy of anticipation. The disadvantage is that knowledge is insufficient to pick out habitual criminals early. Consequently, there would be many false positives, errors concentrated among blacks and Hispanics. By contrast, a policy of resilience catches criminals too late to do society much good but, because after the fact it is more knowledgeable, the injustice of wrongful incarceration, compounded by racial selectivity, is reduced. Is anticipation to be justified on the grounds that the evil prevented outweighs the evil done, as well it might on some scales, or is resilience preferable because it enables society to tailor the punishment to the crime?

Defense policy provides a useful contrast to health and crime. Whereas the administration of President Ronald Reagan supports resilience in the economy, preferring private enterprise to governmental regulation, it favors anticipation towards defense. The Soviet threat is deemed so great that massive efforts must be made to guard against it in advance. Otherwise, it will be too late to avoid destruction or conquest. Should some of these preparations prove unnecessary, or even detract from economic growth, that is believed to be a price worth paying.

Why the difference in strategies between the domestic economy and foreign policy? Because President Reagan supports markets, he favors resilience; because he believes time is running short, he wants to take anticipatory action. His trust in American institutions leads him to support private markets and governmental hierarchies in their respective spheres. No doubt the same sort of criticisms he leveled at anticipatory strategies in domestic policy—throwing money at problems, overinsurance, decline in productivity, organizational rigidity —apply to his defense policy as well. Indeed, the resemblance of the defense budget to a Chinese menu (three from group A, four from group B, two from group C), which is to say its lack of cutting edge, is due to overprovision of resources; doctrine is unnecessary if there is no need to choose.

As a strategy of social choice, anticipation is going to look quite different when it is applied to human health and environmental pollution rather than to national defense. If people prefer anticipatory action to defend what they value most, they may rely on resilience when they are prepared to let things take care of themselves. The ubiquity of unanticipated consequences in human life becomes more understandable on the supposition that if resilience is, on average, superior to anticipation, people are likely to protect what they care about less than what they work so hard to defend.

REQUIREMENTS OF RESILIENCE

The behavior in which we are interested is the intertwining of clashing consequences (for the human body and the natural environment) in the same technology. With good and bad inextricably mixed, it is not possible to have one without the other. If no new costs can be incurred, no new benefits can be gained. Economic progress, and the health benefits it has brought, would come to an end. Since mankind cannot progress by choosing only those consequences that enhance health (of people and nature), the question is how best to balance the costs and benefits so that, over time, health as well as wealth would improve? It is in this context of balancing opposed effects that governmental regulation versus market operations should be viewed.

The optimal arrangement, in my opinion, is for government to intervene only when there is substantial evidence of benefit. By this I mean that there must be more than a finding of actual (or potential) harm. In addition, there should also be knowledge of what to do and how to do it, so that the cure is not worse than the disease. For if anyone who feels threatened by an adverse consequence can stop the proposed technology dead in its tracks, all future benefits will be foregone, making it impossible to discover new arrangements better than those that now exist.

Nations could, of course, license all new technology, requiring its proponents to prove that it will do no (or minimal) harm before it can be tried. This would be the institutionalization of the doctrine of "trial without error" that has been the subject of this chapter.

Suppose, however, that laissez-faire would be the policy of the day, with no exceptions allowed. Evidently, certain opportunities would be foregone. Public health measures, to give the obvious example, are of overwhelming benefit compared to cost. From the standpoint of business, moreover, the costs are socialized over all taxpayers. The same thing occurs, to a lesser but palpable extent, in regard to other infrastructure—education, roads, sewers, among others. Such considerations may explain why there is no pure laissez-faire policy.

Were we to reformulate this market criterion slightly allowing for public goods of immense benefit in whose production government has a decided advantage, it would still leave out intervention to protect against specific disabilities brought about by new technology. Again, I reformulate my question to ask, "Will people be better off, compared to laissez-faire, if there are specific governmental interventions designed to weed out the harmful from the helpful consequences of technology?"

The answer is question-begging: it all depends on whether and to what extent government is able to (a) guess right and (b) act effectively. For if government were to thrust at shadows, seeking to stop or regulate many substances or mechanisms that, if implemented, would turn out to be benign, or even helpful, vast benefits would be foregone. However effective government might be in remedying real ills, it must fail unless it distinguishes the future consequences of current and proposed technology.

Choosing the wrong risks need not be so serious if there are mechanisms for discarding old solutions and trying out new ones. Yet this evolutionary approach (called trial and error) is precisely what advocates of risk aversion are trying to get away from. Political-bureaucratic processes, moreover, are characterized by slow adaptation; it is difficult to get on the list of technologies to be regulated and difficult to get off.

It is the effort to get government to provide guarantees against risk that characterizes domestic developments during the twentieth century. If we substitute security for safety, social policy for technology, the desire for protection may be seen to be widespread. When one extends this protection to industry and its owners—"socialism for the rich"—the protection of the parts appears to be the ubiquitous phenomenon it is.[25]

Since we do not know enough to identify and overcome each and every source of adversity, insurance may substitute for knowledge.

Now the parts may be insured by the whole but who will insure the whole? If the parts are not risk-absorbers or risk-reducers but become risk-expanders and risk-exporters, how will the whole bear the burden? How can we build resilience into government?

The administrative analogue to markets is cybernetics, which originated as the theory of servo-control mechanisms. From the beginning, the role of the designer–adjuster has remained vague. Elements form a system. Within a level of tolerance postulated by this mysterious center, each element is free to operate. Deviations above, below, or outside this level, sometimes called the governor, are initially to be met by each element's own efforts to dampen the oscillations, that is, to return to the accepted level.

Coordination is kept to a minimum. Should one element (a program, an agency) create difficulties for another, this other unit is expected to take action on its own to contain the disturbance. Although units may export their difficulties, this occurrence still accords with the rules of the game so long as there is sufficient variety so that some element of the system is able to cope. Each element gets lots of practice in coping. As the system matures, therefore, its elements should have learned how to manage an increasingly wider range of disruption. So far, so good.

Suppose, however, that disturbances can no longer be contained. Perhaps some elements no longer can carry their burden. Or perhaps the new disruptions are so novel or severe that existing adaptations cannot cope with them. Possibly the elements in the system no longer trust one another, unwilling to accept any redistribution of burdens.

Enter the center. The governor must govern. But how?

Suppose every subgroup in society—farmers, workers, old people, youngsters, on and on—were guaranteed against risk. Supposing their safety had to be secure, no matter what. Who then would pay penalties? Presumably risks would have to be allocated over the remainder. But if guarantees were extended until there were no one left unprotected, how would shocks be absorbed? How could risks ever be taken for causes however good if the losses could not be assigned to anyone? Where would the center get surplus resources to respond to emergencies if it had to pay out to the parts but received no income in return. The system would cease adapting. The implications of legislating to remove risk are major disasters, from flood, famine, and foreign take-over to the material and technical poverty that has no means of climbing out of trouble.

Cybernetic solutions can work only if there is trust in institutions. That they work with minimal trust and coordination is their strength. But can they work without any?

Resilience requires trust. The organizational requirements of resilience are social and political as well as technological. If institutions are to wait until dangers manifest themselves, as resilience requires, they must have freedom to adapt quickly. It follows that resilient institutions are based on public trust; resilient institutions must have high legitimacy. But the risk-averse do not believe their institutions are resilient. They do not believe their institutions can handle future problems. Therefore the "establishment" must be made to anticipate now all the bad things which might happen. The risk-averse demand cash in advance, the palpable evidence that action is being taken to prevent harm. The anticipatory strategy of demanding no trials without guarantees against error is self-fulfilling in that lack of trust lowers the resilience of institutions, thereby making them less effective to deal with problems as they emerge.

Looking back at the past quarter century, living standards have risen dramatically and, along with them, morbidity and mortality have undergone substantial improvements. Why, then, is there so much distrust of the Western institutions that have been, on any criterion of safety achieved anywhere in the world at any time, so successful? For the escalating concern over risk to the human body and natural environment stemming from technology is exactly a referendum on these institutions.[26] Were they trusted to respond resiliently to future dangers, the kinds of concerns we witness every day would not occur. The beginning of wisdom about our controversial subject is that it is, first and foremost, our institutions that are at risk.

REFERENCES

1. John von Neumann, "The General and Logical Theory of Automata," in *Modern Systems Research for the Behavioral Scientist*, Walter Buckley, ed. (Chicago: Aldine Publishing Company, 1968), pp. 97–107. See also, W. Ross Ashby, "Variety, Constraint, and the Law of Requisite Variety," in ibid., pp. 129–136.

2. David W. Pearce, "The Preconditions for Achieving Consensus in the Context of Technological Risk," in *Technological Risk: Its Perception and Handling in the European Community*, Meinolf Dierkes, Sam Edwards, Rob Coppock, eds. (Cambridge, Mass.: Oelgeschlager, Gunn & Hain, Publishers; and Konigstein/TS: Verlag Anton Hain, 1980), p. 58.

3. *The Journal of Gas Lighting, Water Supply, and Sanitary Improvement* (November 14, 1865), p. 807.

4. Pearce, op. cit., p. 63.

5. Robert E. Goodin, "No Moral Nukes," *Ethics* 90 (April 1980), pp. 418-419.

6. Ibid., p. 418.

7. Ibid., p. 421.

8. Ibid., pp. 425-426.

9. Martin Landau, "Redundancy, Rationality and the Problem of Duplication and Overlap," *Public Administration Review* (July/August 1969): 346-58.

10. Mary Douglas, "Environments at Risk," in *Implicit Meanings* (London and Boston: Routledge & Kegan Paul, 1975), pp. 230-249. See also Sanford Weiner and Aaron Wildavsky, "The Prophylactic Presidency," *The Public Interest*, no. 52 (Summer 1978): 3-19.

11. See William C. Clark, "Managing the Unknown: An Ecological View of Risk Assessment," Paper prepared for the SCOPE-MAB Workshop on Identification of Environmental Hazards, held in Shrewsbury, Mass. in January 1977; and Aaron Wildavsky, "No Risk Is the Highest Risk of All," *American Scientist*, Vol. 67 (Jan/Feb 1979): 32-37.

12. C. S. Holling, "Resilience and Stability of Ecological Systems," *Annual Review of Ecology and Systematics*, vol. 4 (1979): 1-23.

13. In *Rights and Regulations*, Tibor Machan and M. Bruce Johnson, eds. (San Francisco: Pacific Institute, 1983).

14. Ibid.

15. Holling, op. cit.

16. John D. Graham and James W. Vaupel, "The Value of a Life: Does It Make a Difference?" *Journal of Risk Analysis*, vol. 1, no. 1 (1981).

17. Friedrich A. Hayek, *Rules and Order*, vol. 1 of *Law, Legislation and Liberty* (Chicago: Univ. of Chicago Press, 1973), p. 59.

18. William C. Clark, "Witches, Floods, and Wonder Drugs: Historical Perspectives on Risk Management," in Richard C. Schwing and Walter A. Albers, Jr., eds., *Societal Risk Assessment: How Safe Is Safe Enough?* (New York: Plenum Press, 1980), p. 298. [Emphasis supplied.]

19. The President's Commission on the Accident at Three Mile Island, *The Need for Change: The Legacy of TMI*, final report, October 1979.

20. My sister tells of observing passengers carrying bathroom plungers on BART in the early days. Since the system was assumed to operate without error (at high speed and with powerful brakes), it was believed that trains would succeed each other with great rapidity so no one would ever have to stand. Hence no provision was made for straps or handles to which passengers might attach themselves. As engines and brakes burned out and the all-seeing computer lost track of trains, passengers piled up in the remaining vehicles. Alas, they could not steady themselves while standing; nothing if not resilient, however, some standees brought plungers, stuck them on the ceilings, and got to their destinations in one piece.

21. Clark, op. cit.

22. Ibid.

23. Aaron Wildavsky, "Richer Is Safer," *The Public Interest*, No. 60 (Summer 1980): 23–29.

24. Stephen Jay Gould, "Darwinism and the Expansion of Evolutionary Theory," *Science*, Vol. 216 (23 April 1982): 380–386.

25. See Robert D. Reischauer, "The Federal Budget: Subsidies for the Rich," in Michael J. Boskin and Aaron Wildavsky, eds., *The Federal Budget: Economics and Politics* (San Francisco: Institute for Contemporary Studies, 1982), pp. 235–262.

26. See Mary Douglas and Aaron Wildavsky, *Risk and Culture: An Essay on the Selection of Technological and Environmental Dangers* (Los Angeles/Berkeley: University of California Press, 1982).

AFTERWORD: A NEW AGENDA

Margaret N. Maxey

The foregoing essays exhibit a seminal as well as an enduring quality. They demonstrate that a new agenda for liberal democracy and for private/free enterprise has now emerged with a higher level of clarity, visibility, and urgency regarding the work that remains to be done. As members of the new agenda-setting class, these authors have not only raised to public consciousness the crucial consequences of issues confronting us, but they also challenge us to a more fruitful debate concerning the purposes to be served by social change, and the methods of responsible control that will more effectively safeguard human rights and structures of fairness in a democratic polity. As representatives of the Four Estates, each author exhibits a deep concern not only for problems raised by the exercise of power in a particular domain, but also for intellectual issues and the choice of ideas which legitimate the wielding of that power. In short, they demonstrate the importance of ideas in establishing the choice of a new agenda, in selecting strategies for their implementation, and in choosing a marketplace to test their validity.

Robert Benne observes that the university does not and should not have a commitment to any one model of political economy. Nonetheless, its time-honored status in medieval and modern society makes it a unique proving ground—a free marketplace—for exchanging and testing the validity of ideas. In the clash of ideas that will come to a head in the near future, the university will undoubtedly become a center for controversy, a place in which ideas and arguments will be tested for their persuasive power among members of a new agenda-setting class. While the university is never going to be decisive in the clash of policy with policy, Pickering observes that it has a great contribution to make in the clash of ideas with ideas.

If this is the case, it is questionable whether our common life is well-served by characterizing our public discourse and honest disagreements as "a war of ideas." Not only does a combative metaphor signal an anti-intellectual approach—as if public discourse were a strategic battle, or an athletic competition, or a wrestling match in which there are winners and losers—but it also implies that ideas are weapons to wound others, or to defeat an enemy in a zero-sum game. To the contrary, ideas are about substantive matters, with the power to heal and reconcile and serve a common good, rather than to win a contest.

It is our hope that these essays have demonstrated why the fate and meaning of one of history's most powerful ideas—liberal democracy sustained by private/free enterprise, unifying democratic political institutions with a market economy—remains worthy of our allegiance as we shape an agenda for a technological society.

INDEX

corn yields, 74
corporate funds and research, 123
cost-benefit analysis, 152
costs and benefits balance, 216
crime and defense, 215
crop yields, 74
cropland loss, *see* farmland loss
cultural climate, 5
cultural theory, of risk selection, 3
cybernetics, 218

dangers, psychology of, 1
dangers and risks, 2
death; causes of, 42; fear of, 57
decentralization, 159
defense, anticipation toward, 215
deforestation, 77–79
deforestation rate, 79
deindustrialization, 153
democracy, 15, 136, 163, 165; in economic life, 165
democratic capitalist: democracy, 169; economic rationality, 169; respect for political order, 170; tension between politics and economy, 169
democratic capitalist approach, 168; to regulation, 159–76; regulation of specific markets, 170
dioxin, 126
disposal facilities, toxic waste, 197
diversity and adaptability, 139
drainage ditch technology, 74

earth preservation, 6
ecology and religion, 8
economic growth, 9
economic planning, 178
economic policy and regulation, 12
economic reasoning, 152
economizing, 169

economy: and environment, 181; government regulation, 177; stationary state, 6
ecosystems, chemicals transport in, 41
education, statistics, 84
efficiency, 159; and growth, 160
Electric Power Research Institute (EPRI), 141
electric power stations, desulfurization equipment, 46
employers insurance, 40
employment, 90
employment of children, *see* child labor
endangered species, 10, 187
Energy, Department of, 197; waste disposal sites, 198
energy industry: hypothetical accidents, 138; self-regulation, 141
energy prices, 203
energy sources, cost, 139
energy supply, 63
entropy, law of, 7
environment: definition of, 33; and evolution, 34; historical perspective, 33
environmental changes: atmospheric changes, 34; by living species on earth, 34
environmental factors, balance of, 35
environmentalism, 33, 177–99; as market externality, 181
environmentalists, 194
environmental legislation: early history, 40; and industry, 50
environmental movement, 37; and regulatory agencies, 103; risk assessment, 101
environmental pollution, 2; American public interest in, 42; and cancer, 42; carbon monoxide,

42; communicable diseases,
36; federal involvement in
control, 44, 62; government's
role in, 181; mercury, 42;
noise pollution, 42; and
Public Health Service, 44;
sulfur oxides, 42; in
underdeveloped countries, 60
Environmental Protection Agency,
33, 45, 118, 183; and inadequate risk assessment studies,
111; and Love Canal issue,
111; registration standards
for pesticides, 116; risk
assessment practice, 102;
Scientific Advisory Board,
122; sulfur dioxide regulation, 46
environmental reforms: through
economic means, 194;
government regulations, 195,
197
environmental regulations, and
health risks, 33–52
epidemic disease, 37
error detection, 205
errors, 202
evolution and environment, 34

famine deaths, 68
fanaticism, 162
farmland loss, 74, 76
Federal Water Pollution Control
Act, 47, 188
feedback, 206
fishery statistics, 66, 68
Food and Drug Administration,
102, 112, 118
food chains, pesticides in, 6
food consumption, 69; meat consumption, 72
food insurance policy, 72
food prices, 68
food production, reduction in, 69

fossil fuel burning, 204
freedom and prosperity, 162
freedom of choice, 164
future and danger, 5

game animals, protection of, 183
General Public Utilities (GPU),
141
genetic-engineering research, 124;
risks, 125
government: intervention into private sector, 160; intervention
into public problems, 179; involvement in environmental
issues, 53, 55; regulation of
investment capital, 166
government and free enterprise,
178
government ownership of resources, 185; protection, 187
government power limitation, 160
government regulation, as social
policy, 12
growth and entropy, 7
growth limits, 6
growthmania, 5
growth stopping and world collapse, 6

health and environment, 37
health improvements, 60
health risks, 33
heating, waste, 171
high school graduates, 85
housing costs, increase in, 89
housing improvements, 90
human beings, positive effect on
environment, 63
human error, 108
human services budget, 160

immigrants, in United States, 91
income, per-capita, 83
income statistics, 88

industrial accidents, 40
Industrial Biotest Corporation, 110
industrialization and pollution, 60
industrial policy, 166
industrial pollution and cancer, 42
Industrial Revolution, 39, 183
industries: and environmental
    pollution, 50; marketable
    rights to pollute, 188; pricing
    of polluting side effects, 173
inequality, 180
Institute of Nuclear Power Opera-
    tions (INPO), 142
insurance as investment, 131
insurance coverage, 31
Interior, Department of, 190;
    mismanagement, 191
international income comparisons,
    88
intuition, 146
investment capital, government
    regulation, 166
irresolvable uncertainties, 203

judgement, 146
justice, 159

laboratory animal experimenta-
    tion, 107
lakes, protection of, 187
landscape deterioration, 181
learning, by trial and error, 202
Leninism, 16
less-developed countries, see un-
    derdeveloped countries
liability law, 173
liberal democracy, 14
liberal democrats, 160
life: condition of, 53; existence on
    earth, 34; and health, 55–60;
    in United States, 54
life expectancy, 55; increase, 57;
    and pollution, 60
Los Angeles, air pollution in, 45

Love Canal problem, 50, 111
lumber prices, 63
lung cancer, 42

man, primitive, 35
Marble Canyon Dam, 190
marginal utility theory, 163
market as preserver of liberty, 163
market economy, 170
market externalities, 180
Marxism, 16, 163
Mediterranen region: climate, 35;
    desertification of, 35
mortality risk, 214
Motor Vehicle Air Pollution Con-
    trol Act, 44

National Academy of Sciences
    (NAS), 121
national toxicological laboratories,
    119; and universities, 120
natural gas, distribution of, 171
natural gas prices: deregulation,
    171; regulation, 170
natural resources, 53–97; allocation
    for risk limitation, 137–39;
    balanced allocation, 135–37;
    depletion of, 6; deterioration
    in capitalist system, 181; fish,
    66; lumber, 63; misallocation
    of, 132; misallocation for risk
    aversion, 136; price, 63; scar-
    city, 63; underdeveloped
    countries, 63
noise pollution, 42
nuclear energy: and conventional
    fuel cost, 203; risks, 203;
    risks of individual harm, 151
Nuclear Energy Insurance Limited
    (NEIL), 142
nuclear power industry, risk as-
    sessment, 102
nuclear power plant operators,
    licensing of, 108

nuclear power plants: accidents, 142; emergency response capability, 141; ignorance about operation, 202; irresolvable uncertainties, 203; Nuclear Regulatory Commission (NRC), 141; regulations, 140; safety measures, 142–144; safety studies for licensing, 107; security technologies, 109; waste disposal problem, 201

Nuclear Regulatory Commission (NRC), 141; interaction with energy industry, 141; licensing reform, 145; policy and planning guidance, 144; regulatory reforms, 145; safety goals, 145

Nuclear Safety Analysis Center (NSAC), 142

nuclear war, 203

nuclear weapons testing, 41

nutrition, improvement of, 38

occupational disease, 41

occupational health and safety, 181

Occupational Safety and Health Administration (OSHA), toxic substances exposure standards, 102

oil prices, 63

opinion, cultural climate of, 5–11

overbreeding, 5

Palestine, land deterioration, 36

patent rights, 206

personal contamination, 2

pesticide regulations, based on inadequate studies, 110

pesticide research, 124

pesticides, carcinogenic risk assessment, 102

pesticide use, by certified people, 108

polar ice, 204

political classes, 19–23

political conflicts, 19

political economy, 9

political economy models, 161; commercial republican, 161; democratic capitalist, 161; social democratic, 161; political passions, violent, 162

politics and social change, 19

pollution and industrialization, 60

pollution control, 11

pollution rights, 187, 188

pollution standards, 195

poor, energy distribution, 172

population growth: by immigrants, 91; positive effect on standard of living, 91; and productivity increase, 91

price control, 165; and conservation, 171; and production cost, 171; protective regulation, 172

price deregulation and competition, 171

private enterprises, 177

private ownership and environment protection, 186

private property, 184

probability, 148; and consequences, 106

productivity loss, insurance, 131

property ownership, 184

property rights, 187

prosperity and private enterprises, 178

public: risk education, 126; risk perception, 151

public health: improvement, 38; social regulation, 104

Public Health Service, United States (USPHS), 44

229

soil erosion, 35, 74; economics of, 74
solar energy, 171, 204
Soviet threat, 215
soybean yields, 74
species extinction, 77–79; rate, 78
stability and resilience, 209
starvation, 6
steel industry, 189; water pollution, 188
streams and lakes, privatizing, 62
sulfur dioxide, control of, 45–47
superstition, 2

technological politics, 15–18; theory of culture, 16
technological risk regulation, 13
technological society, 24; as political agenda-setting class, 20
technology: and natural resources, 6; potential harm, 201; regulation, 18; and risk, 101
Tennessee Valley Authority, 185
thalidomide, 112
theology, 165
theory of culture, 15
thermodynamics, laws of, 7
Three Mile Island accident, 151, 212
tobacco growers, 112
toxic substances, exposure standards, 102
Toxic Substances Control Act, 107
toxic waste disposal facilities, 197
toxic wastes, 197. *See also* chemical wastes; radioactive waste disposal
trans-scientific questions, 117; and university scientists, 122
trial and error, 200
tropical forests, 77

underdeveloped countries: deforestation, 77; education, 86; evironmental pollution, 60; individual income, 87
unemployment, 153
United States: agricultural productivity, 76; farmland loss, 76; food production, 69; free enterprise economic system, 178; housing improvement, 90; income per person, 87; international income comparisons, 88; Public Health Service, 44; Social Democratic party, 163
university community: economic reasoning for risk assessment, 152; as information source, 120; and regulation, 151; risk assessment challenges, 152; role in improving scientific information, 153; role in public perception of risk, 151; role in risk assessment conflicts, 153; role in risk education, 124–28
university-corporate relations, 123; in genetic engineering research, 124
university role, in regulatory risk assessment, 118
university scientists, disclosure of income sources, 124
university specialties, 152

wage control, 165
waste disposal, 151
water pollution, 6, 173; oil, 48; polluting charge for industries, 173
water pollution control, 47–49; cost, 49; sewage treatment plants, 48
Water Pollution Control Act, 48
Water Pollution Control Amendments, 48

ABOUT THE EDITORS AND CONTRIBUTORS

MARGARET N. MAXEY is Professor of Bioethics in the Biomedical Engineering Program and Director of the Chair of Free Enterprise in the College of Engineering, University of Texas at Austin. Formerly, she served as Assistant Director, South Carolina Energy Research Institute and Associate Professor of Bioethics at the University of Detroit. Dr. Maxey is a former consultant for Lawrence Livermore Laboratory, Livermore, California, on the question of ethical issues in nuclear waste disposal. She holds a B.A. degree in Philosophy from Creighton University, M.A.'s from St. Louis University and University of San Francisco and a Ph.D. in Christian Ethics from Union Theological Siminary, New York.

ROBERT LAWRENCE KUHN is a scientist, strategist, scholar, and author at home in the complementary worlds of business and academics. He is Senior Fellow in Creative and Innovative Management at the IC²Institute at the University of Texas at Austin, and is an Adjunct Professor of Corporate Strategy in the Department of Management and Organizational Behavior at the Graduate School of Business Administration of New York University. He holds a B.A. (Phi Beta Kappa) in Human Biology from Johns Hopkins University, a Ph.D. in Neurophysiology from the Department of Anatomy and Brain Research Institute of the University of California at Los Angeles, and an M.S. (Sloan Fellow) in Management from the Sloan School of Management of the Massachusetts Institute of Technology where he was also a Research Affiliate in Psychology. Recent books include: *The Firm Bond: Linking Meaning and Mission in Business and Religion*; *To Flourish Among Giants: Creative Strategies for Mid-Sized Firms*; *Commercializing Defense-Related Technology*; *Corporate Creativity: Robust Companies and the Entrepreneurial Spirit*. Dr. Kuhn is a contributing editor to the *Journal of Business Strategy* and is Senior Editor of *Texas Business*. He is active with several corporations, including Eagle Clothes, and he recently chaired a symposium of leaders from premier intellectual institutions ("Frontiers in Creative and Innovative Management: A Research Agenda").

*   *   *

ROBERT BENNE is the Dennis Fentley Jordan Professor of Religion, Director of the Center for Church and Society, and Chairman of the Department of Philosophy and Religion at Roanoke College, Salem, Virginia. He was formerly Professor of Church and Society, Lutheran School of Theology at Chicago. Honors and awards include a Fulbright Scholarship to Germany, a Woodrow Wilson Fellowship, a Rockefeller Doctoral Fellowship, and the Franklin Clark Fry Post-Doctoral Fellowship. He is author of *Defining America: A Christian Critique of the American Dream* and *The Ethic of Democratic Capitalism*. His B.A. degree is from Midland Lutheran College and Erlangen University in Germany; his M.A. and Ph.D. degrees are from the University of Chicago.

MERRIL EISENBUD is Professor of Environmental Medicine and Director of the Laboratory for Environmental Studies at New York University Medical Center, Institute of Environmental Medicine. He served for 12 years with the Atomic Energy Commission as Director of the Health and Safety Laboratory. Honors and awards include the U.S. Atomic Energy Commission Gold Medal, the Arthur Holly Compton Award of the American Nuclear Society, and the Power-Life Award of the Institute of Electrical and Electronics Engineering. He is a member of The National Academy of Engineering and an honorary life fellow of the New York Academy of Sciences. He is author of *The Environment, Technology and Health: Human Ecology in Historical Perspective* and of *Environmental Radioactivity*. His B.A. degree is from New York University. He holds honorary doctorates from Fairleigh Dickinson University and Catholic University of Rio de Janeiro.

EARNEST F. GLOYNA is currently Dean of the College of Engineering at The University of Texas at Austin while maintaining active teaching, research, and professional interests. He is a member of the National Academy of Engineers, recipient of a dozen medals and special honors. Dr. Gloyna is author of five books on water resources and wastewater treatment; 180 professional papers on industrial wastewater management, water reuse, radiation protection, environmental health engineering, and engineering education. He has served as Chairman of the Science Advisory Board, U.S. Environmental Protection Agency and as consultant or advisor to numerous U.S. governmental agencies, cities, and industries. He received his B.S. degree in Civil Engineering from Texas Technological

College; M.S. in Civil (Environmental) Engineering from The University of Texas at Austin; and Doctor of Engineering degree in Sanitary and Water-Resources Engineering from Johns Hopkins University.

THOMAS O. MCGARITY is Professor of Law at the University of Texas School of Law, Austin. He was formerly Associate Professor of Law at the University of Kansas School of Law, Lawrence. He has served as Attorney Advisor for the U.S. Environmental Protection Agency, 1975-77. He has published numerous articles, including "Public Regulation of Recombinant DNA Gene Therapy," "Contending Approaches to Regulating Laboratory Safety," "The Death and Transfiguration of Mirex: An Examination of the Integrity of Settlements Under FIFRA," and "Substantive and Procedural Discretion in Administrative Resolution of Science Policy Questions: Regulating Carcinogens in EPA and OSHA." His B.A. degree in Physics is from Rice University, and his D.J. degree is from The University of Texas at Austin.

JULIAN L. SIMON is currently a senior Fellow at The Heritage Foundation in Washington, D.C. on leave as Professor of Economics and Business Administration at the University of Illinois in Urbana. Formerly, he served as Lipson Professor of International Marketing and Visiting Professor of Business Administration at Hebrew University, Jerusalem. A businessman before becoming a professor, he has consulted widely with both government and private organizations including Population Planning Associates (N.C.), Westinghouse, Sears Roebuck, Dynamed Corporation, Federal Trade Commission, U.S. State Department, Israeli Ministry of Tourism, and others. He is inventor of the recently adapted CAB policy requiring airlines to use an overbooking system of obtaining volunteers by an auction scheme. He is author of *The Ultimate Resource* which develops themes in his 1977 technical work, *The Economics of Population Growth*. His B.A. degree is from Harvard University; his M.B.A. and Ph.D. degrees are from the University of Chicago.

WILLIAM G. TUCKER has served as a contributing editor to *Harper's* magazine 1977-81 and has been a free-lance writer for seven years. His articles have appeared in *Atlantic Monthly, Life, Fortune, National Review,* the *New Republic, Reason, The Wall Street Journal,* and the New York *Times.* His first book-length publication is *Progress and Privilege: America in the Age of Environmentalism.* His writings have won the Gerald Loeb Award, the John Hancock Award, the Amos Tuck Award. He was a runner-up for the National Magazine Award in 1980. Mr. Tucker is a graduate of Amherst College with degrees in English and economics.

MURRAY L. WEIDENBAUM is Director of the Center for the Study of American Business at Washington University in St. Louis. He has recently served as the first chairman of President Reagan's Council of Economic Advisers and as chairman of the Task Force on Regulatory Reform established by the president-elect in 1980. He has held a variety of business, government, and academic positions such as Assistant Secretary of the Treasury for Economic Policy, Chairman of the Economics Department at Washington University, Fiscal Economist in the U.S. Bureau of the Budget, and the Corporate Economist at the Boeing Company. His publications include *Business, Government, and the Public, The Future of Business Regulation, Government-Mandated Price Increases, Economics of Peacetime Defense,* and *The Modern Public Sector.* He has also published numerous articles and currently writes a column for *Washington Report.* Dr. Weidenbaum holds a B.A. from City College of New York, an M.A. from Columbia University and a Ph.D. in Economics from Princeton University.

AARON WILDAVSKY is Professor of Political Science, University of California at Berkeley. He was formerly President, Russell Sage Foundation in New York City, and Dean of the Graduate School of Public Policy, University of California-Berkeley. Honors include the Dwight Waldo Award from the American Society for Public Administration; the Paul Lazersfeld Award for Research, Evaluation Research Society; The Charles A. Merriam Award from the American Political Science Association; and a Guggenheim Fellowship. He is a Fellow of both the American Society of Arts and Science and of the National Academy of Public Administration. He is author of *Risk and Culture; An Essay on the Selection of Technological and Environmental Dangers* as well as *How to Limit Government Spending* and *The Private Government of Public Money.* His B.A. degree is from Brooklyn College; his M.A. and Ph.D. degrees are from Yale University.

EDWIN L. ZEBROSKI is Chief Nuclear Scientist at the Energy Studies Center of Electric Power Research Institute, Palo Alto, California. He was formerly Vice President of Analysis and Engineering at the Institute of Nuclear Power Operations (INPO) in Atlanta, Georgia. For INPO he oversaw operating experience reports, studies of significant events and accidents, and the development of remedies. He also had responsibility for human factors engineering, and emergency response capability development. His degrees are a B.S. in Chemistry and Physics from the University of Chicago and a Ph.D. in Physical Chemistry from the University of California. He is a registered professional engineer, and a member of the National Academy of Engineering, Phi Beta Kappa, Sigma Xi and many others. Recent publications include "Nuclear Energy in North America—Advantages and Issues," "Inter-&-Intra-National Cooperation on Practical Improvements in Plant Operations and Safety Practices."